AMERICAN
HIGHER
EDUCATION

Recent Titles in
Bibliographies and Indexes in Education

AMERICAN HIGHER EDUCATION

A Guide to Reference Sources

PETER P. OLEVNIK

With the Assistance of Betty W. Chan,
Sarah Hammond, and Gregory M. Toth

Foreword by Philip G. Altbach

Bibliographies and Indexes in Education, Number 12

GREENWOOD PRESS
Westport, Connecticut • London

Library of Congress Cataloging-in-Publication Data

Olevnik, Peter P.
    American higher education : a guide to reference sources / Peter
P. Olevnik ; with the assistance of Betty W. Chan, Sarah Hammond, and
Gregory M. Toth ; foreword by Philip G. Altbach.
        p.   cm.—(Bibliographies and indexes in education, ISSN 0742-6917
; no. 12)
    Includes bibliographical references (p.   ) and index.
    ISBN 0-313-27749-4 (alk. paper)
    1. Education, Higher—United States—Bibliography.   I. Title.
II. Series.
Z5815.U5044   1993
[LA226]
016.378'73—dc20   93-25015

British Library Cataloguing in Publication Data is available.

Library of Congress Catalog Card Number: 93-25015
ISBN: 0-313-27749-4
ISSN: 0742-6917

First published in 1993

Greenwood Press, 88 Post Road West, Westport, CT 06881
An imprint of Greenwood Publishing Group, Inc.

Printed in the United States of America

The paper used in this book complies with the
Permanent Paper Standard issued by the National
Information Standards Organization (Z39.48-1984).

10 9 8 7 6 5 4 3 2 1

CONTENTS

FOREWORD

American Higher Education: A Guide to Reference Sources shows just how vast the literature on higher education has become. The field has developed from a small offshoot of educational studies in the period just after World War II to a significant field of research and scholarship. A number of factors has contributed to the growth of interest in higher education. The academic enterprise in America has, of course, expanded dramatically, now enrolling more than 12 million students. Financial outlays have grown concomitantly. Higher education has become a major national industry—indeed at the present time, it is one of the few industries in America that has a significant export potential in terms of enrolling foreign students and producing research that can be licensed or sold overseas. Because higher education has become so large and so central to American society, it has generated a need to know about the enterprise. One important tradition in American higher education that has contributed to the growth of the literature is institutional research—the desire for academic institutions to collect information about themselves that is used for planning and management. The institutional research idea spread to the major public authorities at the state level which have become important in policy making and funding higher education.

Another source of the literature is the growth of an academic field of higher education studies. This field has developed from very small beginnings prior to the 1950s to a significant scholarly subdiscipline with its own journals, publishers, professional organizations and the like. The main *raison d'être* for the field is the preparation of administrative personnel for colleges and universities as well as policy makers in government. This administrative cadre has grown in the post-war period at a much faster rate than the overall expansion of higher education as academic institutions have become more professionalized and bureaucratized. Professionals in student personnel administration, legal students and a variety of others have emerged within the rubric of higher education studies. Several hundred American universities offer academic specializations in higher education. Faculty and students involved in this enterprise have contributed significantly to the literature and constitute a market for it as well.

The public is also interested in higher education. Guidebooks relating to the selection of colleges, rankings of academic institutions, and discussions and analyses of the American university all attract readers. With about half of American young people in the traditional age groups attending a post-secondary institution and with the proportion of 'non-traditional' older students growing rapidly, it is not surprising that there is considerable interest in learning about higher education.

American Higher Education: A Guide to Reference Sources provides not only a comprehensive overview of the literature that is available on virtually every topic relating to American higher education, it is an indication of the size, scope and diversity of the literature in the field. It is testimony to the importance of American colleges and universities in American society. This book is valuable precisely because it permits ready access to a vast array of literature. Its logical organization not only permits ease of use but provides a kind of benchmark for the field. No doubt, it would be possible to analyze this vast literature and to point to significant changes in its nature over time. When this book is possibly revised in a few years, the number of publications dealing with economic crises and retrenchment will have increased. Yet, the topics included here show considerable stability over time and are indicative of broad trends in a growing and increasingly diverse literature.

PHILIP G. ALTBACH

ACKNOWLEDGMENTS

The authors wish to express their appreciation to Robert Gilliam, who heads our Interlibrary Loan Department at Drake Memorial Library, for his patience with the deluge of interlibrary loan requests and for his help in locating and obtaining a substantial number of needed publications. We also wish to acknowledge the excellent work of Jeanne Saraceni, who directs the State University College at Brockport Document Preparation Center, and her very able staff, who spent many hours preparing the preliminary and final drafts of the work. To George Butler we extend our appreciation for his patience and editorial assistance. Finally, we acknowledge the support and encouragement of our respective families during this long period.

INTRODUCTION

Paralleling the growth in publications related to higher education is the increasing appearance of reference works associated with the field. Yet to date, there has been no comprehensive guide to this growing body of reference sources.

There are a number of bibliographies and guides relating to higher education. Some include reference works among their citations. Others are devoted exclusively to covering reference works, but focus on particular kinds of sources or subjects. Two examples are Richard Quay's Research in Higher Education, 2nd ed., (Oryx Pr., 1985), with his emphasis on bibliographies, and Rodriguez and Charles' Compendium of National Data Sources on Higher Education (State Higher Education Executive Officers, 1991), with their focus on statistical data.

Yet another group of guides to reference works covering education generally includes sources related to higher education. Lois Buttlar, in her Education: A Guide to Reference and Information Sources (Libraries Unlimited, 1989), provides citations to a substantial number of works on higher education.

None of these sources, however, provide the in-depth coverage of higher education that we provide in the present volume.

The impetus for this work was Peter Olevnik's Guide to Reference Sources in Higher Education (Dept. of Higher Ed., State Univ. of New York at Buffalo, 1981). The positive response to his selective guide led the principal author and his collaborators to begin work on this first effort to compile a more comprehensive guide to the literature of higher education.

Our purpose is to provide for a broad range of readers a useful guide to generally available reference works dealing with higher education in the United States. We aim to make these sources accessible, thus opening up the past while providing comprehensive coverage of the present.

This collection is limited to published works. Of the more than sixteen hundred sources considered, we narrowed our selection to approximately eight hundred titles. The bibliographies, encyclopedias, and indexes found in this guide include among their citations and entries references to the entire history of American higher education from the Colonial period to the present. These sources reflect the full range of subjects especially as represented in the periodical abstracts and indexes described.

Directories form a significant part of the guide. They are a valuable source of information about institutions, organizations, and people. As these works generally serve practical needs for current information, they were included only if cited in current issues of Books in Print (R.R. Bowker, 1945--) or Directories in Print (Gale Research Inc., 1989--).

Handbooks and manuals have undergone a similar selection process. Some older works, however, that remain useful for their comprehensive treatment, focus, or uniqueness in subject coverage are included. The decisive consideration for these and other sources listed in this guide is their availability.

In the other chapters, emphasis is on comprehensive coverage or representation of the broadest range of users' subject interests. In the chapters covering bibliographies, indexes, and statistical compilations, sources are considered for their historic or research value, as well as for coverage of current issues and subjects.

Generally included are sources likely to be available in libraries serving users with an interest in education. Such libraries might be found on campuses of small or medium-size colleges, universities or research centers. These sources might also be found in some governmental agency libraries or large public libraries.

Sources included have publication dates that range from 1861 up to and including 1992. While most were published in the 1970s and 1980s, approximately eighty have publication dates in the 1990s.

Throughout the volume users will find books, monographs, government publications, and other reports. Not included are periodicals, pamphlets, unpublished works, and with some exceptions, sources of fewer than forty pages. Excluded as well are works dealing with a single institution, a particular state or region of the United States or a single field of study. If a source deals with a broad area of knowledge (i.e., the humanities, sciences, etc.) it was usually included.

Publications appearing exclusively as documents in the Educational Resources Information Center (ERIC) microfiche collection are generally excluded, as these sources are readily accessible through monthly issues of Resources in Education (Office of Educational Research and Improvement) and via the ERIC computer database. As ERIC and a number of other databases covering higher education are in themselves bibliographic works and have reference value, they are represented together in the final chapter of this guide.

Because of its broad coverage, this work should be useful to an audience with an interest in American higher education and especially valuable to scholars and students. Administrators, government officials and Public Service librarians also should find the works listed useful and important. Prospective college students and their parents will find the chapter on directories especially helpful.

To facilitate access, sources are arranged in chapters according to their form. Eight chapters cover: 1) bibliographies and catalogs, 2) dictionaries and encyclopedias, 3) directories, 4) handbooks and manuals, 5) almanacs and yearbooks, 6) abstracts and indexes, 7) biographical sources, and 8) computer databases.

Within each chapter, general works are listed first, followed by others arranged by more specific topics. Sources in these subdivisions are arranged alphabetically by main entry (i.e., by personal or corporate author, or if lacking an author, by title). Since most directories continue to be published on a regular basis and are commonly recognized and listed by their title, they are all arranged in this form.

Where author and title main entries appear together, they are interfiled alphabetically word-by-word and letter-by-letter. For entries with multiple authors, arrangement is by the first one named. Other authors are ignored for arrangement purposes, but do appear in the author index.   For multiple entries by the same author, arrangement is alphabetical by title. Numbers are alphabetized as though spelled out, whenever they appear in a title.

In addition to a table of contents listing chapters and their subdivisions, access is further facilitated by separate author, title, and subject indexes. Individual source entries are numbered in a single continuous sequence. Index listings refer to these entry numbers.

All entries include descriptive annotations, indicating a source's purpose, scope, treatment, arrangement, and content. Where appropriate, information about former editions or related works is noted. In a few cases, annotations include brief chronologies of former editions and versions of the work along with a record of any title changes. Citations, however, are always to the most recent editions.   For continuing publications, we indicate the first appearance of the work, regardless of the original publisher's identity.   Only the current publisher is reported in the citation.

Another concern was the frequent inconsistency and incompleteness of imprint information given in the bibliographic resources we consulted. In these cases, we turned to the Online Computer Library Center (OCLC) bibliographic database as the final arbiter.

In conclusion, we offer this work knowing of its limitations. The process of identifying, obtaining, and describing sources could easily have continued. Making certain only the latest editions are represented, resolving questions about dates or places of publication, and solving a number of other bibliographic-record puzzles might easily have matched the time it took us to compile the guide. A deadline and a belief in the value of what we had already accomplished compelled us to bring our work to a conclusion.

With an eye to the possibility of a future edition, we welcome readers' comments and suggestions.

AMERICAN
HIGHER
EDUCATION

1.

GUIDES TO THE LITERATURE

INTRODUCTION

This chapter describes a wide range of bibliographies, along with a selection of library catalogs. To facilitate access, sources are arranged in four categories: Bibliographies of Bibliography, General Works, Special Works, and Library Catalogs.

Within these categories, sources are arranged alphabetically by author or main entry. There is one exception -- Special Works. Here bibliographies on a particular topic are grouped in subject categories.

The fourth category, "Library Catalogs," is comprised of lists of books and other materials held by particular libraries or library collections. It seems appropriate to include them in a chapter designed to aid those seeking to identify the literature, or some particular aspect of it, as it relates to higher education.

Thus, this chapter is comprised of approximately two hundred bibliographies and library catalogs. In it we have sought to provide a comprehensive -- though selective --list of books and monographs we believe would be both useful and available. To achieve this we generally excluded (1) superseded sources; (2) sources we considered of secondary importance to works we included; and (3) other sources we judged to be ephemeral or transitory in nature. Specifically, we rejected (1) bibliographies appearing in periodicals; (2) bibliographies of fewer than forty pages; (3) bibliographies appended to dissertations; (4) bibliographies appearing exclusively in the Education Resources Information Center (ERIC) documents collection; (5) similar documents and bibliography collections, such as those of the Council of Planning Libraries, accessible through readily available paper and electronic indexes; and (6) most in-house or unpublished works. However, if we believed a source had a special or unique focus, or was one-of-a-kind, we included it.

BIBLIOGRAPHIES OF BIBLIOGRAPHY

1. Beeler, Kent D. *Source Bibliographies on Higher Education: 1968-1972*. Washington, D.C.: Educational Resources Information Center (ERIC), National Institute of Education, 1972.
An updated, expanded version of the compiler's "Helpful Tools in Higher Education, 1960-1970" (Viewpoints, January 1971, pp. 1-100)including more than one hundred fifty source bibliographies. This is a bibliography of bibliographies appearing separately in booklet, monograph and various other non-journal forms. Sources are arranged by topic and sub-topic, each with complete imprint, description, and listing of major content areas. The text is preceded by an alphabetically arranged keyword index, with the individual source entry numbers. The final part of the work includes a separate listing of eighteen of the more comprehensive bibliographies available.

2. Besterman, Theodore. *Academic Writings: A Bibliography of Bibliographies*. (The Besterman World Bibliographies) Totowa, N.J.: Rowman and Littlefield, 1971. 252p. ISBN 0-87471-044-8.
An international guide to about one thousand bibliographies of theses, university publications and similar writings. Arrangement is according to four sections: periodicals, general sources, subjects and countries. Seventy-six subjects range from advertising and economics, to Japan, radio, and the United States. Bibliographies of publications by or about specific universities are entered by subject or following that are in alphabetical order under the university name. Citations, some of which include brief annotations, are gathered from the five-volume, fourth edition (1965-1966) of A World Bibliography of Bibliographies. A significant number of sources relate to higher education in the United States. Includes a detailed listing of contents, but lacks an index.

3. Besterman, Theodore. *Education: A Bibliography of Bibliographies*. (The Besterman World Bibliographies) Totowa, N.J.: Rowman and Littlefield, 1971. 306p. ISBN 0-87471-047-2.
This is a gathering of citations found under related subject fields throughout the five-volume, fourth edition (1965-1966) of A World Bibliography of Bibliographies. The present work is arranged under thirty major subject sections, ranging from education in forty-seven countries, education of women, and educational administration, to tests and measurements, the teaching of forty-five specific subjects, and university and college teaching. As an indication of its scope, psychology is divided into eleven areas. While entries include only occasional brief annotations, each shows the number of works cited in the bibliography. This is an important work of interest to students and scholars of the history of higher education. Access is by means of a detailed table of contents. Lacks an index.

4. Drazan, Joseph G. *An Annotated Bibliography of ERIC Bibliographies, 1966-1980*. Westport, Conn.: Greenwood Pr., 1982. 520p. ISBN 0-313-22688-1.
Includes more than thirty-two hundred briefly annotated citations to bibliographies available in the Educational Resources Information Center (ERIC) system. Arrangement is alphabetical according to a broad range of subjects, including higher education. Each entry includes the ERIC ED number. A contents page listing the subject sections would have been helpful. Author and subject indexes are provided.

5. Leitner, Erich. "Selected Bibliographies on Research into Higher Education: An International Inventory," *Higher Education*, 7 (August

1978), 311-330.
Includes citations to more than three hundred bibliographies. While international in coverage, most entries are for English language publications. Emphasis is on Anglo-American countries followed by German-speaking countries, Japan and Poland. An attempt was made for completeness in coverage of sources published from 1956 to 1977. Citations are alphabetical by author. Lacks an index.

6. Quay, Richard H. *Research in Higher Education: A Guide to Source Bibliographies.* 2d ed. Phoenix, Ariz.: Oryx Pr., 1985. 133p. ISBN 0-89774-194-3.
Includes over nine hundred citations to sources published mainly during the 1970s, with a substantial number appearing in the 1980s. Sources include books, monographs, journals, ERIC documents, government publications, and other items. Fifteen chapter topics range from four-year and two-year institutions, students, and faculty, to financial management, research, physical plant management, and adult and lifelong learning. Some items include brief annotations. An appendix lists sources covering higher education as a field of study. Includes both author and subject indexes.

7. Reynolds, Michael M. *Guide to Theses and Dissertations: An Annotated International Bibliography of Bibliographies.* Detroit: Gale Research, 1975. 599p. ISBN 0-8103-0976-9.
This annotated bibliography provides an international listing of more than two thousand bibliographies of theses and dissertations published through 1973. Arranged according to nineteen general and specific subject categories, the work is subdivided into appropriate subcategories. Subject categories range from area studies, communication and mass media, and education, to fine arts, language and literature, sciences, and social sciences. One section is devoted to higher education. Includes indexes by institutions, names and titles, and subjects.

8. Shanks, Doreen. *Guide to Bibliographies in Education.* (Monographs in Education, vol. 7) Winnipeg: Univ. of Manitoba, 1982. 144p. ISSN 0709-6313.
A classified, unannotated guide to 947 bibliographies published from 1964 to 1980, on a broad range of topics related to all educational levels. Included are separately published sources chiefly in the English language. The year 1964 was chosen as the initial date as the fourth edition of Besterman's World Bibliography of Bibliographies (1965-1966), on which that author's education compilation is based, covers sources published through 1963. Shank's guide includes sections on higher education, adult education, and teacher education. There is an author-title index, as well as a detailed table of contents, for access to source citations.

GENERAL WORKS

9. Allman, Katherine A. *A Reference Guide to Postsecondary Education Data Sources.* Boulder, Colo.: Western Interstate Commission for Higher Education, 1975. 721p.
Designed as a companion to the National Center for Higher Education Management Systems (NCHEMS) Statewide Measures Inventory (1975). This is essentially an annotated bibliography describing in detail a number of data sources in the Inventory. Included are books, articles, documents, and other published reports available in the United States.

The work is organized into seven parts: an unannotated bibliography, a numeric list of measures contained in the Inventory, an alphabetical index, measures with corresponding data sources, data sources with corresponding measures and two appendices. One appendix includes a brief list of other guides to data on higher education; the other provides an annotated list of NCHEMS documents related to state and national planning and decision making.

10. *Annotated Bibliography of Institutional Research.* Seattle: Univ. of Washington, Assn. for Institutional Research, 1966/1967-1973/1974.
A series of eight classified guides to research reports covering, in the later editions, eighteen subject areas. These range from academic governance, curriculum and instruction, and faculty, to professional and graduate education, planning, and student development outcomes. Abstracts vary in length from a single sentence to a paragraph. Each issue covers approximately two hundred citations, and includes an author index. Of marginal value, but still useful for topics discussed and era covered.

11. Barak, Robert J. *Research in Postsecondary Education, 1974: An Inventory of Research by Professors and Students in the Field of Higher Education.* Iowa City, Iowa: American College Testing Program, 1974. 66p.
This annotated source includes 248 entries, 136 (55 percent) from faculty, researchers, and administrators, and 112 (45 percent) from doctoral students. It updates two previous U.S. inventories (McGraw-Hill, 1968, and Univ. of California at Berkeley, 1972). Tables record research fields and numbers of projects by field. Source citations are alphabetical by author. Includes researcher and topic indexes.

12. Berry, Dorothea M. *A Bibliographic Guide to Educational Research.* 3d ed. Metuchen, N.J.: Scarecrow, 1990. 500p. ISBN 0-8108-2343-8.
An annotated list of reference sources likely to be found in large academic libraries. It includes bibliographies, directories, government publications, ERIC documents, as well as guides to educational materials. The third edition has increased coverage to over one thousand entries, twice the size of the first edition (1976). Arrangement is by author under broad categories such as books, periodicals, indexes, research studies, government publications, media, etc. One half of these entries are new titles not found in the second edition (1980). Includes author, title and subject indexes.

13. *Bibliography of Research Studies in Education.* Detroit: Gale Research Inc., 1974. 4 v. ISBN 0-8103-0975-0.
Reprint of fourteen annual issues of the United States Office of Education Bulletin series published from 1926 to 1940. Forty-eight thousand published and unpublished source entries are included, many with annotations, covering a broad range of subjects. Among subjects found are biography, educational psychology and sociology, methods of instruction, tests and measurement, vocational education, etc. Covered are periodicals, research reports, masters theses, doctoral dissertations, and other studies. Entries include author, title, date and place of publication, and number of pages. Each bulletin is reprinted separately as issued. The first four issues provide author-subject and institution indexes. Beginning in 1930-1931, issues include tables indicating both the number and field of research studies. Lacks a cumulative index.

14. Brewer, Deborah J. *ARBA Guide to Education.* Littleton, Colo.:
Libraries Unlimited, 1985. 232p. ISBN 0-87287-490-7.
A guide to 453 reference works drawn from more than twelve hundred
sources reviewed in American Reference Books Annual (Littleton, Colo.:
Libraries Unlimited, 1970- .) Sources are arranged in twelve chapters
divided into three parts: Sources of Bibliographic Information, Sources
of Factual Information, and Special Topics (i.e., sources of dissertations, instructional material, etc.) Entries include signed, critical-
descriptive annotations. The work is concluded with separate author-
title and subject indexes.

15. Buttlar, Lois. *Education: A Guide to Reference and Information
Sources.* (Reference Sources in the Social Sciences Series, no. 2).
Englewood, Colo.: Libraries Unlimited, 1989. 258p. ISBN 0-87287-
619-5.
An annotated list of more than nine hundred reference sources and databases pertaining to education. A substantial number relate to higher
education. Twenty-five subtopics, from "affirmative action" to "video
courses" are listed in the subject index under "Colleges and Universities." There are a number of other relevant subject headings as well.
All the titles in the guide were published after 1980. These sources are
arranged in twenty chapters by subject field. Chapters cover such topics
as General Reference Sources to Curriculum, Instruction Reference
Sources, and Evaluation in Education Reference Sources, to Higher Education, Research Centers, and Women's Studies. Also provided are lists of
periodicals, indexes and abstracts, research centers, and other organizations. A highly useful source. Includes a general index.

16. Cordasco, Francesco and Alloway, David N. *Sociology of Education:
A Guide to Information Sources.* (Education Information Guide
Series, vol. 2) Detroit: Gale Research, 1979.   266p.   ISBN
0-8103-1436-3.
Drawing from studies of the 1960s and the 1970s chiefly related to
American education, this guide includes more than fifteen hundred
entries. While all levels are covered, a substantial number of source
citations relate to higher education. Contents are arranged according
to four chapters: reference works, the school, levels of education, and
special aspects such as adults, minorities, or the disadvantaged.
Includes separate author, title, and subject indexes.

17. Crabbs, Richard F. and Holmquist, Frank W. *United States Higher
Education and World Affairs: A Partially Annotated Bibliography.*
New York: F.A. Praeger, 1967. 207p.
For those concerned with the international role of colleges and
universities. Begun in 1964 as a service to the members of the Indiana
University Committee on International Affairs, this guide includes 882
citations to books and articles arranged into nineteen categories.
Categories are formed into seven major parts: from a general perspective
on international educational activity, to curricular matters and aspects
of educational exchange. Dated but useful to the student and scholar of
American higher education and world affairs. Includes an author index.

18. Dressel, Paul L. and Pratt, Sally B. *World of Higher Education: An
Annotated Guide to the Major Literature.* San Francisco: Jossey
Bass, 1971. 238p.
Reviews the research relevant to understanding and making decisions about
higher education. Included are some seven hundred citations to sources
divided into seven major topics: institutional research; governance,
administration, management; students; faculty and staff; curriculum and

instruction; research methodology; and related bibliographies and other reference sources. A detailed subject-author-title index concludes the work.

19. Formerand, Jacques, Van de Graff, John H. and Wasser, Henry. *Higher Education in Western Europe and North America: A Selected and Annotated Bibliography.* New York: Council for European Studies, 1979. 229p.

This work cites 786 books, journal articles, dissertations, government publications, international agency documents, and other sources dealing with higher education in non-communist, industrial countries of Western Europe and North America. Emphasis is on works published during the 1970s, although major earlier works are included. Focus is on a limited range of basic, interrelated topics, with critical evaluation of research trends and individual works. Four chapters cover a) higher education's main functions, b) universities and their social environment, c) government of higher education, and d) the economics of higher education. Includes author, subject, and country indexes.

20. Halstead, D. Kent. *Higher Education: A Bibliographic Handbook.* Washington, D.C.: U.S. Dept. of Education, Office of Educational Research and Improvement, National Institute of Education, 1984. 750p.

A major source covering about eight hundred "substantial" and "distinctive" works, with emphasis on practical value. Higher education is here viewed from the aggregate or national perspective. Eighteen chapter topics range from economics and finance to institutional role, policy and student concerns. Lengthy annotations are both critical and descriptive, with many more books being covered than journal articles. Author and title indexes cover this and the author's companion volume, Higher Education Planning (1979).

21. Halstead, D. Kent. *Higher Education Bibliography Yearbook.* Washington, D.C.: Research Associates of Washington, 1987-1988. Annual.

Published for only two years, this source was designed to identify those books and articles considered of "greatest interest and value to the generalists and practitioners." Noted scholars describe, discuss and evaluate the selected works which are grouped into thirty-four topic areas. Emphasis is on both research and works having practical value. Sources included are those published the year preceding the yearbook. The 1987 issue includes 155 source citations with annotations and a listing of several guides or bibliographies of higher education. Includes an author index and a detailed table of contents.

22. Halstead, D. Kent. *Higher Education Planning: A Bibliographic Handbook.* Washington, D.C.: U.S. Dept. of Health, Education, and Welfare, National Institute of Education, 1979. 537p.

The author's purpose is to identify and publicize "high quality, "scholarly and critical references on state and national level planning." Works are chosen with emphasis on practical value. Most of the more than six hundred sources were published during the 1970s. They are arranged in twenty two sections, covering topics ranging from admission, articulation and retention; to demography; faculty; institutional role; and space management. In-depth annotations are both descriptive as well as evaluative and critical. Includes separate author, publisher and sponsoring agency indexes.

23. Hamilton, Malcolm C. *Directory of Educational Statistics: A Guide to Sources.* Ann Arbor, Mich.: Pierian Pr, 1974. 71p.

A classified, annotated guide to sources of educational statistics on a wide range of subjects, with titles dating back to 1870. The table of contents lists eleven sections, from general summaries to elementary and secondary education, and miscellaneous educational statistics. Three sections are devoted to higher education. More than 130 titles are cited. This is a valuable source for librarians, scholars, and students with interest in the history of American education. Includes indexes to titles and subjects.

24. Heckman, Dale M. and Martin, Warren Bryan. *Inventory of Current Research on Higher Education, 1968.* New York: McGraw-Hill Publishing Co., 1968. 198p.
One of the first publications of the Carnegie Commission on Higher Education, this annotated inventory for the period July, 1967-June, 1968 (with some earlier U.S. projects and ninety selected projects worldwide) includes in total more than one thousand entries. By current is meant at the time this inventory was published. Projects are arranged into eight subject chapters covering: students; faculty; administrators; structures; functions; governance; graduate and professional education; and supply and demand, money, and manpower. Includes an inventory taxonomy, index of researchers, and a topical index. While limited in the period covered, this work records research conducted during a period of "social malaise and rapid educational changes".

25. Hefferlin, JB Lon and others. *Inventory of Current Research on Post-secondary Education, 1972: A Guide to Recent and Ongoing Projects in the United States and Canada.* Berkeley, Center For Research and Development in Higher Education, Univ. of California, Berkeley, 1972. 291p.
An annotated guide to approximately 1,130 research projects. This work updates Dale Heckman and Warren Bryan Martins <u>Inventory of Current Research on Higher Education</u> (McGraw-Hill, 1968). Entries are numbered and arranged alphabetically by the name of the principal researcher. The work concludes with a subject index.

26. Kaufman, Martha and Rabineau, Louis. *Perspectives on Postsecondary Education: An Annotated Bibliography.* Denver, Colo.: Education Commission of the States, 1981. 55p.
Covers papers, proceedings, and publications from Inservice Education Program (IEP) State Leadership Seminars, 1974-1980. The work includes about 150 entries related to higher education and the states' responsibilities. Entries are arranged under nine topics, from finance and budget, to minorities in postsecondary education non-traditional and lifelong learning, and state agencies and government relations. A useful source for review of major issues confronting higher education during a period of substantial change, reflecting the insights of an eminent group of administrators and scholars. Includes a separate listing of proceedings and an author index.

27. Kelsey, Roger R. *A Bibliography on Higher Education.* Baltimore: Higher Education Council, Maryland State Teachers Assn., 1969. 175p.
An unannotated list of nearly six thousand books pertaining to higher education. Books were so identified during the years 1964 and 1965 by the compiler during his tenure as book exhibitor for the American Association for Higher Education. Works are arranged under sixteen subject sections. These range from adult and university extension curricula, and evaluation and accreditation, to organization and administration, and teaching methods and media. Lacks an index.

28. Kramer, John E. *American College Novel: An Annotated Bibliography.*
     New York: Garland Publishing, 1981. 286p. ISBN 0-8240-9365-8.
An extensive guide to 425 full-length novels featuring graduate students,
faculty, administrators, and other academic personnel. The chronologically arranged work begins with Nathaniel Hawthorne's *Fanshawe*,
published in 1828, and ends with Gordon Webber's 1979 novel, *The Great
Buffalo Hotel*. Excluded are short stories, anthologies, science fiction,
mysteries, inter-collegiate sports and military institutions. Includes
author and title indexes.

29. Kramer, John E. and Kramer, John E., III. *College Mystery Novels:
     An Annotated Bibliography Including a Guide to Professional Series -
     Characters - Sleuths.* New York: Garland Publishing, 1983. 356p.
     ISBN 0-8240-9237-6.
Essentially a complement to the senior author's *American College Novel*
(Garland, 1981). The 632 citations identify books in paperback and hard
cover, with the first section organized by series characters. Personality profiles of each of the fifty-one series characters are summarized
succinctly. Titles of series are listed after the description. A second
section provides chronological entries of 308 publications, from 1882 to
1982. Includes author and title indexes.

30. Marks, Barbara S. *New York University List of Books in Education.*
     New York: Citation Pr., 1968. 527p.
A selected, annotated guide to nearly three thousand books, some
pamphlets, yearbooks, and a few monographic series compiled from lists
put together by the departments of the New York University School of
Education. Sources are arranged under 178 alphabetically arranged topics
covering everything from academic freedom, and faculty in colleges and
universities, to liberal education, and writing and composition. A
substantial number of sources relate to higher education. Includes a
name and title index.

31. Mayhew, Lewis B. *Literature of Higher Education.* San Francisco:
     Jossey-Bass, 1971. 162p.
Grown beyond its original size from articles published in the *Educational
Record*, this bibliography covers some ninety-six book reviews of "most
significant books on higher education". Reviews are arranged by general
topics ranging from governance, history, and campus unrest, to
institutional differences, teaching and curriculum. An introductory
bibliographic essay covers the literature of higher education from 1965
to 1970. Includes an author-title index. Planned as an annual
publication, unfortunately only one other edition (1972) was published.

32. Olevnik, Peter P. *A Guide to Reference Sources in Higher Education.*
     (Occasional Paper No. 3) Buffalo: Dept. of Higher Education, Faculty
     of Educational Studies, State Univ. of New York at Buffalo, 1981.
     45p.
A selected, annotated guide to one hundred reference works in the field
of higher education. While sources included range in dates of publication from 1895 to 1980, more than sixty percent have been published since
1970. Earlier source dates indicate indexes and abstracts which have
been published continuously to date. Arrangement is by source type,
e.g., bibliographies, encyclopedias, indexes, etc. Remains useful for
students. Includes author and title indexes.

33. Parker, Franklin and Parker, Betty June. *U.S. Higher Education: A
     Guide to Information Sources.* Detroit: Gale Research, 1980. 675p.
     ISBN 0-8103-1476-2.

This guide provides annotated citations to well over three thousand books and reports representing all aspects of American higher education. Emphasis is on twentieth-century works, in particular those published from after World War II to 1979, with inclusion of selected nineteenth-century sources. Includes separate author, title, and subject indexes.

34. Pfinster, Allan O. *Trends in Higher Education in the United States: A Review of Recent Literature*. Washington, D.C.: Lutheran Educational Conference of North America, 1975. 368p.
Actually six monographs combined into one. Each provides a review of selected literature on a single topic: enrollments; students of the 1970s; governance; instructional programs; finance; and implications for the predominantly undergraduate, church-related institution. This work is in bibliographic essay format with sources listed at the ends of chapters. In total there are more than nine hundred citations to books, monographs, articles, and government publications, with substantial coverage of the <u>Chronicle of Higher Education</u>. Emphasis is on works published between 1964 and 1975. The work provides an overview of the status of higher education in the United States, with special attention given to planning for undergraduate colleges in general and Lutheran colleges in particular. Access is by means of the table of contents. Lacks an index.

35. Rodriquez, Esther M. and Lenth, Charles S. *Compendium of National Data Sources on Higher Education*. Denver, Colo.: State Higher Education Executive Officers, 1991. 183p. loose-leaf.
A classified, annotated guide to eighty-seven data sources. All are national in scope. Some describe surveys of all United States institutions of higher education. Others, while national in scope, report surveys of representative samples of institutions, students, and faculty. Included are surveys, databases, reports, statistical digests, and other data sources that are updated and made available on a regular or periodic basis. Sources are arranged into nine subject categories: Institutional Descriptors (i.e., directories); Student Data; Student Longitudinal Data; Student Financial Aid; Financial Data; Tuition and Fee charges; Faculty, Staffing, and Salaries; Physical Facilities, Libraries, and Assets; and Sourcebooks and Comparative Studies. An essential source. This work replaces an earlier source entitled <u>Comparative Data About Higher Education</u> (SHEEO, 1986). The table of contents lists all data sources by category. Lacks an index.

36. Spear, George E. and Mocker, Donald W. *Urban Education: A Guide to Information Sources*. (Urban Studies Information Guide Series, vol. 13) Detroit: Gale Research, 1978. 203p. ISBN 0-8103-1431-2.
An annotated bibliography of books, articles, studies and reports, many of them ERIC documents. Entries are drawn mostly from the mid-1960s onward, when interest in specifically urban issues began to grow. Items are grouped in three major sections: 1) Preschool, Elementary and Secondary Schools, 2) Urban Higher Education and 3) Adult Education. More recent trends have probably increased the relevance of the last section to higher education in general. Author, title and subject indexes are provided.

37. White, Jane N. and Burnett, Collins W. *Higher Education Literature: An Annotated Bibliography*. Phoenix, Ariz.: Oryx Pr., 1981. 177p. ISBN 0-912700-80-7.
A classified guide to 1,618 books dealing with two-year and four-year accredited, degree-offering colleges and universities. Major categories for inclusion are: historical backgrounds and nature and scope of higher

education, the learning-teaching environment, administration and organization, community and junior colleges, comparative systems, and higher education as a field of study. Coverage includes the range of current concerns: finance, enrollments, legal issues, state and federal government controls, administration and faculty tensions, accountability, and collective bargaining. A series of appendices includes short lists of sources, definitions, organizations and associations. Includes author and subject indexes.

38. Zucker, Jacob D. *Annotated Bibliography on Topics of Concern to Higher Education 1974: A Topical Paper.* Gainesville: Institute of Higher Education, Univ. of Florida, 1974. 56p.

Brings together a collection of brief (fifteen to fifty items) bibliographies on a variety of higher education topics: Black Colleges, the New Community College Student, Cooperative Education, College Teaching Internship, the Department Chairman, Financing, Leadership, Organizational Theories, Statewide Planning, Student Personnel Services. Though no statements of scope, purpose or criteria for selection are offered, citations are mainly to U.S. books, chapters, articles and ERIC documents of the 1960s and early 1970s. No indexes.

SPECIAL WORKS

Administration

39. Altbach, Philip G. *Reform and Innovation in Higher Education.* (Bulletin of the International Bureau of Education, Year 56, No. 223, 2nd quarter, 1982) Paris: Unesco, 1982. 59p.

A partially annotated guide which includes among its 336 citations any kind of planned change in higher education, with some focus on underlying causes and stimulants for such change. Thirteen sections deal with broad perspectives and a fourteenth covers geographical areas. The earliest work cited was published in 1956, while the most recent were published in 1981. Includes an author-editor index. While there is no subject index, a table of contents provides access by broad concepts.

40. Askew, Thomas A. *The Small College: A Bibliographic Handbook.* Washington, D.C.: Council for the Advancement of Small Colleges, 1973. 135p.

Responds to the needs of the leaders of small colleges, as expressed in a survey, by providing a comprehensive bibliography of information. The materials, published from 1965 through 1971 and comprising a little more than five hundred items, either are about small colleges or have some indirect application and have been selected for their availability. The annotated bibliography is divided into twelve major sections and is followed by separate subject and author indexes.

41. Baatz, Charles Albert. *The Philosophy of Education: A Guide to Information Sources.* (Educational Information Guide Series, vol. 6) Detroit: Gale Research, 1980. 344p.

Furnishes a structured bibliography of the philosophy of education for both beginners and specialists, covering the works of both known and not-so-well-known authors, and including some foreign and international studies. The literature, starting with 1967, is organized around a schema shown on pages 3 and 4. Each chapter has a short introductory paragraph. Not every item carries a brief commentary. There are author, title, and subject indexes, as well as a highly detailed table of contents.

42. Batkin, Ruth Baron. *Educational Measurement: Subject, Reference & Research Guide.* Washington, D.C.: ABBE Pubs. Assn. of Washington, D.C., 1987. 159p.
Analyzes the subject field through detailed categorization of the included works. The bibliography of over three hundred items published in the 1980s is preceded by a highly organized alphabetical listing of subject and research categories with appropriate item numbers representing the only means of access.

43. *Bibliography on Postsecondary Accreditation.* Washington, D.C.: Council on Postsecondary Accreditation, 1984. 108p. ISBN 0-318-17661-0.
The first part of the work records changes in accreditation practices through a survey of sources published from 1970 to Spring 1984. Each of thirteen subject categories listed in the table of contents is briefly introduced and the 542 citations are arranged alphabetically by author in each chapter. Some items are annotated. Three appendices list names and addresses of accrediting institutions. The second part of this work provides a tool for researchers, students, agency officials, and others including a "complete representation" of the first half-century of dissertations in this area. A brief discussion of how to use this work precedes the bibliography. Includes author, topic, and university indexes. A fourth means of access is provided by the chronological organization of entries and alphabetical listings by author within each year from 1935 through 1984.

44. Blessing, James H. *Graduate Education: An Annotated Bibliography.* (U.S. Office of Education, Bulletin 1961, no. 26) Washington, D.C.: U.S. Department of Health Education and Welfare, Office of Education, 1961. 151p.
Surveys recent studies and communications about graduate education, excluding sources covering single academic or professional fields or higher education in general. There are almost nine hundred items published over the period from 1957 to 1960, with some important earlier works. The material is restricted to American graduate education. There are a table of contents, showing the divisions and subdivisions of the bibliography, and an index which covers authors, editors, organizations, agencies, committee chairs, and some topical headings.

45. Blimling, Gregory S. and others. *An ACUHO-I Bibliography on Residence Halls.* Columbus, Ohio: Association of College and Univ. Housing Officers, 1987. 468p.
The authors have attempted a comprehensive survey of the U.S. literature, resulting in more than four thousand unannotated entries which have been grouped in ten major subject sections; from historical development and financing, to organization and administration, food service, and legal issues. Within each section, entries are arranged by publication type: books, periodicals, newspapers, ERIC documents, proceedings, etc. Materials available from ACUHO-I are listed in a appendix. Indexed by author only.

46. Broudy, Harry S. and others. *Philosophy of Education: An Organization of Topics and Selected Sources.* Urbana: Univ. of Illinois Pr., 1967. 287p.
Sets out to identify and classify the topics and literature in the philosophy of education as a means of affirming the validity of the field in teacher education. Items listed range from the classics of Greece and Rome to works published in early 1967. The material, most of which is annotated, is organized into eight major chapters which are sub-divided

on the basis of a chart facing the table of contents. A short index of topics comprising the penultimate chapter refers the user to the appropriate section.

47. Christensen, Ernest M. *Annotated Bibliography of the College Union.* (Golden Anniversary Monograph Series, *College Unions at Work*, no. 7) Ithaca, N.Y.: Association of College Unions-International, 1967. 268p.

Designed to organize methodically and meaningfully most of the major works published during the period 1950-1966. The work, consisting of twelve hundred items (some are duplicates), is organized into several chapters dealing with such aspects of the college union as its role, planning, operations, programs, and services. An author index is followed by a detailed and highly cross-referenced subject index.

48. Cowley, William Harold. *Personnel Bibliographical Index.* Columbus: Ohio State Univ., 1932. 433p.

A selected, classified and annotated guide to more than two thousand books, articles, monographs, and pamphlets focusing on student personnel issues and problems. The work is in three parts: Part 1 provides a detailed subject index; Part 2, the major section, includes source entries with annotations; Part 3 offers an author index. A system of type styles indicate the sources level of importance. Most entries cover the 1920s, with others covering the preceding decade. A few cover 1930 and 1931. For those with an interest in the history and development of student personnel administration.

49. D'Amico, Louis A. and Brooks, William D. *Spatial Campus: A Planning Scheme with Selected and Annotated Bibliography.* Bloomington: School of Education, Indiana Univ., 1968. 118p.

A classified guide to 761 periodical articles arranged into eleven subject areas, from administration, planning, and finance, to construction, utilization, and parking. An introductory essay "Why Prepare For Growth" explores the subject areas focused on by the authors cited in the bibliography. While dated, many of the studies and reports reflect topics that still occupy higher education planners and administrators. The compilers identify the first 289 articles as substantive, and those remaining as non-substantive. There are no indexes. Arrangement within eleven subject sections is alphabetical by author.

50. Ebbers, Larry H., Marks, Kenneth E. and Stoner, Kenneth L. *Residence Halls in U.S. Higher Education: A Selective Bibliography.* (Series in Bibliography, no. 4) Ames: Iowa State Univ., Library, 1973. 610p.

A classified guide to more than two thousand books, articles, ERIC documents, theses, proceedings, government documents, and other works extending back to the turn of the century. Sources are divided into the following subject areas: history; finance; planning, construction, and facilities; organization and administration; programming; personnel counseling; food service; legal issues; and miscellaneous areas. Within each area works are arranged by form (e.g., books, articles, etc.) Entries, many including annotations, are arranged alphabetically by author. Dated, but important for tracing the development, history, and status of residence halls in American higher education. Concludes with an author index.

51. Eells, Walter Crosby and Hollis, Ernest V. *Administration of Higher Education: An Annotated Bibliography.* (U.S. Office of Education Bulletin 1960, no. 7) Washington, D.C.: U.S. Department of Health,

Education and Welfare, 1960. 410p.
A selected list of 2,708 books, proceedings, dissertations, and articles published chiefly during the 1950s. More than one half of the items are articles. Topics are covered in thirteen main fields, ranging from administration of faculty, students, and instruction, to federal relations, finance, regional organizations, and public relations. Delves into issues related to the rising tide of students and the anticipated growth of higher education in the 1960s. A comprehensive index includes names of authors and others mentioned in titles or annotations, names of educational institutions and organizations, and numerous subjects.

52. Eells, Walter Crosby and Hollis, Ernest V. *College Presidency, 1900-1960: An Annotated Bibliography*. Westport, Conn.: Greenwood Pr., 1978. 143p. ISBN 0-313-20680-5.
Originally published in 1961 by the United States Department of Health, Education and Welfare, Office of Education, this bibliography includes seven hundred sources published during the twentieth century, with about one half appearing during the years 1940 through 1960. Six major fields include reference works, general and composite sources, personal factors, duties and responsibilities, and biographies. Personal factors (including age, degrees, salary, tenure and retirement) and information on duties and responsibilities comprise over one half of all citations. Includes an index of names, institutions, periodicals, organizations, and principal topics.

53. Hall, Wayne C. *An Annotated Bibliography on Graduate Education, 1971-1972*. Washington, D.C.: National Board on Graduate Education, 1972. 151p.
The subject matter is restricted to the traditional areas of graduate education, excluding law, medicine and other professional fields. Annotations are more like abstracts giving summaries of findings. A topical index before the bibliography section provides the key to some fifty subject headings such as quality of faculty teaching versus research. Separate title and author indexes at the end. This work updates a similar one for the period 1950-1971, by the author.

54. Hastings, Anne H. *The Study of Politics and Education: A Bibliographic Guide to the Research Literature*. Eugene: Clearinghouse on Educational Management, Univ. of Oregon, 1980. 302p.
A classified, unannotated guide to more than twelve hundred books, monographs, and selected periodicals. This work cites and describes sources and their contents for the period 1960 through 1979. Sources are arranged into eight major sections and forty-seven subsections. Edited collections list individual authors and generally titles of individual items. One section is devoted to politics, governance, and finance of postsecondary education. Includes a detailed table of contents, name index, and a subject index.

55. Herring, Mark Youngblood. *Ethics and the Professor: An Annotated Bibliography, 1970-1985*. New York: Garland Publishing, 1988. 605p. ISBN 0-8240-8491-8.
An annotated guide to 1,905 sources - chiefly books and articles - published between 1970 and 1985. According to the compiler, to include a source "there had to be some overt ethical mechanism,...some protruding spirit of practice that clearly indicated the author was trying to unveil what he thought was a good or a bad practice." Ten chapters with such headings as "The Fair Round Belly: Justice" are each preceded by brief introductory essays giving an "aerial view" of the chapter. An interesting source for the non-specialist interested in ethics in education.

Includes a detailed contents page, author and title indexes, and a brief keyword-subject index.

56. Hunt, Thomas C. and Carper, James C. *Religious Colleges and Universities in America: A Selected Bibliography.* (Garland Reference Library of Social Sciences, no. 422) New York: Garland Publishing, 1988. 374p. ISBN 0-8240-6648-0.
Includes 2,342 citations to books, articles, dissertations and a range of other published and unpublished reports and documents. Introductory chapters cover general works on religion and higher education, and government aid and regulation. These are followed by twenty-five chapters each arranged by denomination. Chapter treatment and scope reflect both the importance of the denomination and approach taken by the respective chapter authors. The many descriptive annotations range in length from a couple of sentences to a paragraph. Includes both an author and subject index.

57. Kaiser, Leland R. *Designing Campus Environment: A Review of Selected Literature.* Boulder, Colo.: Western Interstate Commission for Higher Education, 1976. 75p.
About three hundred annotated citations to dissertations, articles and ERIC publications. Six chapters cover such topics as student characteristics, housing, measurements, overview, transactions and dysfunction. Use of particular assessment instruments or scales are reported in the abstracts. No index.

58. Layton, Elizabeth N. *Higher Education Administration and Organization: Annotated Bibliography 1940-1950.* Washington, D.C.: Federal Security Agency, Office of Education, Division of Higher Education, 1951. 72p.
A compilation of 357 references to books, chapters, articles, conference proceedings, dissertations and association publications. Arrangement is by author or source with brief descriptive annotations. A combined author/subject index is provided, but no front-matter. Dated, but provides coverage of a decade not well represented elsewhere.

59. Meeth, L. Richard. *Selected Issues in Higher Education: An Annotated Bibliography.* New York: Teachers College Pr., Columbia Univ., 1965. 212p.
Includes more than twelve hundred citations to books, articles and other documents arranged by subjects related to the establishment of policy and the operation of colleges and universities. Subjects range from academic rank, faculty recruitment and selection, to class size, long-range planning, and student participation in college policy formulation and administration. Includes an author index. While the book lacks a subject index, the table of contents with its thirty-nine subject section listings facilitates access to the sources.

60. Parsons, Kermit C. and Lang, Jon T. *An Annotated Bibliography on University Planning and Development.* New York: Society for College and Univ. Planning, 1968. 158p.
Includes 350 entries covering policy, community relations, enrollment, campus planning and architecture. Coverage ranges from readily available publications including articles and government documents to reports by planning staffs of and consultants to State agencies and universities. Previous editions were published as Council of Planning Librarians Exchange Bibliography (No. 22 and No. 30). Includes author and title indexes.

61. Peterson, Marvin W. and Mets, Lisa A. *Key Resources in Higher Education Governance, Management, and Leadership: A Guide to The Literature.* San Francisco: Jossey-Bass, 1987. 515p. ISBN 1-55542-052-A.
The twenty-one chapters are the combined efforts of the editors and twenty-eight contributors with expertise in the subjects they treat. An overview and discussion of the development of the topic are provided for each chapter. Classic works are identified by asterisks. The editors cover the history of academic governance from the founding of Harvard College and the continuing evolution of the field. This is a comprehensive resource. Name and subject indexes with a listing of associations in higher education.

62. Sontz, Ann H.L. *The American College President, 1636-1989: A Critical Review and Bibliography.* (Bibliographies and Indexes in Education, no. 10) Westport, Conn: Greenwood Pr., 1991. 176p. ISBN 0-313-27325-1.
A selected guide to books, articles, and doctoral dissertations divided into three major divisions: background sources covering higher education and leadership, historical works, presidential selection, finance and fund-raising, and minority and women's issues. A second part includes biographies arranged alphabetically by institution, then by president. The third and largest section covers presidential works also arranged by institution, then by president. Introductory pages include a review essay and statistical tables. This source updates Walter C. Eells and Ernest V. Hollis's The College Presidency, 1900-1960 (Greenwood Pr., 1978.) Includes author and subject indexes.

63. Stickler, William Hugh. *Institutional Research Concerning Land-Grant Institutions and State Universities: A Report Prepared for the Joint Office of Institutional Research of the American Association of Land-Grant Colleges and State Universities and the State Universities Association.* Tallahassee: Office of Institutional Research and Service, Florida State Univ., 1959. 142p.
The author presents a description and the results of a study of institutional research done by or concerning member institutions of AALGSU-SUA. Relevant published literature was surveyed for 1954-1959, and questionnaires surveying in-house studies were sent to member institutions for 1958-59. One appendix provides an unannotated list of the published studies, grouped by topic, and another a list of the in-house studies identified, arranged by topic and institution. A very thorough work limited in value by its age and the narrow time span it covers.

64. Szekely, Kalman S. and Jones, James L. *Higher Education: Its Mission, Goals and Problems.* Bowling Green, Ohio: Bowling Green State Univ. Libraries, 1969. 26p.
A classified, unannotated list of about 350 books, articles, and a few unpublished theses and dissertations. Emphasis is on works appearing in the 1960s. While dated, this bibliography remains useful as a record of writings pertaining to processes and events taking place on college and university campuses of the era. It is useful also for its particular emphasis on the mission and goals of institutions of higher education.

65. Testerman, Jack, Blakemon, Robert and White, Terry. *Institutional Research: A Comprehensive Bibliography.* (Research Series, no. 12) Fayetteville: Univ. of Southwestern Louisiana, Office of Institutional Research, 1972. 131p.
An unannotated list of 1,202 references to works of or about institu-

tional research. Most items date from the 1960s and are grouped by type
of publication: books and pamphlets, chapters and conference papers,
articles. Focus is on administration, decision making, and planning in
higher education. Lacks an index.

66. Tice, Terrence N. *Resources on Campus Governance and Employment
     Relations, 1967-1977, With Essay, Annotations and Indexes.* Washing-
     ton, D.C.: Academic Collective Bargaining Service, 1978. 135p.
Lists more than eleven hundred items, covering both the U.S. and Canada,
in two sections: 1) books, booklets, monographs and dissertations; and
2) articles, chapters, papers, and other items. Within each section
items are grouped by year, with some entries including brief annotations.
Name and subject indexes are provided. The author, who has written
extensively on employment issues in higher education, describes and
critiques the literature in this area in an introductory essay, also
offering a separate list of non-bibliographic sources of information.

67. Tice, Terrence N. *Resources on Campus Governance and Employment
     Relations, Supplement, 1977-1979, With Essay, Annotations, and
     Indexes.* Washington, D.C.: Academic Collective Bargaining Service
     Project on Educational Employment Relations, 1980. 59p.
A supplement to the author's 1978 publication of the same title, this
source covers more than five hundred items, covering both the U.S. and
Canada. The work is in two sections: 1) books, booklets, monographs and
dissertations; and 2) articles, chapters, papers, and other lesser items.
Within each section items are grouped by year, with some entries
including brief annotations. Name and subject indexes are included.

68. Van Antwerp, Eugene I. *Accreditation in Postsecondary Education:
     A Sometimes Annotated Bibliography.* Washington, D.C.: Federation
     of Regional Accrediting Commissions in Higher Education, 1974. 20p.
A compilation, in pamphlet form, of references to some 250 books,
commission reports, conference publications and journal and magazine
articles. An introductory note claims selection was limited to the last
ten years, but older items do appear. Arrangement is by author. The few
annotations are very brief. Publications of the Federation and the
regional accrediting commissions are listed separately. No indexes.

69. Widdall, Kenneth R. *Selected References for Planning Higher Edu-
     cation Facilities.* Columbus, Ohio: Council of Educational Facility
     Planners, 1968. 95p.
An annotated guide to nearly two hundred books, reports, articles, and
other documents arranged according to five major categories: orientation
to facility planning, developing a master plan, planning for specific
institutions, technical aspects, and administering the plant expansion.
Coverage includes schools, community colleges, four year colleges, and
universities. Perhaps dated regarding applications, but still useful in
terms of concepts and principles. Lacks an index.

70. Willingham, Warren W. and others. *The Source Book for Higher Educa-
     tion: A Critical Guide to Literature and Information on Access to
     Higher Education.* New York: College Entrance Examination Board,
     1973. 481p.
This annotated guide has as its primary objective the creation of a
conceptual framework for dealing with the subject of access. A second
purpose is to identify the most critical literature published over the
previous decade, as well as provide a secondary reference to sources
covering all aspects of access. Included are 1,519 representative books,
articles, and reports. A taxonomy provides two conceptual framework for

the content and organization of the work, with each major division, section, and subsection clearly shown. The final two sections describe approximately four hundred organizations, programs, and sources of information important to the access process. Includes separate author and subject indexes. Now somewhat dated, this work remains useful for study of the issue of access.

Collective Bargaining

71. *Collective Bargaining in Higher Education and the Professions.* New York: National Center for the Study of Collective Bargaining in Higher Education, 1973-   . Annual. ISSN 0738-1913.
A selective, classified guide to hundreds of books, articles, speeches, dissertations, research reports, and other published and unpublished works. This is a major source for the researcher and practitioner in the field. With its changing emphasis and coverage, and topics added and dropped, this annual publication serves as a barometer of major issues and events over the years. Unannotated entries are arranged in two major parts: Part I covers the faculty, while Part II covers the professions and professionals. Another part lists selected reference sources, periodicals, and organizations. Includes both author and subject indexes.

72. Marks, Kenneth E. *Collective Bargaining in U.S. Higher Education; 1960-1971: A Selective Bibliography.* (Series in Bibliography, no. 1) Ames: Iowa State Univ. Library, 1972. 64p.
Surveys the literature of labor negotiations related to the faculty in higher education. Works are included that provide a history of collective bargaining and the evaluation of the laws governing labor relations. Included are about four hundred books, articles, ERIC documents, statutory citations and court decisions. Selectively, briefly annotated. Access is provided by means of a topical table of contents. No index.

73. Wayne State University, Detroit. Archives of Labor and Urban Affairs. *An American Federation of Teachers Bibliography.* Detroit: Wayne State Univ. Pr., 1980. 222p. ISBN 0-8143-1659-X.
A guide to material on the history and development of the AFT from its founding in 1916 to 1979. The 1,475 entries and their brief descriptive annotations are grouped by type of source: books, articles, dissertations and theses, selected AFT documents and lastly, archival materials held in the Archives of Labor and Urban Affairs (AFT's official depository) and other research collections. AFT's activities in higher education are well represented. Topical index included.

Community Colleges

74. Boss, Richard and Anderson, Roberta. *Community/Junior College: A Bibliography.* 2d ed. Corvallis: Division of Continuing Education of the Oregon State System of Higher Education, 1967. 184p.
Updates an earlier bibliography designed for use by students of the developing field of the community/junior college movement. The entries have been selected mainly from material published after 1956, and higher education in general has been omitted. The table of contents lists twelve subject areas and four categories of materials cited. An author index constitutes the sixteenth chapter.

75. Burnett, Collins W. *The Community Junior College: An Annotated Bibliography with Introductions for School Counselors.* Columbus: Ohio
State Univ., 1968. 122p.
Provides information to high-school counselors, admissions personnel,
faculty, administrators in the community college, admissions counselors
in four-year colleges and universities, and graduate students in order
to overcome hostility and ignorance about the significance of the
community-junior college in higher education. The articles included are
said to be the "best published" between 1961 and 1967. Each chapter is
introduced by an interpretative discussion of its material. There are
no indexes. There is a table of contents with subheadings.

76. Cohen, Arthur M., Palmer, James C. and Zwemer, Diane K. *Key
Resources on Community Colleges.* San Francisco: Jossey-Bass, 1986.
522p. ISBN 1-55542-020-6.
An annotated guide to the "major literature that has contributed to the
field over the past twenty years," represented in more than 680 books,
monographs, articles, and reports. Fifty or so works considered
"seminal" are marked for ready access. There are thirteen chapters, the
first of which provides a brief introduction to the history, development,
and literature of the community college. The last chapter identifies
additional selection aids. The middle chapters form the bibliography,
ranging in topics from students, faculty, governance and administration,
to remediation, occupational education, and the college function. This
is a major work designed for community college faculty and adminis-
strators, as well as students of higher education. In addition to
appendices listing community college journals and reference works, there
are both author and subject indexes.

77. Conley, William H. and Bertalan, Frank J. *Significant Literature
of the Junior College, 1941-1948: An Annotated Bibliography.* Washington, D.C.: American Association of Junior Colleges, 1949. 40p.
Includes 212 items divided into three categories: articles, doctoral
dissertations, books and pamphlets. Now dated, but of use to those
interested in the community-college movement during the post-World War
II period. An index is arranged under twenty-two general topics with
entries in alphabetical order by author under the respective topics.

78. Eells, Walter Crosby. *Bibliography on Junior Colleges.* (Office of
Education, Bulletin 1930, no. 2) Washington, D.C.: U.S. Department
of the Interior, Office of Education, 1930. 167p.
An annotated guide to about sixteen hundred published and unpublished
works, including books, journal articles, selected master's theses and
doctoral dissertations, and other sources. More than half of these
appeared from 1927 through 1929. Most items cover junior colleges in
California. This work is cited for its comprehensive coverage and, thus,
its value to the scholar and student of the junior-college movement.
Includes subject index.

79. Engleman, Lois E. and Eells, Walter Crosby. *Literature of Junior
College Terminal Education.* Washington, D.C.: American Assn. of
Junior Colleges, 1941. 322p.
Annotated and classified bibliography of more than fourteen hundred
citations covering the years from 1900 to 1940. Emphasis is on
publications of the 1930s. Source titles and annotations provide a
glimpse of the major issues and trends associated with the early phases
of this significant aspect of the junior college movement. Ten chapters
cover a broad range of subjects, from organization and administration to
guidance and personnel services, the library, faculty, and the

curriculum. Includes a general index to names, sources, and subjects.

80. Keller, Rosemary Henderson and Anderson, Kenneth E. *An Annotated Bibliography of Books and Monographs Pertaining to the Community/ Junior College*. Lawrence: Univ. of Kansas, 1977. 94p.
Provides historical treatment of the subject from before 1945, while covering the period through 1965 and after. This is one of the few sources that includes references to libraries and learning resource centers. No index.

81. Morrison, D.G. and Martorana, S.V. *The 2-Year Community College: An Annotated List of Studies and Surveys*. (U.S. office of Education Bulletin 1958, no. 4) Washington, D.C.: U.S. Dept. of Health, Education and Welfare, Office of Education, 1958. 33p.
Lists 208 studies, mostly theses, dissertations and unpublished reports, completed since 1953 or still in progress. Books on community colleges and projects reported in the periodical literature are not included. Entries are grouped under broad subject areas and briefly annotated. There is also a brief subject index to the completed projects.

82. Morrison, D.G., Brunner, Ken August and Martorana, S.V. *The 2-Year Community College: An Annotated List of Unpublished Studies and Surveys, 1957-61*. (U.S. office of Education Bulletin 1963, no. 28) Washington, D.C.: U.S. Dept. of Health, Education and Welfare, Office of Education, 1963. 41p.
Continues the 1958 work by the authors. The present work covers studies completed or underway from 1957 to mid-1961. Unpublished dissertations are now not included since they are accessible through <u>Doctoral Dissertations</u>. Of limited value, but useful in the documentation of research and scholarship about community colleges in the U.S. Indexes by subject and by author or study director.

83. Padfield, William T. *A Bibliography of Selected Publications Related to Junior College Education*. Sacramento: California State Dept. of Education, 1965. 75p.
Includes articles from sixty-five journals published from 1950 to the mid-1960s. Annotations are grouped into five parts identifying evaluation, grading practices, motivation, learning theories, and counseling. A list of Journals is provided. Index not included.

84. Parker, Franklin and Bailey, Anne. *The Junior and Community College: A Bibliography of Doctoral Dissertations, 1918-1963*. Washington, D.C.: American Assn. of Junior Colleges, 1965. 47p.
A classified, unannotated guide to more than six hundred dissertations. Thirteen subject sections range from administration and history to instructional programs, staff, and student personnel services. Includes a brief list of sources consulted and separate author and subject indexes.

85. Rarig, Emory W. *The Community Junior College - An Annotated Bibliography*. New York: Columbia Univ. Teachers College Pr., 1966. 114p.
This source arose from the need to identify publications in the community junior college field when Columbia University established a program for training of administrators for these colleges in 1960. It traces the history, function, organization, students, programs, facilities and personnel. Approximately three hundred books and journal articles are included. Author index is provided.

86. University Microfilms International. *Dissertations Relating to Community, Junior, and Two-Year Colleges.* Ann Arbor, Mich.: Univ. Microfilms Int., 1975. 41p.
An unannotated list of more than two thousand doctoral dissertations accepted by North American universities since 1938. Dissertations are listed alphabetically by author under twenty-six general subject categories. Each entry includes the full title, degree earned, granting institution, date of degree, number of text pages, citation to *Dissertation Abstracts International*, and the University Microfilms purchase order number. No index.

Comparative Education

87. Altbach, Philip G. *Comparative Higher Education.* (ERIC/Higher Education Research Report no. 5) Washington, D. C.: American Association for Higher Education, 1973. 81p.
This work is in two parts: Part 1 consists of an essay on some key areas of comparative higher education research and analysis, and on the value of a comparative perspective in the discussion of U.S. higher education. Of special interest is the focus on higher education reform, a major issue of the 1960s and 1970s. Part 2 provides an unannotated biblio-graphy of more than eighteen hundred citations to books, articles and reports published chiefly during the 1960s and 1970s. Emphasis is on cross-cultural materials of interest to American readers. Bibliography entries are in alphabetical order by author. Lack of an index or table of contents hampers access.

88. Altbach, Philip G. and Kelly, David H. *Higher Education in Inter-national Perspective: A Survey and Bibliography.* London: Mansell Publishing, 1985. 583p. ISBN 0-7201-1707-0.
A classified, unannotated bibliography of nearly seven thousand entries, including books, articles, and doctoral dissertations. It is strongest on materials published in North America. Worldwide in coverage, it in-cludes items for the years 1970 through 1983. There are twenty-three subject chapters, ranging in coverage from access and history to reform, teaching, and theories of higher education. The work is supplemented by two essays: one providing discussion and analysis of the development of research in an international context, while the second covers research on higher education in European socialist countries. Access is by means of a detailed table of contents. Lacks an index.

89. Berdahl, Robert O. and Altomare, George. *Comparative Higher Edu-cation: Sources of Information.* (Occasional Paper no. 4) New York: International Council for Educational Development, 1972. 115p.
Brings together sources of material on comparative higher education which are both inside and outside the field of education. Five sections list relevant journals, abstracts, indexes, bibliographies, organizational publications, and centers and associations of higher education around the world. Content analysis is given for the twelve English-language journals in the first section. Four appendices provide mailing addresses for the listings in the last four sections.

90. Bristow, Thelma and Holmes, Brian. *Comparative Education Through the Literature: A Bibliographic Guide.* Hamden, Conn.: Shoe String Pr., 1968. 181p.
A selective bibliography "primarily intended for librarians and lecturers in university departments and colleges of education". Items include only works in English. The United States is included throughout the volume

within various subject headings (imaginative writing and comparative education, national area studies in comparative education, cross-cultural and case studies, library tools and research in comparative education). Includes a person-title index and a subject index.

91. Lulat, Y. G.-M., Altbach, Philip G. and Kelly, David H. *Governmental and Institutional Policies on Foreign Students: Analysis, Evaluation and Bibliography.* (Special Studies in Comparative Education no. 16) Buffalo: Comparative Education Center, Faculty of Educational Studies, State Univ. of New York at Buffalo, 1986. 114p. ISBN 0-937033-05-7.
Focuses on the development of policy relating to foreign students by governments and institutions of higher education in two parts: An "extensive essay that provides an evaluatory overview, from a comparative perspective;" and a classified, unannotated bibliography of 388 citations to books, articles, and other reports. A separate, unannotated bibliography of 108 citations follows the essay. The work supplements the authors' Research on Foreign Students and International Study: An Overview and Bibliography (Praeger, 1985).

92. Nitsch, Wolfgang and Weller, Walter. *Social Science Research on Higher Education and Universities: Part II: Annotated Bibliography.* (Confluence; Surveys of Research in the Social Sciences, vol. 10) The Hague: Mouton, 1970. 802p.
This classified guide to more than eight thousand book and periodical citations forms part of a three-volume work of the International Committee For Social Sciences Documentation. Other parts are: Part I: Trend Report (Confluence 9), and Part III: Supplement. This bibliography emphasizes the "socio-economic, historical and socio-cultural conditions and foundations, and the basic structure of higher education and universities" world wide. Sources are arranged in seven chapters covering reference works, historical and interpretative studies, sociological and interdisciplinary empirical research economics, law and government, sociographic survey research and statistics and social psychiatry. Sources are arranged in a regional classification system, with a regional index. Lacks additional indexing.

93. Von Klemperer, Lily. *International Education: A Directory of Resource Materials on Comparative Education and Study in Another Country.* Garrett Park, Md.: Garrett Park Pr., 1973. 202p. ISBN 912048-09-3
The author, an authority in this field, presents citations to more than thirteen hundred items. Entries are grouped in two sections, the first including descriptive and comparative works arranged geographically, the second focusing on issues related to international students. While not limited to higher education, this work includes much that is relevant. An author index and broad subject index are provided.

Economic Factors

94. Blaug, Mark. *Economics of Education: A Selected Annotated Bibliography.* 3d ed. (Series in Library and Information Science) Elmsford, N.Y.: Pergamon Pr., 1978. 421p. ISBN 0-08-020627-1.
Includes nearly two thousand items to September 1975, and deals with education as it impacts on economics and is affected by economics. The book consists of two parts dealing separately with developed and developing countries. Includes coverage of U.S. higher education, but lacks access according to educational levels. Items within each chapter

are arranged alphabetically by author within annual groupings. Indexes of authors, continents and countries (other than U.S. and U.K.). Lacks a subject index.

95. Frank, Ira Stephen. *Economic Impact of Institutions of Higher Education on Local Communities: An Annotated Bibliography.* Berkeley: Univ. of California, Systemwide Administration, 1976. 99p.

A guide to seventy-four published and unpublished reports and studies covering the period 1958 to 1974. Includes books, articles, theses, and local, state, and federal reports. The first section provides information on the distribution of faculty, staff and student spending (includes tables). Three following sections comprise the bibliography, covering general background studies, special purpose studies, and general economic impact studies. This brief but useful source includes three indexes: names; institutions; and states, regions, and cities.

96. Hines, Edward R. and McCarthy, John R. *Higher Education Finance: An Annotated Bibliography and Guide to Research.* (Garland Bibliography in Contemporary Education, vol. 4) New York: Garland Publishing, 1985. 357p. ISBN 0-8240-9054-3.

Covers nearly one thousand citations to works appearing from 1970 to June 1983. Books, journal articles, reports, and other studies were selected if they were found in university library catalogs, or were found in the computer-accessed ERIC database. Eight chapters cover topics from general trends and economics, government support, and institutional development to fiscal planning and reductions and retrenchments. Author and subject indexes are included.

97. Hufner, Klaus, Hummel, Thomas R. and Rau, Einhard. *Efficiency in Higher Education: An Annotated Bibliography.* (Okonomische Theorie der Hochschule, band 2) New York: Verlag Peter Lang, 1987. 340p. ISBN 3-8204-1501-7.

A guide to 1,354 publications on the internal economics of higher education. Only sources published from 1960 through 1985, in English and German (with English annotations), are cited, including monographs, articles in journals and in collected volumes, and contributions with no identifiable single author or editor. A substantial number of sources include American imprints. It is divided into seven chapters, covering the following: inputs and outputs, costs and returns, productivity, cost-benefits, and cost-effectiveness and analysis. There are also chapters on business administration and efficiency, and cost and performance indicators. A concluding chapter describes bibliographies and other sources. Includes an author index.

98. Powel, John H. and Lamson, Robert D. *An Annotated Bibliography of Literature Relating to the Costs and Benefits of Graduate Education.* Washington, D.C.: Council of Graduate Schools, 1972. 59p.

Annotations are grouped under Behavioral Models, Planning and Budgeting, Finance of Higher Education, and General References. The approximately two hundred items include unpublished materials and commission reports. Includes an author index. Dated, but here included as this work contributes to the body of publications dealing with the cost-benefits question.

99. Quay, Richard H. and Olevnik, Peter P. *The Financing of American Higher Education: A Bibliographic Handbook.* Phoenix, Ariz.: Oryx, Pr., 1984. 142p. ISBN 0-89774-047-5.

Documents the principal issues and trends in the published scholarship on the financing of American higher education. Included are more than one thousand annotated source citations for publications from 1960 through 1981. The work is organized around four general topics divided into nineteen chapters covering such subjects as federal and state support; private versus public institutions; financial issues; faculty workload; students as consumers of higher education; and development, operation, and maintenance of the physical plant. Two appendices include related bibliographic sources and financial data sources. Includes author and subject indexes.

100. Wittstruck, John R. *Comparative Data About Higher Education: A Resource Directory*. Denver, Colo.: State Higher Education Executive Officers, 1986. 66p.
Lists fifty sources of comparative data of use at the state or regional level. The various surveys, reports and compilations are grouped in ten sections that cover such areas as: state appropriations and expenditures, salaries, tuition and fees, financial aid, finances, taxes. Annotations range from one-half to two pages and include contact and purchase information as well as descriptions of the data provided. Access is through a detailed table of contents only.

History

101. Beach, Mark. *A Bibliographic Guide to American Colleges and Universities: From Colonial Times to the Present*. Westport, Conn.: Greenwood Pr., 1975. 314p. ISBN 0-8371-7690-5.
Brings together works relating to the history of specific institutions to provide both access to the material for interested persons and a subject guide to the historical writing about higher education in the United States. Identifying works from the nineteenth century through the early 1970s, the 2,806 sources cited describe the growth of the institutions, persons associated with the institutions, and other matters. The cited books, journals, and dissertations are organized alphabetically by state and then by institutions within the state. A general index concludes the work.

102. Beach, Mark. *A Subject Bibliography of the History of American Higher Education*. Westport, Conn.: Greenwood Pr., 1984. 165p. ISBN 0-313-23276-8.
A companion volume to the author's Bibliographic Guide to American Colleges and Universities (Greenwood, 1975). Its scope is limited to historical writing over the last five decades, excluding, in the main journalism, polemics, and autobiography. The bibliography of 1,325 items is organized by topic with cross-references to both the initial volume and the present one. An author index and a subject index complete the work.

103. Beauchamp, Edward R. *Dissertations in the History of Education 1970-1980*. Metuchen, N.J.: Scarecrow Pr., 1985. 259p.
Extracts from Dissertation Abstracts International materials on the history of education so that the historian of education may have access not only to those works subsumed under that classification but also those relevant works to be found under other headings (more than half of those discovered). Items, published and unpublished, in the chosen period are cited alphabetically by author in each of the sub-sections of eight chapters designating geographical areas of the world. A subject index provides access to the more than twenty-four hundred numbered citations,

almost seventy-five percent of which are found in the chapter relating to the United States.

104. Brookhart, Edward. *Music in American Higher Education: An Annotated Bibliography* (Bibliographies in American Music, no. 10). Warren, Mich.: Harmonie Park Pr. 1980. 245p. ISBN 0-89990-042-9.
Compiles materials on the history of music in American higher education. This selective work is designed to give an "overall impression" of the topic from ca. 1830 to 1985. The work excludes archival materials, but references to such sources are noted in the preface. Most of the thirteen hundred items are annotated. Materials are organized under eight headings (each with a brief introduction), and further topical subdivisions. Access is provided by a table of contents, an author index, and a subject index.

105. Chambers, Merritt Madison. *A Brief Bibliography of Higher Education in the Middle Nineteen Sixties.* Bloomington: School of Education, Indiana Univ., 1966. 52p. (In: Bulletin of the School of Education of Indiana University vol. 42, no. 5, Sept. 1966.)
Addresses the need for knowledge of higher education generally with emphasis on administrative and financial aspects. Entries, numbering more than six hundred, cover literature of the middle-1960s, with earlier standard books noted. The list is divided into twelve categories, including two-year colleges. There are both topical and author indexes.

106. Cordasco, Francesco, Alloway, David N. and Friedman, Marjorie Scilken. *History of American Education: A Guide to Information Sources.* (Education Information Guide Series, vol. 7) Detroit: Gale Research, 1979. 313p. ISBN 0-8103-1382-0.
Covers about twenty-five hundred books and periodical articles. In addition to reference works, other sections cover source citations to historiography; the American college and university; the expansion of American education; teachers, teaching, textbooks, and curriculum; and numerous other topics. The authors include a significant number of citations related to higher education. Topics range from accreditation and philanthropy, to textbooks and women in higher education. Includes some brief annotations. Separate author, title, and subject indexes are included.

107. Cordasco, Francesco and Brickman, William W. *A Bibliography of American Educational History: An Annotated and Classified Guide.* New York: AMS Pr., 1975. 394p. ISBN 0-404-12661-8.
Includes about three thousand citations to books, articles, government publications and other documents. Sources are arranged into twenty-one chapters, divided into three sections. Section 1 covers bibliographies, encyclopedias, collections of sources, historiographics, and comprehensive histories. Section 2 is divided into thirteen subject chapters covering educational levels, the connection between church or state and education, women, biographies, foreign influences, and contemporary issues. Section 3 arranges sources according to historical periods, from the Colonial era to the twentieth century. In addition to a chapter on higher education, the field is represented in a number of other chapters. Includes a detailed table of contents and an author index.

108. Durnin, Richard G. *American Education: A Guide to Information Sources.* (American Studies Information Guide Series, vol. 14) Detroit: Gale Research, 1982. 247p. ISBN 0-8103-1265-4.
A selected, classified guide to about fifteen hundred books recording the

history and development of American education. Source citations extend
in publication dates from the seventeenth century to the late 1970s. An
especially interesting section of bibliographic essays traces the history
of education from Roger Ascham's The Scholemaster (London, 1570) to the
Carnegie Commission on Higher Education's publication Priorities for
Action (New York, 1973). Provides a substantial listing of sources in
higher education, including sections on general historical works by state
and by major institutions. Includes both a lengthy contents listing of
more than one hundred subject sections and a separate name index.

109. Eells, Walter Crosby. *Survey of American Higher Education*. New
      York: Carnegie Foundation for the Advancement of Teaching, 1937.
      538p.
Provides critical analysis of 578 surveys of higher education in the
United States appearing after 1900. Emphasis is on 230 published
reports, while 70 mimeographed surveys and another 278 typed documents
are considered. Eleven chapters analyze the surveys according to their
classification, techniques, methods of presentation, contents and
results, and a number of other factors. Appendices include a listing of
institutions surveyed, agencies conducting the studies, cost factors, and
a bibliography of surveys of higher education. Of special interest to
those concerned with turn-of-the-century American higher education is an
annotated list of the surveys (printed, mimeographed, and in manuscript
form). Also includes a detailed topical index to the surveys.

110. Fusonie, Alan and Jacobs, Marilyn. *Land-Grant Colleges: A
      Selective Historical Bibliography and Legislative Chronology*.
      Beltsville, Md.: Historical Program, National Agricultural Library,
      1983. 26p.
A selective guide to 137 books, articles, and documents (published 1858-
1982), and a legislative chronology, relating to the historical
development of land-grant colleges. Some items include brief
annotations. For the student of higher education or others interested
in this milestone of U.S. higher education. No index.

111. Herbst, Jurgen. *A History of American Education*. (Goldentree
      Bibliographies in American History) Northbrook, Ill.: AHM Pubns.,
      1973. 153p.
A selective, classified, unannotated guide to about twenty-five hundred
books and articles. Coverage extends from the Colonial Period to the
crisis of the 1960s. Chapters begin with general works and continue by
historical periods. Among an array of topics, each chapter includes a
section on higher education. The table of contents provides subject
access. An author index is included.

112. McCarthy, Joseph M. *An International List of Articles on the
      History of Education Published in Non-Educational Serials, 1965-
      1974*. New York: Garland Publishing, 1977. 228p. ISBN 0-8240-
      9909-5.
An unannotated bibliography of more than twenty-eight hundred entries,
with citations arranged by country, and, under each, by author. Among
sources searched for citations were America: History and Life (Clio Pr.)
and the American Historical Review (Macmillan). The section covering the
United States includes nearly one thousand entries, many of which are
related to the history of American higher education. Includes an author
index.

113. Park, Joe. *The Rise of American Education: An Annotated
      Bibliography*. Evanston, Ill.: Northwestern Univ. Press, 1965.

216p.
A selective guide to about nine hundred books and other items on the history of American education. Eleven sections cover such topics as European backgrounds, studies in the development of education, and biographies. One section is devoted to higher education. Two other units cite dissertations and reference works. A special feature is the list of sources found in the American Antiquarian Society microprint collection.   Made available through the Readex Corporation, the collection contains texts of books, pamphlets and broadsides published in America from 1639 to 1800. An important source for the student and scholar. Brief outline of section contents is the only means of access. Does not include an index.

114. Sedlak, Michael W. and Walch, Timothy. *American Educational History: A Guide to Information Sources*. (American Government and History Information Guide Series, vol. 10) Detroit: Gale Research, 1981.   265p.   ISBN 0-8103-1478-9.
Intended more for the undergraduate or generalist than for the historian, this work includes a forty-page chapter specifically on higher education. Though references to significant older works are included, most items date from the early 1960s onward, and the majority are provided with brief evaluative annotations. While the higher education section of this work cannot be as comprehensive as book-length compilations, the authors claim to have sought out especially items that had not been listed in other sources. Author and subject indexes.

115. Songe, Alice H. *The Land-Grant Idea in American Higher Education: A Guide to Information Sources*. New York: K.G. Saur, 1980. 62p. ISBN 0-89664-272-0.
A revision of a 1962 bibliography by the author, this work is a selective listing of sources on the background and development of the federal land-grant program and schools.   The six hundred unannotated entries are arranged alphabetically and include books, articles, government and congressional materials, theses and dissertations from the mid-1800s on. Some general histories of the U.S. and of U.S. higher education are included for context and background. A subject index and a list of the land-grant institutions are appended.

116. Sparks, Linda. *Institutions of Higher Education: An International Bibliography*. (Bibliographies and Indexes in Education, no. 9) Westport, Conn.: Greenwood Pr., 1990. 470p. ISBN 0-313-26686-7.
An unannotated compilation of books, booklets, theses, dissertations and ERIC documents (though no ED numbers are given) on the histories of individual post-secondary institutions of all types.   Entries are arranged by country, with references given in their original languages. Although the author's intention is to create a comprehensive source, worldwide in scope, some 280 pages of this work are devoted to U.S. institutions, making it very useful for researching American higher education. Author and subject (i.e., institution) indexes are provided.

117. United States. Office of Education. *Bibliography of Publications of the United States Office of Education, 1867-1959*. Totowa, N.J.: Rowman and Littlefield, 1971. pp. 57, 158, 157. ISBN 0-87471-011-1.
A valuable record of the history and development of education in the United States, covering all educational levels. This reprint brings together three separate lists of publications divided by period of coverage: Part 1: 1867-1910 (U.S. Bureau of Education Bulletin no. 3, 1910); Part 2: 1910-1936 (U.S. Bureau of Education, Bulletin no. 22,

1937); Part 3 (U.S. Office of Education, Bulletin no. 3, 1960). Each part "has been cumulated to make for easy chronological review," and includes a separate author and subject index. The index for Part 2 is divided into two sections; one covers U.S. Office of Education publications, while the other covers publications included from the Federal Board for Vocational Education (1917-1933), and the Vocational Division of the Office of Education (1933-1936). Long out of print, these lists provide an invaluable resource and research tool.

118. Young, Arthur P. *Higher Education in American Life, 1636-1986: Bibliography of Dissertations and Theses.* (Bibliographies and Indexes in Education, no. 5) New York: Greenwood Pr., 1988. 431p. ISBN 0-313-24352-8.
Brings together references to 4,570 items of an historical nature on American higher education. The entries are unannotated except for brief biographical notes when the subject is a person. The work is in two parts: the first groups items related to individual institutions by state and then by institution. The second organizes topical works into sixty-nine subject categories. Both author and detailed subject indexes are also provided. The author has succeeded admirably in achieving his goal of increased access to this literature.

119. Zubatsky, David S. *The History of American Colleges and Their Libraries in the Seventeenth and Eighteenth Centuries: A Bibliographical Essay.* (Occasional Papers no. 140) Urbana, Ill.: Univ. of Illinois, Graduate School of Library Science, 1979. 66p.
In essay format, citing books, doctoral dissertations, articles, and other reports representing approximately six hundred authors. An introductory survey covers Higher Education in Colonial and Early National America, with coverage by source type (i.e., bibliographical guides, biographies, readings, etc.), and by topic (religious education, college selection, student life, etc.); General Library History, and Early American College Libraries. A second survey covers nine individual colleges. Two others focus on colleges founded after the Revolutionary War, and Undergraduate Literary Society Libraries to 1800. This is followed by a concluding essay and a list of authors covered. Access is by means of the table of contents. Lacks an index.

Institutional Advancement

120. Constantine, Karen Krall. *Annotated and Extended Bibliography of Higher Education Marketing.* Chicago: American Marketing Association, 1986. 71p. ISBN 0-87757-184-8.
A useful guide to more than two hundred books, reports, and articles on such marketing functions as audits and pricing, coupled with marketing applications from admissions to public relations. Coverage extends from 1980 through the summer of 1985. Entries are in alphabetical order. An elaborate coding system arranges sources according to marketing function and area of higher education. Two indexes provide entry number codes with subject codes according to either of the two major categories mentioned above.

121. Muller, Leo Claude. *Selected Bibliography on the Advancement and Support of Higher Education.* 2d ed. Washington, D.C.: American College Public Relations Assn., 1962. 68p.
A wide-ranging survey of literature useful for practitioners in the field, this work lists about two hundred books, reports and government publications, mostly from the previous ten years. Entries are briefly

annotated and some are coded to indicate level of treatment. Arrangement is by broad subject areas: nature and financing of higher education, fund raising, public relations, and communications. A separate section for booklets and addresses is also arranged by these topics. Three concluding sections list reference works and bibliographies, pertinent periodicals, and organizations. No indexes.

122.   Pride, Cletis.   *Securing Support for Higher Education: A Bibliographical Handbook.* New York: Praeger Pubs. 1972. 403p.
Provides access to more than seventeen hundred sources including articles published from 1966 through mid-1971; relevant books, regardless of publication date; and other selected materials. Arranged in four parts: a key-word or topic index; a selected, annotated bibliography of books, articles and other documents judged to be of "fundamental value"; an alphabetical key-word-in-context index; and a final bibliography arranged by author.   Dated but useful to those engaged in institutional advancement.

123.   Rowland, A. Westley. *Key Resources on Institutional Advancement: A Guide to the Field and its Literature.* (Jossey-Bass Higher Education Series) San Francisco: Jossey-Bass, 1986. 251p. ISBN 1-55542-014-1.
The author, a longtime practitioner in the field, begins this work with an overview of institutional advancement. Subsequent chapters provide lengthily annotated lists of significant works in the field, starting with basic resources. Other chapters cover areas such as fund raising, government relations, publications, two-year and independent colleges, and legal considerations. A separate, annotated list of periodicals in the field is provided, as well as name and subject indexes.

124.   Rowland, A. Westley. *Research in Institutional Advancement: A Selected, Annotated Compendium of Doctoral Dissertations.* Washington, D.C.: Council for Advancement and Support of Education, 1983. 136p. ISBN 0-89964-215-2.
This thoroughly researched compilation includes 2,609 items which range in date from the 1920s to the early eighties. Entries are arranged by author within six major subject sections: institutional relations, educational fund raising, alumni administration, government relations, publications and executive management. Two final unannotated sections list additional dissertations and a selection of master's theses. No indexes.

125.   Ryans, Cynthia and Shanklin, William L. *Strategic Planning, Marketing and Public Relations, and Fund-Raising in Higher Education: Perspectives, Readings and Annotated Bibliography.* Metuchen, N.J.: Scarecrow, Pr., 1986. 266p.
Authors' emphasis is on currency (nothing before 1979 is included) and immediate usefulness to administrators. The work is arranged in three chapters corresponding to the topics in the title. Each chapter includes the authors' overview of the topic ("Perspectives"), reprints of selected articles, with references, and a selected list of books and articles. Separate author/title and subject indexes are provided, along with a directory of publishers/associations and their publications.

Minority Groups and Women

126.   Bengelsdorf, Winnie. *Ethnic Studies in Higher Education: State of the Art and Bibliography.* Washington, D.C.: American Association

of State Colleges and Universities, 1972. 260p.
Based on material collected in 1972, from over two hundred higher education institutions, ethnic associations, government agencies, publishers, and libraries. The project sought to "identify and summarize recent material on Ethnic Studies in higher education and to determine the state of the art or trend of these studies". Each ethnic group (Black, Asian-American, Chicano, Indian, Puerto Rican and other Spanish-speaking groups, white ethnic groups (designations are the author's) has a chapter which is subdivided into categories, which include research, sources, bibliography, and institutional listings. Author index, title index, as well as access to subjects through the table of contents.

127.   Brown, Charles I. and Speller, Benjamin F. *Desegregation and the White Presence on the Black Campus: A Bibliography for Researchers.* (ID/IRG Monograph, no. 80-1) Durham: Institute on Desegregation, North Carolina Central Univ., 1980. 46p.
Brings together research and related literature from the social and behavioral sciences addressing the question of the white presence, particularly the white student, and the problems of desegregation on traditionally Black campuses. Most entries were published after 1954, and some are annotated. The six major chapters are subdivided according to publication type. The table of contents provides the only access to the material.

128.   Chambers, Frederick. *Black Higher Education in the United States-A Selected Bibliography on Negro Higher Education and Historically Black Colleges and Universities.* Westport, Conn.: Greenwood Pr., 1978. 268p. ISBN 0-313-20037-8.
Gathers extensive references on the subject, selected basically from generally available sources. More than three thousand items cover the years 1857-1976. The citations, which are not annotated, are organized into six chapters: dissertations, institutional histories, periodical literature, masters' theses, selected books and general references, and other miscellaneous items. Citations are organized alphabetically by author, with the exceptions of institutional histories, which are listed geographically and by institution, and the miscellaneous items, which are separated into various categories, such as autobiographies, biographies, and reports. Includes a general index.

129.   Donovan, Mary. *Sex Discrimination in Higher Education and the Professions: An Annotated Bibliography.* New York: National Center for the Study of Collective Bargaining in Higher Education and the Professions, Baruch College of the City Univ. of New York, 1989. 32p. ISBN 0-911259-25-2.
Includes 124 citations to monographs and articles appearing in professional journals from 1984 through 1988. Citations are arranged according to four chapter topics: compensation and pensions, hiring practices, promotions, and the work environment. Includes an author index.

130.   Farley, Jennie. *Academic Women and Employment Discrimination: A Critical Annotated Bibliography.* (Cornell Industrial and Labor Relations Bibliography Series, no. 16) Ithaca: New York State School of Industrial and Labor Relations, Cornell Univ., 1982. 103p. ISBN 0-87546-092-5.
Describes 179 items mostly published from the mid-1970s to the early 1980s. Emphasis is on professional journal articles and books, but also includes newspaper articles, newsletters, other periodicals and study

reports. The author has included summaries of fifty court decisions, covering 1971 to 1981. A brief general index concludes the work.

131. Franzosa, Susan Douglas and Mazza, Karen A. *Integrating Women's Studies into the Curriculum: An Annotated Bibliography.* (Bibliographies and Indexes in Education, no. 1) Westport, Conn.: Greenwood Pr., 1984. 100p. ISBN 0-313-24482-0.
A compilation of briefly annotated references to more than five hundred selected books and articles, mostly from 1976-1983. Entries are arranged in nine chapters, the first listing bibliographic resources, the second works on Women's Studies in the curriculum generally. The remaining chapters list works related to major disciplinary areas, such as literature, science and technology, and fine arts. Author index, but no subject index.

132. Harmon, Linda A. *Status of Women in Higher Education: 1963-1972; A Selective Bibliography.* Ames: Iowa State Univ., 1972. 124p.
Women, in this annotated guide, refers to women faculty and staff, administrators, librarians, and students. More than five hundred sources are listed, including books, articles, as well as ERIC documents, government publications, dissertations, and other miscellaneous sources. The author concludes with texts of selected major documents concerning women's rights. While there is no index, entries are coded as they relate to seventeen general topics outlined in the table of contents.

133. Kelly, David H. *Women in Higher Education: A Select International Bibliography.* (Special Studies in Comparative Education, no. 25) Buffalo: Comparative Education Center, Graduate School of Education Publications, State Univ. of New York at Buffalo, 1990. 64p. ISBN 0-937033-15-4.
Over five hundred unannotated references to scholarly books and articles published in the eighties are arranged by author in twenty-seven topic sections. North American materials are more heavily represented than those of Europe, Asia and Africa. No indexes.

134. Krichmar, Albert. *Women's Movement in the Seventies: An International English-Language Bibliography.* Metuchen, N.J.: Scarecrow, Pr., 1977. 875p. ISBN 0-8108-1063-8.
A partially annotated bibliography of articles, books, reports and dissertations on the status of women internationally. Of the eighty-six hundred items cited, fifty-eight relate to women in higher education in the United States. The arrangement by countries renders this a useful source for comparative study. Includes an author index and a comprehensive subject index.

135. McGee, Leo and Neufeldt, Harvey G. *Education of the Black Adult in the United States: An Annotated Bibliography.* Westport, Conn.: Greenwood Pr., 1985. 108p. ISBN 0-313-23473-6.
Traces the history in four periods: pre-Civil War 1619-1860, Civil War and Reconstruction 1860-1880, 1880-1930, and the Modern Era from 1930 and beyond. Some 367 books and articles and dissertations are cited. An important source for the history of Black adult education, with some coverage of higher education. Includes both author and subject indexes.

136. Moore, Kathryn and Wollitzer, Peter A. *Women in Higher Education: A Contemporary Bibliography.* Washington, D.C.: National Assn. of Women Deans, Administrators, and Counselors, 1979. 114p.
Summarizes the scholarship on women's roles and experiences in academia during most of the 1970s (i.e., 1970-1977). Includes women admin-

istrators, faculty and students.   Emphasis is on discrimination.   A
special feature is the listing of ERIC publications by states. Includes
an author index.

137. Parker, Franklin and Parker, Betty June. *Women's Education - A
      World View: Annotated Bibliography of Doctoral Dissertations.*
      Westport, Conn.: Greenwood Pr., 1979. 470p. ISBN 0-313-20891-3.
Over two thousand dissertations are selected from sixteen sources and the
library of the University of California at Berkeley.   Entries are
alphabetical by author with brief annotations. Major emphasis is on the
United States, with extensive coverage of subjects such as higher
education, history of women's education, women faculty, nursing
education, physical education, sex differences and sex roles. Includes
a subject index.

138. Swanson, Kathryn. *Affirmative Action and Preferential Admissions
      in Higher Education: An Annotated Bibliography.* Metuchen, N.J.:
      Scarecrow Pr., 1981. 336p. ISBN 0-8108-1411-0.
Written as a guide to the literature since 1970 on this controversial
topic in four-year colleges and professional schools, this work gathers
together references to nearly twelve hundred books, articles, government
publications and chapters in collected works.   Entries are grouped in
three sections: The Law and the Courts, The Academic Community Response
and The Philosophical Debate. An analytic essay introduces each section.
Especially useful is an overview of major legislation and regulations.
Name and title indexes are provided.

139. Westervelt, Esther Manning and Fixter, Deborah A. *Women's Higher
      and Continuing Education: An Annotated Bibliography With Selected
      References on Related Aspects of Women's Lives.* New York: College
      Entrance Examination Board, 1971. 67p.
Presents about three hundred book and article references selected for
their currency and quality.   Items are grouped in several chapters
representing broad and somewhat overlapping subtopics (e.g., women's
status, college students, women and employment).   Subject and author
indexes would have been a helpful addition.

140. Wilkins, Kay S. *Women's Education in the United States: A Guide
      to Information Sources.* (Education Information Guide Series, vol.
      4) Detroit: Gale Research, 1979. 217p. ISBN 0-8103-1410-X.
A very useful compilation of selected references to more than eleven
hundred books, articles and ERIC documents with brief descriptive
annotations. Entries are grouped in nineteen topical sections, including
"Higher Education," "Women's Colleges," "Women in Academia," and
"Continuing Education". Most of the materials listed are from the early
1960s through 1978, with items of historical importance drawn from as far
back as the eighteenth century. Author, title and subject indexes are
provided.

       Publishers and Publishing

141. Camp, William L. and Schwark, Bryan L.   *Guide to Periodicals in
      Education and Its Academic Disciplines.* 2d ed. Metuchen, N.J.:
      Scarecrow Pr., 1975. 552p. ISBN 0-8108-0814-5.
A classified, annotated guide to 602 nationally distributed and
education-related periodicals issued in the United States. Within each
subject section, entries are arranged alphabetically by title. Included
are thirty-five titles related specifically to higher education. While

much of the information is dated, this source remains useful to those interested in the history of periodical literature as it relates to education in general and higher education in particular. In addition to subject and title indices, includes a master list of subjects covered.

142. Diener, Thomas J. and Trower, David L. *An Annotated Guide to Periodical Literature: Higher Education.* Athens, Ga.: Institute of Higher Education, Univ. of Georgia, 1969. 35p.
A selected guide to about one hundred nationally or internationally distributed periodicals having higher education as their major focus. Descriptive annotations range from a couple of sentences to a couple of paragraphs in length. While dated, this remains a useful guide to a range of major publications for students and scholars. Includes a title index.

143. Dyer, Thomas and Davis, Margaret. *Higher Education Periodicals: A Directory.* Athens, Ga.: Institute of Higher Education, Univ. of Ga.: 1981. 148p.
An annotated guide to 269 periodicals "which regularly publish articles and other items of interest to higher education professionals, professors, and students." Included are scholarly and professional journals, newsletters of professional associations, magazines, and other related serial publications. Arrangement is alphabetical by periodical name. Entries provide title and former title (where appropriate), sponsoring agencies and publishers, editors and their addresses, descriptions, subscription and circulation information followed by manuscript requirements. Includes an index of titles. A useful source in need of updating.

Students

144. Altbach, Philip G. and Kelly, David H. *American Students: A Selected Bibliography on Student Activism and Related Topics.* Lexington, Mass.: Lexington Bks., 1973. 537p. ISBN 0-669-85100-0.
Provides comprehensive coverage of sources on student political activism, while including selected items on other aspects of student life, from student attitudes and educational reform to minority group students. The work is in two parts: an introductory bibliographic essay followed by brief commentary on cited sources and an extensive bibliography of books, doctoral dissertations and articles. While the bibliography of some nine thousand listings is unannotated, sources are arranged according to a rather extensive array of topics and subtopics. Sources are mainly from the 1960s and early 1970s. This source updates and expands upon Altbach's <u>Student Politics and Higher Education in the United States</u> (1968). While there is no index, sources are accessible via the table of contents.

145. Altbach, Philip G. and Wang, Jing. *Foreign Students and International Study: Bibliography and Analysis, 1984-1989.* New York: Univ. Pr. of America, 1989. 201p. ISBN 0-8191-7371-1.
Includes a short essay discussing current trends in the literature on foreign students and international exchanges, and an annotated bibliography of 519 books, doctoral dissertations and theses, articles, magazine reports, and selected government documents. While international in scope, the large majority of listings are in English. Sources are listed alphabetically, with books and theses covered first and articles following. The bibliography updates the author's <u>Research on Foreign Students and International Study: An Overview and Bibliography</u> (Praeger,

1985). Entries are arranged under thirty-one topics, beginning with a unit covering reference and bibliographic materials. Lacks an index.

146. Altbach, Philip G., Kelly, David H. and Lulat, Y. G.-M. *Research on Foreign Students and International Study: An Overview and Bibliography*. New York: Praeger Pubs., 1985. 403p. ISBN 0-03-071922-4.
A partly annotated bibliography of 2,811 items published in English, French, Spanish, German and Russian. Its exploratory essay provides historical and comparative perspectives on international students and foreign policies. Statistical data are included. The bibliography section has thirty-seven categories, from policy of host countries, legal issues, language problems, and the Eastern bloc to women international students and brain drain. A scope note is given for each category in place of a subject index. This is a valuable resource to policy makers concerned with large numbers of foreign students.

147. Altbach, Philip G. *Student Politics and Higher Education in the United States: A Select Bibliography*. St. Louis, Mo.: United Ministries in Higher Education, 1968. 86p.
Covers materials from the late nineteenth century to July 1968, on the subject of student political activism. More than one thousand items including books and articles (unpublished material and dissertations are excluded), cover, among other topics, the university, the society, sociological and psychological aspects of student activism, radical student politics, and the civil rights movement. The final chapter lists journals published by students or student organizations and those which deal with student issues regularly. No index. Access is by means of a detailed table of contents.

148. American College Testing Program. *An Annotated Bibliography in Student Financial Aid 1960-1973*. Iowa City, Iowa: American College Testing Program, 1974. 98p.
Selects and annotates publications and studies related to the role and practice of student financial aid in post-secondary education. Each of the five chapters listed in the table of contents is subdivided by publication type. There is no index.

149. Aptheker, Bettina. *Higher Education and the Student Rebellion in the United States 1960-1969: A Bibliography*. (Bibliographical Series, no. 6) New York: American Institute for Marxist Studies, 1969. 50p.
Encompasses materials from all political positions, with greatest emphasis on the left, and the rebels' own critiques, that are considered "coherent, relevant, provocative and influential." The bibliography is selective, confined to the United States, and is only occasionally annotated. The table of contents indicates general divisions of the material on the basis of form. There is a one-page addendum. Lacks an index.

150. Brickman, William W. *Foreign Students in the United States: A Selected and Annotated Bibliography*. Princeton, N.J.: College Entrance Examination Board, 1963. 24p.
Samples materials dealing with the background and current status of foreign students in the United States for the benefit of college and university officials concerned with them. This short bibliography is limited to published works considered of major significance, with the exception of those classed as historical works, in the 1950s and 1960s. Access is provided by the table of contents.

151. Brooks, Gary D. and Brooks, Bonnie S. *The Literature of Student Unrest*. Englewood Cliffs, N.J.: Educational Technology Pubns., 1972. 70p.
Compiles the literature on student unrest. Items, essentially covering the 1960s, include books, signed and unsigned articles, papers, reports, and proceedings. This unannotated bibliography is organized according to the form of publication and alphabetically by author in each section. There is no index. The table of contents merely indicates the sections dealing with each publication type.

152. Campus Order Project. *Campus Order: Problem Solving Without Violence*. Atlanta: Georgia State Univ., 1973. 344p.
Reports the work of a project seeking to develop methods of dealing with campus problems by peaceful means. There is a twenty five hundred item bibliography of material published mainly in the 1960s, selected from both scholarly and popular literature. Entries are in alphabetical order and are not annotated. There are no indexes.

153. Davis, Jerry S. and Van Dusen, William D. *Guide to the Literature of Student Financial Aid*. New York: College Entrance Examination Board, 1978. 166p.
This annotated sourcebook lists about eight hundred books, articles, dissertations, and other documents generally making their appearance after 1969. Sources are arranged in seven major categories, ranging from general guides to the history, philosophy, and purpose of aid to aid administration and management. Other categories include financial aid administration as a profession, federal and state issues, financing post-secondary education, and research on financial aid. Categories and subcategories are preceded by summaries of major themes and contents of items included. While dated, some sections will be of interest to students and researchers of financial aid. The work includes a detailed table of contents but no index.

154. Eells, Walter C. and Hollis, Ernest V. *Student Financial Aid in Higher Education: An Annotated Bibliography*. (Office of Education, Bulletin 1961, no. 3) Washington, D.C.: U.S. Department of Health, Education, and Welfare, Office of Education, 1961. 87p.
Updating an earlier source in the series (1957, no. 59), this work includes 451 titles, the vast majority published after 1954. While now dated, this publication is useful in the study of such major developments as the National Defense Education Act of 1958 and the National Merit Scholarships. Intended as a practical guide, the work is divided into nine sections, ranging from costs, scholarships, and fellowships, to loans, part-time employment, and foreign study. A general index covers names, institutions, organizations and major topics.

155. Feldman, Kenneth A. and Newcomb, Theodore M. *The Impact of College on Students, Volume I: An Analysis of Four Decades of Research, Volume II: Summary Tables*. San Francisco: Jossey-Bass, 1969. 2v. ISBN 87589-036-9.
The first volume surveys the results of more than fifteen hundred published and unpublished studies from the mid-twenties to the mid-sixties in eleven chapters with titles such as The Sequence of Experiences, The Diversity of Major Fields, Student Culture and Faculty, and Persistence and Change After College. Tables in Volume II summarize and compare the research discussed and, along the seventy-five page bibliography and name and subject indexes, give this work considerable value as a guide to this literature.

156. Funkenstein, Daniel H. and Wilkie, George H. *Student Mental Health: An Annotated Bibliography, 1936-1955.* London: World Federation for Mental Health, 1956. 297p.
Prepared for the International Conference on Student Mental Health, Princeton, N.J., this source includes 1,803 source citations appearing over two decades on college students and mental health. Omitted are sources dealing with special groups of students such as veterans, adults, medical or law students, etc. Coverage is international, while the great majority of books, articles and other documents and reports have American imprints. Access is limited as the contents are not classified (arrangement is alphabetical) and no subject index is provided. A personal and association index is included.

157. Hood, Albert B. and Arceneaux, Cathann. *Key Resources on Student Services: A Guide to the Field and its Literature.* San Francisco: Jossey-Bass, 1990. 263p. ISBN 1-55542-230-6.
Designed for the practitioner, this annotated guide presents an overview of 616 principal works related to student services, including such special fields as academic advisement, career service, financial aid, and placement. Presented are books and monographs published since 1980. Journals are also described, but specific articles appearing in them have typically not been included. There are thirteen chapters, with chapter introductions. The first four contain references useful in all the different specialties, while the next eight relate to particular specialties. The final chapter examines emerging issues and trends. Works considered of "indispensable value" are so marked. Includes name and subject indexes.

158. Keniston, Kenneth. *Radicals and Militants: An Annotated Bibliography of Empirical Research on Campus Unrest.* Lexington, Mass.: Lexington Bks., 1973. 219p. ISBN 0-669-85381-X.
More than three hundred empirical studies reported in books and articles from 1945 on are abstracted according to a standardized format including: the institutional setting, subjects, research method, findings, and comments. Entries are rated as valuable, extremely important, or mandatory reading. Reports are on young American activists or radicals, or on institutions where protests occurred. Excluded are studies of single individuals. Institutional studies involve comparisons among several institutions. Indexes for authors and editors; events, groups, institutions and settings studied; and topics.

159. Lenning, Oscar T. and others. *The Many Faces of College Success and Their Nonintellective Correlates: The Published Literature Through the Decade of the Sixties.* (Monograph 15) Iowa City, Iowa: American College Testing Program, 1974. 552p.
Compilation of the literature on factors that correlate with nonacademic criteria of college success (e.g., intellectual development, personality development, motivational, cultural, moral development, etc.). Similar in scope, organization and treatment to its companion volume, Lenning's Nonintellective Correlates (American College Testing Program, 1974).

160. Lenning, Oscar T. and others. *Nonintellective Correlates of Grades, Persistence and Academic Learning in College: The Published Literature Through the Decade of the Sixties.* (Monograph 14) Iowa City, Iowa: American College Testing Program, 1974. 276p.
A thorough survey of the literature on variables that correlate with academic measures of success. Nonacademic criteria are addressed in Lenning's The Many Faces of College Success (American College Testing Program, 1974). Individual chapters cover related factors such as per-

sonality, adjustment and anxiety; interests and activities; and biographical and demographic correlates. Each chapter presents a survey essay
describing some noteworthy works in the literature, followed by a lengthy
unannotated list of books, articles, proceedings and reports. Author
index.

161. Miller, Albert J.   *Confrontation, Conflict, and Dissent: A
      Bibliography of a Decade of Controversy, 1960-1970*. Metuchen,
      N.J.: Scarecrow Pr., 1972. 567p. ISBN 0-8108-0490-5.
An important source for the study of conflict during the 1960s. More
than six thousand items are represented, including diaries, documents,
interviews, journals, letters, pamphlets, and reports. Included are a
number of the "underground" or alternative press tabloids. Ten chapters
range in coverage from the control and regulation of firearms, police-
community relations, and sex education, to student dissent and military
service. Here are citations to such topics as the Black Panthers, coffee
houses, the crisis of colleges and universities, drugs and the drug
culture, Students for a Democratic Society, and the war in Vietnam.
Includes an index.

162. Parsons, Algene and Saxton, Kenneth D.   *Rights and Respons-
      ibilities of College Students: An Annotated Bibliography*. Pasadena,
      Calif: Western Personnel Institute, 1962. 32p.
Attempts to address the student movement on campuses in the early 1960s.
Some one hundred annotations reflect the prevailing views on academic
freedom, legal issues, discipline and the role of student presses. Of
use to those interested in student issues during the Vietnam era.

163. Pascarella, Ernest T. and Terenzini, Patrick T.   *How College
      Affects Students: Findings and Insights from Twenty Years of
      Research*. (Jossey-Bass Higher and Adult Education Series) San
      Francisco: Jossey-Bass, 1991. 894p. ISBN 1-55542-304-3.
Noteworthy for its scale and scope, this work surveys the literature of
the late sixties, seventies and eighties, covering some twenty-six
hundred studies. Individual chapters deal with specific student outcome
areas, such as cognitive skills and intellectual growth, self concept,
attitudes and values, career choice and development, and quality of life
after college. Other chapters examine theories and models of student
change in college and the implications of the research for policy and
practice. Also included are an appendix on methodological issues and
a 154-page bibliography. The latter, along with detailed name and
subject indexes, imparts a substantial reference value to this work.

164. Professional Information Service, American Personnel and Guidance
      Association. *Professional Resource Bibliography: College and Post-
      Secondary Student Personnel Services*. Falls Church, Va.: American
      Personnel and Guidance Assn., 1983. 34p.
An unannotated bibliography divided into sections dealing with
counseling, peer counseling, counseling the handicapped, student
orientation, student life and housing, etc. No index. Addresses an
important area generally not well covered.

165. Rosenthal, Carl F.   *Social Conflict and Collective Violence in
      American Institutions of Higher Learning, vol. 2: Bibliography*.
      Kensington, Md.: Center for Research in Social Systems, American
      Institute for Research, 1971. 496p.
Sponsored by the National Institute of Law Enforcement and Criminal
Justice, this is a classified, annotated, cross-cultural bibliography on
the social values and political behavior of students. Periodical indexes

were searched for relevant materials. Two-thirds of the work covers historical and contemporary works on United States higher education. Foreign sources relate generally to the post-World War II era. Volume 1 includes reports on the nature of collective behavior on campuses, with suggested operational implications. The bibliography's first objective is to compile "incidents of collective behavior on American campuses" from the beginnings of the institutions to the 1960s and 1970s. Lacks an index.

166. Samson, Mary S. and others. *Student Housing in Colleges and Universities: Abstracts of the Literature, 1961-1966.* Claremont, Calif.: College Student Personnel Institute, 1966. 85p.
Prepared for the Association of College and University Housing Officers (ACUHO) and intended to be a comprehensive bibliography on college food services as well as housing, this work provides lengthy signed abstracts of about 250 books, articles, studies, statistical reports and unpublished papers. Entries are grouped by twenty-one broad subject areas, such as Design and Construction, Off-Campus Housing, Regulations and Student Development. An author index is provided. This work extends coverage of the field begun by two previous works, by ACUHO (1956) and Western Personnel Institute (1960).

167. Spaulding, Seth and others. *World's Students in the United States: A Review and Evaluation of Research on Foreign Students.* N.Y.: Praeger Pubs., 1976. 522p. ISBN 0-275-56130-5.
A substantial survey of the research done on foreign students in U.S. institutions of higher education since 1967. Nearly two hundred pages are devoted to a lengthily annotated bibliography of the studies discussed and to an unannotated list of additional references. Both a subject index and a page index to the studies cited are included.

168. Stark, Matthew. *An Annotated Bibliography on Residence Counseling.* Ann Arbor, Mich.: Assn. of College and Univ. Housing Officers, 1964. 99p.
The author has attempted to compile all relevant literature up to 1964. All titles are in English and nearly all are of U.S. origin. The 339 items include books, articles, reports, dissertations, conference proceedings and in-house guides and training manuals and are given brief evaluative annotations. Arrangement is by author with an index to broad subject areas. Age may limit its usefulness to historical research.

169. Suljak, Nedjelko D. *Campus Disorder and Cultural Counter Revolution: A Bibliography.* Davis: Univ. of California, Davis, Institute of Governmental Affairs, 1970. 40p.
This work offers a list of some 650 books and magazine and journal articles on campus unrest. While the brief foreword makes no statement about scope or criteria for inclusion, most items come from the 1960s, with a few from the 1950s and earlier, and are mainly U.S. in origin and focus. Entries are arranged in a single author-alphabetical list. No annotations or indexes: really a bare-bones checklist.

170. Tice, Terrence N. *Student Rights, Decision-Making and the Law.* (ERIC/Higher Education Research Report no. 10) Washington, D.C.: American Assn. for Higher Education, 1976. 98p.
This work is about evenly divided between a lengthy essay on its topic and bibliographies of books and articles on students' rights issues in the U.S. college context. Over three hundred items are cited, many with annotations, from the early 1960s through 1976. In addition to name and subject indexes, a very helpful index of cases is included.

Teaching and Learning

171. Aker, George F. *Adult Education Procedures, Methods and Techniques: A Classified and Annotated Bibliography 1953-1963.* Syracuse, N.Y.: Syracuse Univ. Pr., 1965. 1963p.
Represents an attempt to compile the majority of work on the methodology of adult education during the decade covered. All reported research and theoretical writings, as well as other selected relevant writings and some earlier significant works, are included among the 704 items. There is an author index, but no subject index. The five parts of the table of contents are highly sub-divided with notations of the number of citations in each section.

172. Burnett, Collins W. and Badger, Frank W. *Learning Climate in the Liberal Arts College: An Annotated Bibliography.* (Morris Harvey College Curriculum Series, no. 2) Charleston, W. Va.: Morris Harvey College, 1970. 87p.
Review of both the journal literature and selected monographic literature designed to help college teachers, administrators, and graduate students. Items are arranged alphabetically by author under four major headings: the liberal arts approach, curriculum, teaching methods and new media, and the teaching-learning process. Index not included.

173. Childs, Gayle B. *An Annotated Bibliography of Correspondence Study, 1897-1960.* Minneapolis: National Univ. Extension Program, 1960. 111p.
Includes nearly one thousand citations to books, articles, proceedings, theses and dissertations, and other documents. Arrangement is chrono-logical. Sources are listed in two categories: "general" and "research". Not all citations include annotations; those that do range from a sentence to several paragraphs. This source would be important to those interested in the history and development of adult education and correspondence study in the United States. Includes neither a table of contents nor an index.

174. Clarke, John L. *Educational Development: A Select Bibliography With Particular Reference to Further and Higher Education.* New York: Nichols Publishing, 1981. 207p.
Surveys the literature in the broad area of educational development for both professionals and tutors. According to the compiler, the work is "a first select bibliography" covering materials produced in the 1960s and 1970s in the United Kingdom and the United States. Ten chapters range in coverage from educational technology and curriculum development to evaluation of teaching and learning, staff development, and the student in adult and higher education. Items are arranged alphabetically by author in each of the subsections of the ten chapters, and are accessible only through the table of contents. A separate section lists relevant periodicals.

175. Eells, Walter Crosby. *College Teachers and College Teaching: An Annotated Bibliography on College and University Faculty Members and Instructional Methods.* Atlanta, Ga.: Southern Regional Education Board, 1957. 282p.
With the 1959 supplement, this source lists more than thirty-seven hundred books, chapters, dissertations, and articles about teachers as persons, as well as covering the subject of teaching. Emphasis is on the 1950s, with coverage back to 1920. Six chapters cover general and reference works, recruitment and scholarship, institutional status, teaching conditions, and teaching methods in general and in special

fields. For those interested in the post-World War II era, as well as
those interested in how planners and practitioners anticipated, planned,
and prepared for the expansion of the 1960s. Includes both a detailed
table of contents and a general index.

176. Flaugher, Ronald L., Mahoney, Margaret H. and Messing, Rita B.
*Credit by Examination For College-Level Studies: An Annotated
Bibliography.* New York: College Entrance Examination Board, 1967.
233p.
The authors provide more than three hundred citations to books, articles,
dissertations, and other documents arranged under three major topics:
transfer students, credit by examination, and the unaffiliated student.
Emphasis is on publications of the 1950s to the mid 1960s. Prepared at
the Developmental Research Division of Educational Testing Service, this
bibliography was developed to support program and research planning of
the College Board to learn about the transfer student credit by
examination, and the unaffiliated student. Publications dated before 1945
are grouped separately. Includes a detailed table of contents in place
of a subject index. Also a brief author index.

177. Good, Carter V. *Teaching in College and University: A Survey of
the Problems and Literature in Higher Education.* Baltimore, Md.:
Warwick and York, 1929. 557p.
Describes more than three thousand publications dealing with the problems
and literature of teaching in the post-World War I era. The author
identifies major works, organizing and summarizing their contents or
conclusions, using extensive footnote citations. Eight chapters range
in subject from objectives and standards, the curriculum, and psychology
of learning, to the conduct of classes, and measurement of achievement.
An extensive, briefly annotated bibliography follows, covering problems,
methods, and curriculum of twelve subject-matter fields. Includes author
and subject indexes to all cited sources.

178. *Internationalizing Undergraduate Education: Resources From the
Field.* New York: Global Perspectives in Education, 1987. 175p.
Looseleaf.
A classified, annotated bibliography of more than four hundred source
citations to international studies materials produced in United States
higher education institutions during the years 1979 to 1984. These
sources "incorporate a global/international dimension into courses which
were not normally global in scope." They are arranged into the following
subject chapters: Business Education, Economics, Education, Foreign
Languages, Global Issues, Humanities, Political Science, Science and
Technology, and Social Sciences. Each chapter includes its own index,
while a cumulative index concludes the work.

179. Knox, Alan B. and others. *Adult Learning.* Lincoln: Adult
Education Research, Univ. of Nebraska, 1961. 76p.
An early attempt to identify research studies. Each of the fewer than
one hundred source citations provides an abstract, which generally
includes a problem statement, concept, technique of analysis, hypothesis
and findings. Subject coverage ranges from ability, motivation and age
role to anxiety and psychometrics. Does not include an index.

180. Layton, Elizabeth N. *General Education: Bibliography.* (U.S.
Office of Education Bulletin, 1954, no. 3) Washington, D.C.: U.S.
Dept. of Health, Education and Welfare, Office of Education, 1954.
22p.
A list of references to 144 items, mainly articles and books, published

from 1949 to 1953 on college and university general education programs. Entries are arranged by author and provided with brief descriptive annotations. A combined author and subject index is included. For those interested in general education during the post-World War II era.

181. Little, Lawrence C. *A Bibliography of Doctoral Dissertations on Adults and Adult Education.*   Rev. ed.   Pittsburgh: Univ. of Pittsburgh Pr., 1963. 163p.
Lists some twenty-five hundred doctoral level dissertations from U.S. universities, mostly in the fifties and sixties. Entries are in author order and unannotated, but include references to abstracts in Dissertation Abstracts and other periodical sources. Lack of indexing limits usefulness.

182. Menges, Robert J. and Mathis, B. Claud. *Key Resources on Teaching, Learning, Curriculum, and Faculty Development: A Guide to the Higher Education Literature.*   San Francisco: Jossey-Bass, 1988. 406p. ISBN 1-55542-118-0.
An annotated guide to 685 relatively recent "key resources" in the areas covered, along with earlier "seminal works." Sources cited relate to four-year colleges and universities. They do not deal with community colleges, administration and organization, or student personnel services. Topics included range from higher education as a field of study, and evaluation and improving instruction, to learning processes, the college and university curricula, and relevant periodicals and reference works. About ten percent of the entries are marked by stars, indicating their selection as "seminal." Includes both name and subject indexes.

183. Menges, Robert J.   *Teaching-Learning Experiences For College Students and Other Adults: A Selected Annotated Bibliography.*   5th ed. (Occasional Paper no. 12) Evanston, Ill.: Center for the Teaching Professions, Northwestern Univ., 1985. 136p.
Presents over four hundred briefly annotated references to books, articles and reports, most from within the previous twenty years. Works cited are primarily U.S. in origin, but some Canadian publications also appear. Entries are organized under section headings derived from a systems model of instruction: Preconditions, Plans, Procedures, and Products. Items that cover more than one of these categories appear in a General Resources section along with lists of periodicals and bibliographies. Author index.

184. Mezirow, Jack D. and Berry, Dorothea. *Literature of Liberal Adult Education, 1945-1957.* New York: Scarecrow Pr., 1960. 308p.
A dated but useful guide which begins with more than eighty pages of detailed annotations of articles on the philosophy and trends in adult education. Other chapters cover courses, curricula and the roles of universities and other agencies such as libraries and businesses. Of the one thousand items selected, a majority are articles, but government publications, books, pamphlets and dissertations are also represented. For those interested in adult education in the post-World War II era. Includes author/title and subject indexes.

185. Office of Scientific Personnel. National Research Council. *An Annotated Bibliography on Graduate Education, 1950-1971.* Washington, D.C. Office of Scientific Personnel, Nat. Research Council, 1971. 215p.
Summarizes approximately five hundred books, monographs, articles, proceedings, and other published and unpublished sources dealing with

traditional areas of graduate education. Excluded are references to other professional fields, degrees, and programs, such as law, medicine, theology, etc. Sources are classified into the following: History and Development, Students, Administrators and Faculty, Structure and Functions, Instruction and Research, Manpower, Costs and Financing, and Recommendations. Sources are arranged alphabetically by author within each topic and subtopic. Annotations cover the purpose of the study, methodology used, results, and major conclusions and recommendations. A topical listing with subtopics follows the table of contents. Includes an author index.

186.   Smith, Robert G., Jr. *An Annotated Bibliography on the Design of Instructional Systems.* Washington, D.C.: George Washington Univ., Human Resources Research Office, 1967. 131p.
Prepared for the Office of Research and Development of the Department of the Army, this work presents annotated references to 449 articles and reports dating from 1950 to 1965. Items were selected for their relevance to military training but may have value for instructional design and technology in higher education contexts. Author and KWIC title indexes.

LIBRARY CATALOGS

187.   *Bibliographic Guide to Education.* 1978-   . Boston: G.K. Hall, 1979-   . Annual. ISSN 0147-6505.
Serves as an annual supplement to the Dictionary Catalog of the Teachers College Library, Columbia University (Boston: G.K. Hall, 1970). The guide includes selected publications in the field of education cataloged by the Research Libraries of the New York Public Library. All aspects and levels of education are covered, including the field of higher education. Also covered are administrative reports of departments of education for selected countries and for U.S. states and cities. While not including serial publications, other non-book materials and theses are cited. Access is by main entry (personal author, corporate body, etc.), titles, series titles, and subject headings, all in one alphabetical order.

188.   Columbia University. Library. *Dictionary Catalog of the Teachers College Library.* Boston: G.K. Hall, 1970. 36v. 1st suppl., 1971, 5v. 2d suppl., 1973, 2v. 3d suppl., 1977.
Provides author, title, and subject access in one alphabetical order, to a collection of more than four hundred thousand books, periodicals, and a range of audiovisual materials. While covering "basic reference resources dealing with approximately two hundred distinct educational systems in the world," the catalog provides exceptionally comprehensive coverage of American elementary and secondary education. The catalog, a photo reproduction of the library's card catalog, also provides substantial coverage of higher education, with nearly one thousand card entries under that heading. Supplements extend coverage with more than twenty-four thousand entries.

189.   *Educational Film and Video Locator of the Consortium of College and University Media Centers and R.R. Bowker 1990-1991.* 4th ed. New York: R.R. Bowker, 1990. 2v. ISBN 0-8352-2624-7.
A massive listing of over fifty thousand titles held in the consortium's member media centers. The briefly annotated entries are arranged by title and also indicate running time, format, size, audience level and subject headings. The other major sections are a very useful series

index and a subject/title/audience level index. An alphabetical list of producers and distributors, with addresses, is also provided, and the participating media centers are listed in an introductory section, along with their rental and loan policies.

190. Harvard University. Library. *Education and Education Periodicals.* (Widener Library Shelflist, 16-17) Cambridge, Mass.: Harvard Univ. Library, 1968. 2v.
Represents more than thirty thousand works in the Widener Library education collection. Coverage includes periodicals, general treatises, treatises on special types of education and special types of schools, works on the theory and methods of teaching, and on the training of teachers, and, especially, histories of education. Not covered are histories, reports, and other works on individual institutions. Also not included are the extensive holdings of the Harvard Graduate School of Education Library. The Widener Library's holdings in education "are primarily valuable from historical point of view and are strong until about 1940." This computer-generated catalog lists sources in volume 1 by call number. Volume 2 arranges entries alphabetically by author or title with a chronological arrangement covering from 1504 through 1967.

191. King, Cornelia S. *American Education, 1622-1860: Printed Works in the Collection of the American Philosophical Society, the Historical Society of Pennsylvania, the Library Company of Philadelphia.* New York: Garland Publishing, 1984. 354p. ISBN 0-8240-8966-9.
Includes approximately five thousand monographs and serials printed before 1861. While broad in subject coverage, materials related exclusively to religious instruction are not included. Excluded as well are textbooks, dissertations, and catalogs of library holdings. Arrangement is alphabetical by author or main entry. Entries include location symbols. A series of appendixes list institutions and organizations, and a listing of sources arranged by publication date.

192. U.S. Department of Health, Education, and Welfare. Library. *Author/Title Catalog of the Department Library.* Boston: G.K. Hall, 1965-1967. 29v.
Provides a photo reproduction of about 540,000 card entries from the library's catalog. The collection comprises collections from the Office of Education and Public Health Services, to the Vocational Rehabilitation Administration and the Welfare Administration. While especially strong in the fields of education and social sciences, higher education is well represented. The collection includes books, pamphlets, documents, and serial publications.

193. U.S. Department of Health, Education, and Welfare. Library. *Subject Catalog of the Department.* Boston: G.K. Hall, 1965. 20 vols.
Records a collection of more than five hundred thousand volumes representing agencies from the Office of Education and Public Health Services, to the Vocational Rehabilitation Administration and the Welfare Administration. This photo reproduction of cards from the library's catalog shows that the collection is especially strong in the fields of education and social sciences. There is substantial coverage of higher education, with more than fifteen hundred card entries under that heading. The catalog includes books, pamphlets, documents, and serial publications arranged alphabetically by subject. Headings in general follow the Library of Congress system.

194. University of London.   Institute of Education.   *Catalog of the
      Comparative Education Library.* Boston: G.K. Hall, 1971. 6 vols.
      1st suppl., 1974, 3 vols.
A photo reproduction of about 159,000 catalog cards (including the
supplement).   The collection, begun in the early 1930s, contains
materials from most countries of the world, with special emphasis on the
British Commonwealth. The compiler notes that "apart from materials on
the educational theory and practice in each country, the library collects
books and pamphlets on related subjects," i.e., history, sociology,
anthropology, religion, demography, and geography. Also included are many
references to periodical articles and collections. Resources on American
higher education are represented. On the subject "Higher Education-U.S.,"
nearly three hundred card citations are found. The work is in three
parts: authors and titles, subjects, and regions (includes continents,
regions, etc.) The subject catalog headings are subdivided by country
after a general section.

2.

DICTIONARIES AND ENCYCLOPEDIAS

INTRODUCTION

Essential for researching the history, meaning, or significance of a concept, event or association related to higher education is a relevant and reputable encyclopedia. Equally important to the scholar, student, and practitioner is the availability of a reliable dictionary of higher education. Concomitant with the increase in research and publication of recent decades has been the introduction of a number of critically acclaimed encyclopedias and the appearance of equally valuable and useful dictionaries associated with higher education.

This chapter cites and describes thirty such works, one half of which made their appearance after 1980, four in the 1990s. All should be readily available in libraries supporting education in general or higher education in particular.

Since they are general in coverage and treatment, these works are simply grouped by form (dictionaries and encyclopedias) rather than by subject. They are, of course, also covered in the separate author, title, and subject indexes, at the conclusion of this book.

While they share common traits of comprehensive coverage and broad scope, a number of these works are unique in treatment or purpose. These include a dictionary of quotations, a source of college nicknames, a dictionary of acronyms and a one-volume international encyclopedia devoted exclusively to teaching and teacher education.

DICTIONARIES

195. Aitchison, Jean. *Unesco Thesaurus: A Structured List of Descriptors for Indexing and Retrieving Literature in the Field of Education*, Science, Social Science, Culture and Communication. Paris, France: Unesco, 1977. 2v. ISBN 92-3-101469-2.
Modeled after the <u>Thesaurus of ERIC Descriptors</u> (Phoenix, Ariz.: Oryx Pr.), this source presents terms in a permuted index, hierarchical

display list, and an alphabetical list. The alphabetical list which comprises the entire second volume includes scope notes, "use for" references, narrower terms, broader terms, related terms, and class numbers for cross references. This highly classified thesaurus provides a "controlled vocabulary" for computerized indexing and retrieval of documents processed through Unesco's Computerized Automation System.

196. Barrow, Robin and Milburn, Geoffrey. *A Critical Dictionary of Educational Concepts.* 2d ed. New York: Teachers College, Columbia Univ., 1990. 370p. ISBN 0-8077-3058-0.
Unlike other educational dictionaries, simply defining and describing, this source probes and critically assesses some of the key concepts in education. The work "sets out to provide comment and discussion on expressions that crop up a lot and that seem to have some significance for, or emotive impact upon, people." Its treatment is more theoretical than practical, while avoiding essentially specialist terms and concepts. Here are explored such concepts or notions as computer literacy and deschooling, multiculturalism and topic-centered education. Arrangement is alphabetical, covering some 150 main entries with numerous cross references. Many entries are followed by brief references. Full citations are found in a separate bibliography at the end of the volume.

197. Beach, Mark. *Words for the Wise: A Field Guide to Academic Terms.* Portland, Oreg.: Coast to Coast Books, 1979. 124p. ISBN 0-9602664-0-2.
Defines more than three hundred terms. Most entries include two types of information: a) word origins, and b) advice about the decision or action to which the term refers. This is a basic, practical guide for those not familiar with higher education or some of its special vocabulary. This work is to be enjoyed both for its many humorous illustrations, as well as for its sometimes terse, cogent, and clear definitions.

198. Cloud, Sherrill. *A Glossary of Standard Terminology for Postsecondary Education.* Boulder, Colo.: Nat. Center for Higher Education Management Systems, 1980. 121p.
Developed by NCHEMS to "promote awareness and use of a common language of terms, definitions, and procedures at the institutional, state, and national levels." This work includes more than 360 entries and subentries reflecting established standards for data exchange among the various levels and types of associations, organizations, and other units that comprise higher education. A term found in the glossary, which is part of a category or classification structure, is listed in one of six appendices as a subcategory under the appropriate category or classification structure.

199. Dale, Edgar. *The Educators Quotebook.* Bloomington, Ind.: Phi Delta Kappa, 1984. 107p.
An entertaining, informative, and practical "collection of thoughts" arranged under 103 general topics, ranging from "Adolescence," "Education," and "Knowledge," to "Professors," "Teaching," and "Writing." While most quotations covered include their authors, citations to works of origin are not provided. According to the compiler, most entries deal with human affairs, stressing important ideas on teaching. A list of topics, with page numbers, appears in the front of the book. It does not include an index or list of authors represented.

200. Gatti, Richard D. and Gatti, Daniel J. *New Encyclopedic Dictionary of School Law.* West Nyack, N.Y.: Parker Publishing Co., 1983.

400p.   ISBN 0-13-612580-8.
A comprehensive useful source for those unskilled in law but concerned about lawsuits, legal rights and personal liability. This work is arranged in dictionary form, but treatment of many subjects is similar to that of an encyclopedia. Coverage extends from administration, church and state, and constitutional rights, to dismissals and tenure, equal protection and governing boards. Emphasis is on school law, but this source is useful for explaining in clear, simple terms topics of concern and interest to educators, administrators and others involved in all levels of education. A categorical index arranges entries into thirteen general categories. Includes a table of cases cited and a general index.

201.   Good, Carter V.   *Dictionary of Education*.   3d. ed.   New York: McGraw-Hill Publishing Co., 1973. 681p. ISBN 0-07-023720-4.
A comprehensive guide to professional and technical terms and concepts covering the entire field of education. Best known of the education dictionaries, this source enlists more than one hundred recognized expert-advisors in thirty-eight fields. This edition includes about thirty-three thousand entries covering English language terms, with brief separate sections for Canada, England, and Wales. Not included are persons, institutions, school systems, and titles of publications, with some exceptions. It claims its first purpose is to be the "first instrument of the profession as a whole which is dedicated to the exactness of words and the artistry of precision."

202.   Hills, P.J.   *Dictionary of Education*.   London, England: Routledge and Kegan Paul, 1982. 284p. ISBN 0-7100-0871-6.
While a definite British emphasis, this is a generally useful source for the informed American reader or student. Definitions cover basic statistical concepts and other terms related to educational research. Entries include cross references and references to further readings. An opening section includes fifteen brief essays covering areas of education such as administration, curriculum development and sociology of education, but focus is on the British educational system.

203.   Moore, John Alexander.   *Academic Abbreviations and Acronyms*. Riverside: Univ. of California at Riverside, 1981. 87p. (ERIC ED 225 493)
This document includes more than two thousand acronyms and abbreviations. Arrangement is alphabetical by acronym or abbreviation. Two final lists cover airports and "official" two-letter abbreviations for states and territories of the United States. While appearing essentially as an ERIC document and outside our stated criteria, we decided to accept this somewhat dated source because of its scope and somewhat unique focus assisting those struggling with what the list's author notes as his (and our) "frustration at finding so many official documents and reports incomprehensible because of the plethora of unfamiliar acronyms and abbreviations."

204.   Page, G. Terry, Thomas, John B. and Marshall, Alan R. *International Dictionary of Education*.   New York: Nichols Pub., 1977. 381p. ISBN 0-89397-003-4.
A comprehensive, practical source, in one alphabetical order, on the international language of education from pre-school to post-doctoral levels. It includes more than ten thousand entries, covering the broadest range of fields and subjects, including some persons, organizations (national and international), associations, terms, and concepts.   Two   appendices   list   abbreviations   for   national   and

international associations and organizations, and U.S. honor societies, fraternities, and sororities.

205. Palmer, James C. and Colby, Anita Y. *Dictionary of Educational Acronyms, Abbreviations, and Initialisms.* 2d ed. Phoenix, Ariz.: Oryx Pr., 1985. 97p. ISBN 0-89774-165-X.
Includes more than four thousand acronyms and other shortened forms representing current educational terms and phrases. The work is arranged in two sections: acronyms arranged alphabetically, and the unabbreviated forms arranged alphabetically. Entries generally provide only acronyms and their unabbreviated versions. Occasionally modifiers usually indicate geographic places or parent organizations. The work is not exhaustive, nor are entries considered authoritative, but it remains a useful reference work.

206. Rosenberg, Kenyon C. and Elsbree, John J. *Dictionary of Library and Educational Technology.* 3d ed. Englewood, Colo.: Libraries Unlimited, 1989. 196p. ISBN 0-87287-623-3.
Aims to provide specific information for educators to make informed decisions when choosing education equipment. Approximately one thousand terms are defined in the second half of the book, with cross references especially for abbreviations. In addition, descriptive essays explain various kinds of equipment from computers to projectors in the remaining pages of the dictionary. It was formerly entitled <u>Media Equipment: A Guide and Dictionary</u> (1976). There is always a need for current sources as new technology is introduced.

207. Rowntree, Derek. *Dictionary of Education.* Totowa, N.J.: Barnes and Noble, 1981. 354p. ISBN 0-389-20263-0.
A practical guide, in one alphabetical order, for the English-speaking generalist reader. It includes limited coverage of associations, committees, and organizations, with some mention as well of educational credentials of the world. Covered are selected educational theorists and practitioners - "the sort of names many authors feel free to sprinkle unexplained in their texts as if assuming that all readers will have met them before." Definitions are brief, sometimes a single sentence, with use of abbreviations "US" and "UK" to indicate terms applying to one country or the other.

208. Shafritz, Jay M., Koeppe, Richard P. and Soper, Elizabeth W. *Facts on File Dictionary of Education.* New York: Facts on File, 1988. 503p. ISBN 0-8160-1636-4.
A current, comprehensive, readily understandable and accurate source for the layperson and the professional. It covers all levels of education, administration, and state and local government agencies connected with education. Included is a scattering of names, major court decisions, important pieces of legislation, acronyms, selected tests, major associations and organizations. While in one alphabetical order, the five thousand entries are of two types: brief glossary definitions, and terms given more extensive treatment. The work includes a selected number of charts and tables.

209. Songe, Alice H. *American Universities and Colleges: A Dictionary of Name Changes.* Metuchen, N.J.: Scarecrow Pr., 1978. 264p.
Lists alphabetically the names of all four-year degree-granting universities and colleges in the continental United States and territories that have had name changes since they were founded. These are accompanied by the former names along with the years in which these names were adopted. Also included are the names of universities and colleges that

have closed since the 1964/1965 school year, along with the date of closing. Nearly four thousand entries include the names of institutions that have name changes, and names formerly held by these institutions. An appendix indicates the location of records for institutions listed as closed.

ENCYCLOPEDIAS

210. Altbach, Philip G. *International Higher Education: An Encyclopedia.* New York: Garland Publishing, 1991. 2 v. ISBN 0-8240-4847-4.
Provides comprehensive coverage of fifty-one countries and regions of the world "that have seen some particularly significant developments in higher education." There are also chapters on most of the world's regions. These are presented in fifty-two essays that include statistical and other factual information, along with each contributing author's interpretation of the factual matters. Arrangement is by region and countries within regions. A second set of fifteen essays deals with topics of general interest in a comparative framework. These range in coverage from Academic Freedom and Foreign Students, to Private Higher Education and Women in Higher Education. Not covered are changes in Eastern Europe and the Soviet Union since the latter part of 1989. Access to the essays is by means of the table of contents. Volume two includes a topic and name index.

211. Blishen, Edward. *Encyclopedia of Education.* New York: Philosophical Library, 1970. 882p. ISBN 8022-2308-7.
An attempt to cover in a single volume information about educational administration; teaching methods; legislation and reports; examinations; teaching aids; primary, secondary, further, and higher education; history and philosophy of education; and a range of related subjects. The work is designed for the layperson and the professional. Arrangement is alphabetical, including associations and organizations, persons, legislation, terms and concepts. While dated, with a strong British emphasis, the work remains useful.

212. Burns, Ruth Ketchum. *NASFAA Encyclopedia of Student Financial Aid.* Washington, D.C.: Nat. Assn. of Student Financial Aid Administrators, 1984. Looseleaf.
The focus of this encyclopedia is on administrative terms associated with the training, management, history, and requirements for student financial aid. Its coverage by topic with historical reviews of programs, legislation, and operating details renders this an excellent source for the beginning financial aid officer. The work is published in looseleaf format. An index is included.

213. Clark, Burton S. and Neave, Guy. *The Encyclopedia of Higher Education.* Pergamon Pr., 1992. 4v. ISBN 0-0803-7251-1.
Includes more than three hundred critical review articles from an international perspective. Volume 1 provides a description and analysis of 135 national systems of higher education. Volume 2 is arranged around four central themes: higher education and society; institutional framework of higher education systems; governance, administration, and finance; and faculty and students: teaching, learning and research. Volume 4 focuses on academic disciplines. Includes comprehensive author and subject indexes.

214. Deighton, Lee C. *Encyclopedia of Education.* New York: Macmillan

Publishing Co., 1971. 10v.
With more than one thousand signed articles, this encyclopedia deals with
the history, theory, research, and philosophy, as well as with the
structure, process and products of education. While emphasis is on
American education, coverage includes international education, comparative education, exchange programs, and the educational systems of more
than one hundred countries. There is substantial coverage of higher
education. There are few biographies, however. Articles are arranged
alphabetically, while those related in content appear together in
clusters. Most of the articles include bibliographies. The final volume
includes a "Guide to Articles" which provides article titles with cross
references, and a topical index which contains groupings of articles
under more general conceptual headings. A valuable reference work in
need of revision.

215. Dejnozka, Edward L. and Kapel, David E. *American Educators'*
      Encyclopedia. Rev. ed. New York: Greenwood Pr., 1991. 716p. ISBN
      0-313-25269-6.
A ready-reference of almost two thousand entries "based on the names and
terms frequently found in the literature of professional education."
Coverage extends to all levels of education. Appendices include useful
lists of award recipients, past presidents of major associations, past
chief executives of federal agencies and other national organizations,
as well as listings of higher education institutions and other major
educational bodies. Articles, arranged alphabetically are short, from
a few sentences to several paragraphs. Many include short reference
lists. A general index concludes the work.

216. Dunkin, Michael. *The International Encyclopedia of Teaching and*
      Teacher Education. Oxford, England: Pergamon Pr., 1987. 878p.
      ISBN 0-08-030852-X.
This work enables "readers to learn about key concepts from scholarly,
comprehensive and systematic expositions." It is comprised of 131
articles and summaries grouped under six broad themes: Concepts and
Models, Methods and Paradigms for Research, Teaching Methods and
Techniques, Classroom Processes, Contextual Factors, and Teacher
Education. No articles are included on the teaching of specific
curriculum areas. Readers are advised to consult the parent work
(International Encyclopedia of Education: Research and Studies, 1985).
Each broad section begins with an overview of articles covered and
indicates associations between articles in the same section and in other
sections. Articles conclude with reference lists. For an overview and
source of access to articles, readers are directed to the table of
contents. Includes both author and subject indexes.

217. Eraut, Michael. *The International Encyclopedia of Educational*
      Technology. (Advances in Education) Oxford, England: Pergamon Pr.
      1989. 654p. ISBN 0-08-033409-1.
Designed as both a reference work and a textbook covering all levels of
education and all "areas of knowledge that are either taught in at least
some educational technology courses or used by practicing educational
technologists."   The book includes 114 articles arranged in five
interrelated parts: Part 1 covers Educational Technology as a Knowledge
Field and Occupation; Part 2 includes the hardware aspects of new
technology and the media; Part 3 discusses Media Potential, Utilization
and Impact; Part 4 discusses Instructional Development from general
approaches to evaluation; and Part 5 includes the Distribution and
Organization of Knowledge and Resources. While international in
treatment, nearly one half of the authors are from the United States;

twenty-seven percent are from the United Kingdom. General topics are best covered through the table of contents, while detailed coverage is offered through the subject index. Other indexes cover contributors and names.

218. Husen, Torsten and Postlethwaite, T. Neville. *International Encyclopedia of Education: Research and Studies.* with supplements. Oxford, England: Pergamon Pr., 1985. 10v. ISBN 0-08-028119-2. This set attempts to "present a well-documented, international overview of the major aspects of the educational enterprise by taking into account the various practices and research paradigms in different socioeconomic, cultural, and political contexts." In its 1,448 articles, it covers all educational levels. A valuable feature is the inclusion of 160 articles describing essential features of the educational systems in countries throughout the world. Articles include bibliographies and are arranged alphabetically with concepts and themes linked by cross references. Less coverage is given to higher education, with focus on the curriculum, impact of higher education, teaching methods, faculty training and development, and teaching support services. An index volume arranges articles alphabetically into broader fields, subdivided into appropriate subheadings, lists contributors, and includes a subject index.

219. Knowles, Asa S. *International Encyclopedia of Higher Education.* 10v. San Francisco: Jossey-Bass, 1977. ISBN 0-87589-323-6. Attempts to serve as a single source for all major aspects of international higher education. It covers, in a world-wide perspective, national systems, academic fields of study, educational associations, research centers, institutes, documentation centers, academic and administrative policies and procedures, as well as current issues and trends in higher education. The encyclopedia does not include biographies, nor does it provide coverage of individual colleges and universities. Arrangement of articles is alphabetical, with groupings of certain materials of related subject content. Most articles include bibliographical references. Separate name and subject indexes comprise the final volume. The subject index covers more than ten thousand major entries and approximately forty thousand subentries, and provides "see" and "see also" references.

220. Kurian, George T. *World Education Encyclopedia.* New York: Facts on File, 1988. 3v. ISBN 0-87196-748-0. Selected by the American Library Association as one of the outstanding reference sources of 1988, this work provides the history and overview of the educational systems of 181 countries in the world. It addresses issues related to levels, characteristics, legal matters, political and social foundations of the systems, problems of growth, curricular development, etc. Entries are organized into the following standard headings by country: history and background, constitution, system overview, pre-primary and primary education, secondary education, higher education, administration, non-formal education, teaching professions, and summary. Data on third world countries are considerably shorter than entries for other countries. Finding aids include a subject index. An appendix covers educational rankings and organization names. Statistics, drawn primarily from the UNESCO Statistical Yearbook (New York: United Nations), are provided.

221. Lewy, Arieh. *The International Encyclopedia of Curriculum.* (Advances in Education) Oxford, England: Pergamon Pr., 1991. 1,064p. ISBN 0-08-041379-X. Presents 332 essays, by an international body of experts, summarizing

published curriculum literature. Covering all levels of education, the essays are divided into two parts: "those dealing with the curriculum in general and representing theories, principles, and generalizations;" and "those which examined curricular considerations pertaining to a particular study area." Part 1 includes four sections: Conceptual Framework, Curriculum Approaches and Methods, Curriculum Processes, and Curriculum Evaluation. Part 2 is arranged according to nine curriculum areas, from art to social studies. These sections are subdivided as well. Each essay included a bibliography. Includes separate indexes of contributors, names, and subjects. Additional access is by means of the table of contents.

222. Mitzel, Harold E., ed in chief. *Encyclopedia of Educational Research.* 5th ed. New York: Free Pr., 1982. 4v. ISBN 0-02-900450-0.
For administrators, scholars, students and other interested professionals and nonprofessional readers, this work offers "a critical synthesis and interpretation of reported educational research." It includes 256 signed articles arranged alphabetically. Each includes a bibliography and appropriate "see" and "see also" references. An organizing scheme arranges the article titles under eighteen broad subject headings. These range from "Agencies and Institutions," "Education of Exceptional Persons," and "Instruction Systems and Techniques" to "Measured Characteristics of Learners," "Organization and Administration," and "Teachers and Teaching." Under each heading, entry titles are listed "at either one or two levels of specificity." Includes an index.

223. Monroe, Paul, ed. *Cyclopedia of Education.* New York: Macmillan Publishing Co., 1911. 5v.
Now out of date, this work remains useful especially for historical and biographical information. Comprehensive in coverage, the cyclopedia covers education in all countries and periods. As an indication of its scope, volume five provides an analytical index with the following general outline: History of Education, Philosophy of Education, Educational Psychology, Teaching Methods, Educational Sociology, Educational Administration, Physical Education, School Architecture, as well as sections related to Elementary, Secondary and Higher Education. Arranged alphabetically by topic, this work includes signed articles by specialists in the fields. Articles include cross-references (where appropriate), and listings of selected references, and, to a limited extent, tables and illustrations.

224. Unwin, Derick and McAleese, Ray. *Encyclopedia of Educational Media Communication and Technology.* 2d ed. Westport, Conn.: Greenwood Pr., 1988. 568p. ISBN 0-313-23996-7.
Combining definitions with articles by seventy specialists, this source's target audiences is educational technologists. The title reflects its heavy British emphasis. Other sources should be consulted for more commonly used terms in the United States. Some sixty-two broad topics are treated in depth as articles, along with tables and illustrations. Articles range from copyright in the U.K. and the U.S., cybernetics, research methodology, holography, to language labs, simulation, telesoftware, and visual literacy. References to further readings are copiously included. There is an alphabetical index of terms that lack their own entries.

3.

DIRECTORIES

INTRODUCTION

This chapter brings structure and organization to a wide range of directories covering everything from college fairs and campus lodgings for tourists to nationally recognized accrediting agencies and financial aid programs primarily or exclusively for the disabled. Well over two hundred such works are listed and arranged in broad subject categories. Within these, sources are arranged alphabetically by author and title. As a substantial number of these sources are widely recognized by their titles, we decided that title entries rather than author entries would be more useful. Other works are listed by author or compiler.

We also considered the availability of sources. Most are included if they are listed in the latest editions of such sources as <u>Books in Print</u> (New York: R.R. Bowker), or <u>Directories in Print</u> (Detroit: Gale Research, Inc.). Where sources are judged to be unique or of special interest, and they are relatively recent publications, they are included.

Some works appearing in recent editions of <u>Books in Print</u> or <u>Directories in Print</u> are not unlike other sources we already included. If these additional works were more than four or five years old, we excluded them.

In compiling this chapter, we frequently encountered sources which blurred the distinction between directories and handbooks, i.e., works in which the number of entries is limited and the information provided is extensive. If we determined the primary purpose of the source to be that of providing a systematically arranged list of persons, institutions, or organizations, we included it. If users do not find a particular item in this chapter, they are reminded of the separate title and subject indexes at the end of our compilation.

Another problem we encountered on searching the various print and computer-assisted databases was the disagreement among them concerning certain bibliographic details - and with some, the lack of it. This was especially true regarding publication dates: determining whether a directory was a continuing (serial) publication or a one-time effort, determining the beginning date for a serial publication, and determining whether a source had ceased being published.

Where available, we accepted information provided through the Online Computer Library Center (OCLC) system. Where such data were lacking, we accepted that found in such print sources as Directories in Print or the Encyclopedia of Associations, both published by Gale Research, Inc.

Over the years, certain continuing (serial) directories were produced by different publishers. Citations found in this chapter include the current publisher, but with the date of first appearance of the work.

Of the wide range of sources included are those providing information about individuals. These are in the form of membership lists. Other works that go beyond simply listing persons (and providing addresses, telephone numbers, job titles, etc.) are found in Chapter 7: Biographical Sources.

Not included are pamphlets (works of fewer than forty pages), and items readily accessed through the Educational Resources Information Center (ERIC) system. Excluded as well are directories limited to regional or single state coverage, or to a specific discipline or field of study other than higher education.

Thus, in this chapter we have sought to include current, published directories focusing exclusively, or in substantial part, on higher education. Some works may not be as readily available as others (especially membership directories), but they are listed in recent sources, and they will be of value and importance to those seeking information about particular organizations of constituency groups.

The result is a gathering of a substantial number of publications covering a very broad range of interests and needs.

GENERAL WORKS

225. *College Catalog Collection: Catalogs Reference Guide*, San Diego: Career Guidance Foundation, 1971 -   . Microfiche. Annual.
An annual subscription service which includes catalogs from institutions recognized as accredited by the U.S. Department of Education. The series includes approximately thirty-six hundred catalogs from twenty-nine hundred institutions. The index lists all the colleges and catalogs in the current and prior year collections. Catalogs are listed in numerical order within a state. Entries include the institution name, location, catalog microfiche number, whether graduate or undergraduate, and microfiche number for the previous year's catalog. Separate sections cover U.S. Territories, special bulletins, and selected foreign catalogs. A separate index provides access by college name.

226. Klein, Barry T. *Guide to American Educational Directories*. West Nyack, N.Y.: Todd Publications, 1992. 350 p. ISBN 0-915344-29-7. Intended for those directly or indirectly involved in education at all levels, this broad selection lists nearly twenty-five hundred items grouped into more than a hundred subject areas. Included are bibliographies, indexes, guides and handbooks, as well as more conventional

directories. Entries include title, length, contents and frequency, along with publisher name, contact information and price. A title index is provided.

227. *Micrologue: College Catalogs on Microfiche.*   Bolder, Colo.: Micrologue, 1984 -   . Monthly.
Provides microfiche copies of academic course catalogs (with monthly updates) from all accredited institutions in the United States and its territories. This includes undergraduate, graduate, and professional schools from colleges, universities, junior, technical, and community colleges. The collection is organized alphabetically by state, then by institution, within each state, with only one catalog per microfiche sheet. With this arrangement, an index is not required. A list of institutions covered, however, would assist uninformed users seeking information about institutions found to be unaccredited.

228. Schlachter, Gail A. *How to Find Out About Financial Aid: A Guide to Over 700 Directories Listing Scholarships, Fellowships, Loans, Grants, Awards, Internships.* San Carlos, Calif.: Reference Service Press, 1987. 334 p. ISBN 0-918276-05-5.
Arrangement is by type of aid with geographical, discipline, and special recipient group subsections. Each entry includes an annotation, full bibliographic information and price. A directory of publishers with full addresses and telephone numbers is included. Name, title, subject and geographic indexes are also provided.

229. *State Education Directories.* San Diego, Calif.: Career Guidance Foundation, n.d. Microfiche. Annual.
Reproduces in microfiche format directories published by State education departments. Although format and contents vary, most provide listings and addresses of state education officers and of schools at the elementary, secondary and post-secondary levels. Access to the directories is provided in the annual index College Catalog Collection: Colleges Reference Guide (San Diego: Career Guidance Foundation). Directories are found under "Education Directory" alphabetically listed among the college entries. The directories are found among the catalogs produced in microfiche. Entries include current and previous year's microfiche item number for location in the collection. The annual index arranges entries in two sections: by State, and by college name and directory title.

230. *The World of Learning.* London, England: Europa Publications, Ltd., 1947 -   . Annual. ISSN 0084-2117.
A unique directory that attempts to amass, in a single volume, information on educational institutions of the world. Its scope includes academies, research institutions, learned societies, libraries, archives, museums, and colleges and universities. An introduction section covers international organizations. The rest of the volume is devoted to individual countries. For each institution, the address, phone number, founding date and name of director are provided together with brief descriptive summaries. A total of three hundred pages cover the United States, with inclusion of member names for academies such as the National Academy of Sciences. Universities and colleges are arranged alphabetically by states in the U.S. section. Institutional periodicals available for exchange are identified. There is an index of institutions.

SPECIAL WORKS

Administration

231. *Directory of Graduate Deans at United States Universities*, 1872-
     1970. Washington, D.C.: U.S. Dept. of Health, Education, and
     Welfare, Office of Education, 1970. 47p.
Provides historical and biographical information about more than one
thousand administrators at 240 institutions awarding the Ph.D. or similar
degree, with the exception of those institutions conferring only the
Doctor of Theology Degree. Institutions are listed alphabetically by
state. Each entry indicates the year the first earned doctorate degree
was conferred, the year in which a separate unit for the administration
of the graduate program was established, and a chronological list of
persons in charge, together with their academic fields and years of
tenure. Includes an index of Deans.

232. *HEP Higher Education Directory*. Falls Church, Va.: Higher Education
     Publications, 1983-   . Annual. ISSN 0736-0797.
This comprehensive and authoritative work provides basic information and
a listing of administrative officers for over thirty-five hundred
accredited postsecondary institutions that meet U.S. Dept. of Education
guidelines.   Entries for each institution in the main section are
arranged by state and include contact information, affiliation or control, calendar system, highest degree offered, accreditations, data on
enrollment and tuition, and the names and titles of administrators.
Other sections list accrediting agencies, state higher education agencies
and consortia of institutions. Indexes of institutions, administrators,
and accrediting bodies are also provided.

233. *National Council of University Research Administrators Directory*.
     Washington, D.C.: National Council of University Research
     Administrators, n.d. Annual.
Lists almost two thousand administrators of sponsored research, training
and education programs in colleges or universities, in organizations
wholly organized and administered by colleges or universities, and in
consortia of colleges and universities. Entries are arranged alphabetically, with the name, affiliation, address, and telephone number provided
for each individual.

Associations

234. *Directory for National College Fairs*. Skokie, Il.: National Assn.
     of Coll. Admissions Counselors, n.d. Semiannual.
Provides basic information (location, costs, majors, required admissions
tests, admission and financial aid application deadlines) for the five
hundred to seven hundred institutions that recruit at the Spring or Fall
National College Fairs. Includes an index by fair.

235. Directory of College Stores.   New York: B. Klein Publications,
     1985-   . Irregular. ISSN 0084-988X.
Lists about three thousand stores which cater mainly to a college student
population providing books, stationery, personal care items, gifts, etc.
Entries are arranged geographically and include the following: store
name, address, manager's name, kinds of goods sold, college name and
enrollment, numbers of females and males served, and whether college-
owned or privately owned.

236. *Directory of Computing Facility in Higher Education.* Austin: Texas
     Computation Center, Univ. of Texas at Austin, 1985-   . Annual.
     ISSN 0749-1999.
Lists more than fourteen hundred computing facilities in colleges and
universities. Arranged geographically, the entries include the following
information: facility name; institution name, address, and phone number;
name of director or contact; type of equipment and service; size of
staff; and financial data. Three indexes provide personal names,
institution names, and type of equipment.

237. *Directory of Education Associations.* Washington, D.C.: U.S. Dept.
     of Health, Education, and Welfare, 1977-   . Annual.
Lists names, addresses, and telephone numbers of education associations,
their chief officers, and the titles and frequency of their official
publications. The material is divided into six sections: National and
Regional Education Associations; National Honor and Professional Associations; State Education Associations; Foundations; Religious Education
Associations; and International Education Associations. The volume is
indexed alphabetically by association and by the key word in its name.

238. *Guide to Campus-Business Linkage Programs.* 2d ed. New York:
     American Council on Education/Macmillan, 1986. 278p. ISBN 0-02-
     910600-1.
The first section, about fifty pages, of this work is a handbook- style
guide to developing, implementing, maintaining and evaluating a wide
range of campus-business relationships. The remainder of the work is a
listing, mostly by company name, of such agreements or programs. Entries
give company and institution contact information and indicate the location, purpose, size and duration of each program. Indexes by subject,
state and college are provided.

239. *Guide to COPA Recognized Accrediting Bodies.* Washington, D.C.:
     Council of Postsecondary Accreditation. 1988-   . Biennial.
     ISSN 0897-3628.
A directory of approximately fifty nongovernment accrediting organizations in alphabetical order. The work was formerly entitled Guide to
COPA Recognized Accrediting Associations. In addition to name and
address, this source specifies the agency's accrediting responsibility,
procedures, and fees. Three major sections focus on: 1) national
institutional accrediting bodies (e.g., National Home Study Council); 2)
regional institutional accrediting bodies (e.g., Middle States Association of Colleges and Schools); and 3) specialized bodies (e.g., American
Dietetic Association).

240. *Higher Education Directory.* Washington, D.C.: Council for Advance-
     ment and Support of Education, 1979-   . Biennial. ISSN 0740-
     9230.
A brief directory of more than fifty national education associations that
have headquarters or offices in Washington, D.C. Lists each body's
address and telephone number, total membership, activities, and publications. Includes an acronym index.

241. *The Hillel Guide to Jewish Life on Campus.* Washington, D.C.: B'nai
     B'rith Hillel Foundations, 1990-   . Annual.
A geographical listing of Hillel foundations and other Jewish organizations on about 450 campuses in the U.S. and Canada. In addition to the
name, address and telephone number of each organization and the names of
its staff, information is provided on the schools' total and Jewish enrollments, Judaic studies courses and degrees offered, Jewish residence

houses, religious services, cooking facilities and Kosher menus. Institution and staff member indexes are provided.

242. *International Directory of Research Institutions on Higher Education.* 2d ed. Paris, France: European Center for Higher Education (UNESCO), 1987. 134p. ISBN 92-3-002516-X.
Research centers throughout the world are listed by country from Argentina to Zambia. Each entry contains standard directory information of name, address, phone number, as well as publications by year and author in the country's language with English translations. A total of twenty-eight U.S. centers and programs are identified. While selection criteria are not spelled out, included are well-known research centers at the University of Michigan, Pennsylvania State University, ERIC, Carnegie Foundation, University of Connecticut, University of Massachusetts at Amherst, etc. Surveys trends in higher education research related to minorities, quality, and social awareness. Lacks an index.

243. *Nationally Recognized Accrediting Agencies and Associations.* Washington, D.C.: Office of Postsecondary Education, Department of Education, 1989. 25p.
A recent issue of this irregularly published but very useful source covers about eighty accrediting agencies and associations recognized by the Secretary of Education. Regional associations are arranged by name. Other associations are arranged by the academic area accredited by them. Listings include the name of the accrediting committee, name of the organization, address, telephone number, name of director, kinds of schools or programs accredited or, in the case of regional associations, the states covered, year of recognition by the Dept. of Education, year of last full review, and year of next review by the Education Office. A discussion of criteria and procedures used by the Secretary of Education for accepting accrediting agencies is presented.

244. Olson, Stan, Kovacs, Ruth and Haile, Suzanne. *National Guide to Foundation Funding in Higher Education.* New York: Foundation Center, 1992. 1,012 p.
Provides a state-by-state listing of nearly three thousand foundations with over $1 million in assets and at least $100,000 annual funding. Entries include such information as the foundation's name and address, program interests, type of support, giving restrictions, application information, contact persons, along with fund directors and listings of recent grants awarded. Similar to the Foundation Directory, this source focuses on higher education exclusively. Included is a selected bibliography for further research and a general introduction to foundation-administered grants in the field, and a table analyzing grants by subject area. Four indexes cover donors, officers, and trustees; geographic areas; types of support and foundation names.

245. *Research Centers Directory.* Detroit, Mich.: Gale Research, 1960-
. Irregular. ISSN 0080-1518.
A major source of information about research institutions in the United States and Canada that are non-profit or based in colleges and universities. The 1990 (14th) edition includes 11,726 entries in two volumes, identifying the directors, fields of study and publications. Institutions are grouped into four sections: life sciences, physical sciences and engineering, private and public policy, and social and cultural studies. The subject index enables cross referencing by state under specific headings. Alphabetical listing of research centers is provided in the master index which also gathers university-related centers under the educational institutions where the research activities are carried out.

A supplement, New Research Centers, is available between editions of the directory.

246.   Smallwood, Imelda H. *OERI Directory of Computer Data Files.* U.S. Dept. of Education, Nat. Center for Education Statistics, 1990. 30 p.

The office of Educational Research and Improvement's (OERI) National Center for Education Statistics has been collecting data on all levels of education for over twenty years. This directory provides descriptive information and purchase prices of some seventy computer databases available. They are grouped under five categories: Elementary and Secondary Education; Post Secondary Education; Vocational and Adult Education; Libraries; and Longitudinal Studies. These data files are available on tape and diskette under titles: Public High Schools, School Districts, Private High Schools, Colleges and Universities, Higher Education Revenues and Expenditures. This directory supersedes the 1987 edition entitled OERI Directory of Computer Tapes.

247.   *Society for Values in Higher Education - Directory of Fellows.* New Haven, Conn.: Society for Values in Higher Education, 1976-   . Triennial.

Lists in alphabetical order about sixteen hundred society members with backgrounds in teaching or administration. Entries provide the following: name, title, affiliation, and address; personal and educational data; fields of study or interest; type of fellow and year of election to membership. Includes both geographical and field of study or interest indexes.

Colleges

248.   *Accredited Institutions of Postsecondary Education.* Washington, D.C.: American Council on Education, 1976/1977-   . Annual. ISSN 0270-1715.

Lists institutions which have been accredited or are candidates for accreditation. Data on both institutional and program accreditation are provided by the accrediting bodies. Institutions are listed alphabetically by state. Entries contain the following: name and address, control type, type of institution (four-year college, university, etc.), type of student body, and branch campuses or affiliates. Also included are dates of first accreditation or of candidacy and of latest renewal or affirmation, accrediting body, type of calendar, level of degrees offered, specialized accreditation, name and title of chief executive officers, and fall enrollments. A list of public systems of higher education, their addresses, telephone numbers, and chief executive officers is provided, along with a list of accrediting bodies recognized by the Council on Postsecondary Accreditation. An institutional index is included.

249.   *American Universities and Colleges.* New York: Walter de Gruyter, 1928-   . Quadrennial. ISSN US0066-0922.

Provides detailed descriptions of more than nineteen hundred accredited (or recognized candidate) institutions of higher education offering baccalaureate or higher degrees. An introductory section briefly covers such topics as the evolution of American higher education, its structure, undergraduate and graduate education, relations with government, and foreign students. The major section is devoted to describing the institutions. Arrangement is alphabetical by state then by institution. Entries include customary information for such works, along with such features as the number and rank of faculty by department, the institution's publications, and "distinctive and educational programs". Appendices include several tables, list of ROTC units, summary data for the institutions, and general and institutional indexes. A major source produced in collaboration with the American Council on Education.

250. *America's Lowest Cost Colleges.* Barryville, N.Y.: NAR Publications. 1977- . Biennial.
Identifies approximately seven hundred accredited, low-cost colleges and universities. Entries are arranged by state, including Puerto Rico, Guam, and Washington, D.C. In addition to institution name and address, entries include in-state and out-of-state tuition costs and the degrees offered. Many of the institutions listed are two-year colleges. Useful to those whose primary concern is tuition cost.

251. *Barron's Compact Guide to Colleges.* Woodbury, N.Y.: Barron's Educational Series, 1978- . Biennial.
Covers more than three hundred colleges and universities. Entries include institutions' names, addresses, telephone numbers, degrees offered, tuition, admission requirements, and application deadlines. Also covered are the school calendar, financial aid available, housing, enrollment, and other descriptive information in a coded format. Institutions are arranged alphabetically.

252. *Barron's Guide to the Best, Most Popular, and Most Exciting Colleges.* 4th ed. Hauppauge, N.Y.: Barron's Educational Series, 1986. 472p. ISBN 0-81203-652-2.
Lists about four hundred colleges with high admission standards, enrollments of more than fifteen thousand, or unconventional academic programs, teaching methods, or philosophies. The following information is provided: institution name, location, and telephone number; contact name; description of facilities and programs; admission requirements; costs; financial aid data; enrollment; rating; faculty information; and accessibility to the handicapped. The entries are arranged alphabetically. There are college maps for each state, a glossary, and a selector rating index. Based on information provided in Profiles of American Colleges (Barron's Educational Series).

253. *Barron's Profiles of American Colleges.* Hauppauge, N.Y.: Barron's Educational Series, Inc., 1964- . Biennial. ISSN 0533-1072.
The seventeenth edition (1990) of this work is subtitled Descriptions of the Colleges. It provides the following information about more than fifteen hundred colleges and universities: name and address, application deadline, tuition, programs offered, facilities, comments on student life, rating of faculty, student-faculty ratio, housing, athletic programs, student organizations, requirements, financial aid, transfer, accessibility for the handicapped, computer facilities, admissions contact, etc. The institutions are listed under geographical headings. Some students might find another feature of this directory useful: the "College Admissions Selector", which arranges colleges in seven groups according to the estimated competition in admissions. Under separate cover, Barron's publishes an Index of College Majors. Includes an index of institutional names.

254. *Barron's 300: Best Buys in College Education.* 2d ed. Hauppauge, N.Y.: Barron's Educational Series, 1992. 658 p. ISBN 0-8120-4860-3.
Profiles institutions selected for the excellence of their academic

programs and lower-than-average costs. Entries are arranged alphabetically by state and address each school's strong and weak points, financial aid opportunities, and graduates' academic, business and professional prospects. Students' opinions and comments are also included. Schools selected represent a broad range of curricula and are drawn from all fifty states. Some expensive schools are included if their tuition and fee charges are low relative to those of comparable prestigious institutions.

255. Bear, John. *Bear's Guide to Earning College Degrees Non-Traditionally.* 11th ed. Benicia, Calif.: C & B Publishers, 1991. 304 p. ISBN 0-962931-20-9.
This guide serves as an introduction to and examination of the issues and possibilities presented by non-traditional postsecondary education. There are chapters on the nature and types of non-traditional programs, the meaning and value of degrees and accreditation, and how to evaluate non-traditional schools. The author also discusses the alternative methods of earning college credit, such as equivalency examinations, correspondence courses, and credit for life experience. A sizable portion of the work is a listing of about one thousand institutions, accredited and not, that offer non-traditional approaches to academic and professional degrees. The entry for each school includes its name, address and telephone number, founding date, name of a contact person, fields of study and degrees offered, residency requirements, accreditation and legal status, and tuition charges. A separate chapter lists institutions the author has found to be phony "degree mills." A glossary, bibliography and institution indexes are also provided.

256. *The Best Buys in College Education.* New York: Times Books, 1987. 473 p. ISBN 0-8129-1701-4.
Lists more than two hundred colleges and universities which, in the authors' opinion, offer a high standard of education for a reasonable price. The institutions are arranged alphabetically with the following information provided: name and address; tuition and room and board fees; availability of financial aid, scholarships,and other cost-reducing programs; academic strengths and weaknesses; facilities; sports programs; and a description of social life. Two indexes: geographical and price.

257. *Best Dollar Values in American Colleges.* New York: Arco Publishing, 1990. 320 p. ISBN 0-13-083494-7.
First published in 1988 as <u>Dollarwise Guide to American Colleges</u>, this work lists some three hundred selected institutions whose tuition charges are lower than average. Entries provide basic information about each school and also include tuition, room and board, fees, enrollment figures, faculty, academic, programs, admission requirements and a selectivity rating.

258. Birnbach, Lisa. *New and Improved College Book.* Englewood Cliffs, N.J.: Prentice-Hall, 1990. 640p. ISBN 0-13-538240-8.
The emphasis of this informal guide is on campus life and atmosphere at about two hundred schools, as determined from questionnaires, interviews and campus visits. Students' favorite courses, professors and majors, preferred places to live, eat, drink and recreate, and attitudes toward minorities and gays are reported in varying detail. That and the limited number of institutions covered mean this work is best used as a supplement to more comprehensive guides.

259. *Callahan's College Guide to Athletics and Academics in America.* New York: Harper and Row Pubs., 1984. 259p. ISBN 0-06-015249-4.

Surveys athletic and academic information concerning only about 240 of the more commonly known or attended colleges and universities in the United States, despite the title's use of the designation "in America." Institutions were selected as being broadly representative of the six hundred originally chosen for examination. Information about each covers the usual data about degrees offered, tuition, etc., followed by intercollegiate sports information for men and women. Institutions are arranged alphabetically by name.

260. *Campus Vacations Directory.* Miramar, Fla.: Campus Vacations, 1989. 30p. ISBN 0-94506-324-5.
Lists more than fifty colleges in the U.S. and Canada which offer non-credit summer classes for adults, families, and high school students, with some advance credit courses for high school students. The adults/families section is arranged geographically, while an alphabetical listing by college name is provided in the high school student section. Entries include: institution name, address, and telephone number; program names and dates; admission requirements; courses offered; and descriptions of housing, costs, and special activities offered.

261. Cass, James and Birnbaum, Max. *Comparative Guide to American Colleges for Students, Parents, and Counselors.* 15th ed. New York: Harper Collins Publishers, 1991. 351p. ISBN 0-06-271513-5.
Seeks to provide a sound basis for college selection by students and parents. Institutions are listed alphabetically with the following information: introductory statement, admission, academic environment, faculty, student body, religious orientation, campus life, annual costs. This work includes two abbreviations lists, and a comparative list of majors (with colleges listed alphabetically under each major, or with number of degrees conferred in that major). Includes indexes for selectivity, states, and religions.

262. Christian College Coalition. *Consider a Christian College: A Guide to 78 Private Liberal Arts Colleges and Universities Combining Academic Excellence and Enduring Spiritual Values.* 2d ed. Princeton, N.J.: Peterson's Guides, 1990. 127p. ISBN 1- 56077-019-9.
A guide, assembled by the Christian College Coalition, covering about eighty accredited liberal arts colleges that take an evangelical approach to education. The schools are spread over some thirty states and encompass thirty different denominations. Arrangement is by institution name, and entries include contact information, academic programs, costs, financial aid, student life, and school religious affiliation. Geographical index.

263. *Chronicle Four-Year College Databook.* Moravia, N.Y.: Chronicle Guidance Publications, 1979/80-   . Annual. ISSN 0191-3670.
Similar in purpose, organization and format to the <u>Chronicle Two-Year College Databook</u>, this work covers over two thousand institutions. The volume comprises two major sections: 1) a listing of schools by programs or major areas of study, with an indication of the level of degrees or other certification offered, and 2) basic information on the characteristics of the institutions, presented in tabular form and arranged by state. Entries in this "chart" section include name, address and telephone number, academic calendar, control, enrollment, admissions selectivity and requirements, costs and financial aid. Appendices provide additional information about individual schools, a listing of accrediting bodies and an index to the charts section by school name.

264. *College Admissions Data Handbook.* Concord, Mass.: Orchard House,

n.d. Annual. ISSN 0738-9582.
This directory, published in a national edition and four regional editions (Northeast, Southeast, Midwest, and West), lists nearly sixteen hundred accredited four-year undergraduate institutions offering bachelor's degrees. The following information is provided: institution name, phone number, location, names of president and admissions officer, accreditation, number of students, admission policies, SAT and ACT board score distribution, costs, and financial aid available. Also covered are advanced placement policy; subject majors offered; degrees offered; extracurricular activities; academic calendar; religious requirements; and policies on housing, cars, alcohol, attendance, and marriage. Items are arranged geographically by region, then by school name. Indexes are in a separate volume, entitled College Admissions Index of Majors and Sports (Orchard House, 1988-   .). The index includes college names, majors and sports, religious affiliations, and fees.

265. *The College Blue Book*. New York: Macmillan Publishing Co., 1923-
      . Biennial. 5v. ISSN 0069-5572.
One of the major standard college directories. Its first three volumes cover some three thousand two and four-year institutions in the U.S. and Canada. The Narrative Descriptions and Tabular Data volumes are both arranged by state and province, with indexes by college name, and both provide basic information on each school. The former volume offers more detailed description and background in each entry; the latter's entries emphasize quantitative data. Degrees Offered by College and Subject provides a section arranged by college with the degrees each offers and another arranged by fields of study indicating which colleges offer them. The Scholarships, fellowships, Grants and Loans volume is a listing of over twenty-six hundred sources of financial aid, mostly private, grouped by field of study. Occupational Education is a geographically arranged directory giving basic information on over seventy-five hundred U.S. business, trade and technical schools. It has a detailed index to curricula and programs of instruction. (Based on examination of the 23d ed., 1991.)

266. *College Directory of Cooperative Education*. Philadelphia, Pa.:
      S.B. Collins, Drexel University, 1986. 355p.
Lists over six hundred U.S. and Canadian colleges and universities with programs that include employment related to students' fields of study. Entries are arranged geographically and include: school name, enrollment and contact information; name of program director; program description, eligibility and requirements, and number of students and employers participating. Alphabetical, geographical and field of study indexes are provided.

267. *College Facts Chart*. Spartanburg, S.C.: National Beta Club, n.d.
      Annual. ISSN 0069-5688.
Provides basic information on some thirty-five hundred U.S. institutions. Entries are arranged geographically and include school name and contact information, date of founding, control or affiliation, enrollment, degrees offered, faculty, and costs for tuition, room and board. Indexed by institution.

268. *The College Handbook*. New York: College Entrance Examination
      Board, 1963-   . Annual. ISSN 0069-5653.
Provides information on more than thirty-one hundred two- and four- year institutions in the United States, its territories and six foreign countries. Institutions are listed alphabetically within each state with the following information included: institution type, degrees awarded, ma-

jors, academic programs and requirements, freshman admissions (and class profile for preceding year), fall-term applications, student life, athletics, student services, annual expenses, financial aid, address and telephone number. Introductory sections provide advice on college decisions and separate indexes of general and specialized colleges, campus environments (urban, suburban, rural), open admissions colleges, and colleges with special admissions programs. Also provided is information on application priorities and closing dates. Includes an alphabetical index of colleges.

269. *College Handbook for Transfer Students, 1993.* All New Annual Ed. New York: Coll. Entrance Examination Board, 1992. 544p. ISBN 0-87447-435-3.
Provides information on transfer policies at almost three thousand two- and four-year colleges in the U.S. For each institution, general information is offered on costs, degrees offered, and size. College descriptions include: admission and residency requirements; Fall, 1991, application deadlines; number of transfer applicants accepted; articulation program with other colleges; services for transfer students; financial aid availability and deadline for applying; and percentage of students transferring from two-year to four-year programs. A guidance section explains the transfer process and provides advice on planning ahead for maximum transfer of credit, choosing transfer destinations, budgeting resources, and deciding to apply for transfer. Special sections are devoted to the needs of community-college students and to suggestions on how high-school students can plan for transferring from a community college to a four-year institution. Indexes.

270. *College Planning/Search Book.* Iowa City: American College Testing Program. Annual. ISSN 0147-8826.
Provides information on more than three thousand U.S. two and four-year institutions. Two-year schools are arranged by state, four-year schools by region and admissions selectiveness. Entry for each school includes address, accreditation, admissions policies, costs, financial aid, characteristics of the student body, academic majors and distribution of students among them, and presence of ROTC programs. Indexes of school names, academic majors and career programs are provided.

271. *College Price Book.* Falls Church, Va.: Higher Education Publications, 1990. 427 p. ISBN 0-914927-12-4.
Intended for parents, students or advisors needing basic comparative academic and financial data. Covering about seventeen hundred four-year colleges, this work presents its data in single-line chart form. Entries are arranged by majors, then by state, and by colleges arranged from highest tuition costs to the lowest. They include such data as total enrollment, in-state and out-of-state tuition costs, test score averages, retention rate beyond the freshman year, the percent of students receiving financial aid, and other comparative information. Includes an index of majors, list of institutions by program, and an alphabetical list of institutions. Data are provided from the U.S. Department of Education and the College Research Group. A useful preliminary tool for college selection, but data are now several years old.

272. *College 'Scope.* Boston: Financial Publishing Co., 1985. 48p. ISBN 0-87600-655-1.
Lists about fifteen hundred four-year colleges and universities accredited by regional accreditation agencies. Entries, in tabular form, include: institution's name and address, undergraduate enrollment, entrance tests required, average SAT score of entering freshmen, number

and total dollar value of undergraduate scholarships available, tuition, board and room costs, major fields of study (coded), deadlines for entrance and aid applications. Entries are arranged geographically.

273.   *Common-Sense Guide to American Colleges 1991-92.*   Lanham, Md.: Madison Books, 1991.   448p.   ISBN 0-8191-8244-3.
A range of institutions are assessed from a "traditional" point of view in this very selective guide.   Each entry provides basic contact information and statistics, plus a four- to eight-page evaluative profile that covers the school's history, student body, curriculum, athletics and campus life as well as its distinctive character and its strong and weak points.   Graphs present data on each school's tuition, fees and financial aid.

274.   De la Croix de Lafayette, Jean-Maximillien.   *Directory of Non-Traditional Colleges and Universities in the United States.* Washington, D.C.: American Council for University Planning and Academic Excellence, 1986.
Lists some six hundred institutions which offer such non-traditional approaches to learning as independent study, external, or non-residential degree programs, and extension courses.   Entries are arranged by academic subject area and include institution or program, address, telephone number, contact persons, and program description. Also includes section on "schools to avoid."   Similar and related titles by this prolific author which appear to overlap significantly in their coverage are simply listed here:

The Best and Worst Non-Traditional and Alternative Colleges and Universities in the United States. 3d. ed. Washington, D.C.: ACUPAE, 1991. 161p. ISBN 0-939877-14-7.

The Black List of United States Non-Traditional and Alternative Colleges and Universities. 3d. ed. Washington, D.C.: ACUPAE, 1991. 162p. ISBN 0-939877-33-3.

Directory of United States Adult and Continuing Postsecondary Education.   3d ed. Washington, D.C.: Elite Associates Internat., 1991.   145p. 0-939893-08-8.

Lafayette's Encyclopedia of American Non-Traditional Higher Education.   3d. ed. Washington, D.C.: ACUPAE, 1991. 498p. ISBN 0-685-30550-3.

National Directory of Recognized Alternative and Non-Traditional Colleges and Universities in the United States.   3d. ed. Washington, D.C.: ACUPAE, 1991. 160p. 0-939877-16-3.

National Index of Recognized and Unrecognized Alternative and Non-Traditional Colleges and Universities in the United States. 3d. ed. Washington, D.C.: ACUPAE, 1991. 164p. ISBN 0-939877-32-5.

275.   De la Croix de Lafayette, Jean-Maximillien.   *Directory of the Best Colleges and Universities in the United States.* Washington, D.C.: American Council for University Planning and Academic Excellence. 2v.   n.d.   Biennial.
Some five hundred non-traditional institutions and programs and six hundred conventional colleges and universities are listed in separate volumes.   Entries are grouped by program and include name, address,

telephone number and description of institution, selected officers or contact persons, and academic programs. Subject and institution indexes are provided. Contents overlap with this author's <u>Directory of Non-Traditional Colleges and Universities in the United States</u> and <u>National Register of Social Prestige and Academic Ratings of American Colleges</u>. Also very similar is his <u>Comprehensive Guide to the Best Colleges and Universities in the United States</u>. Washington, D.C.: ACUPAE, 1990. 136p. ISBN 0-939877-01-5.

276. De la Croix de Lafayette, Jean-Maximillien. *United States Colleges and Universities Legally Empowered to Grant Academic Degrees*. Washington, D.C.: American Council for University Planning and Academic Excellence, 1990. ISBN 0-317- 90352 -7.
A geographical listing of about twenty-seven hundred institutions legally sanctioned, usually by their state, though not necessarily accredited by any other body. Entries include each school's address and telephone number, name of contact person, programs and degrees offered, and costs, indexed by institution name and program. This work adds little to what is found in the standard college guides. Appears to be very closely related to this author's <u>Directory of United States Postsecondary Education: U.S. Register of Nationally Accredited, State Approved Institutions and Colleges Without Official Recognition</u> (Washington, D.C.: ACUPAE, 1990. 138p. ISBN 0-939877-34-1).

277. De la Croix de Lafayette, Jean-Maximillien. *National Register of Social Prestige and Academic Ratings of American Colleges and Universities*. Washington, D.C.: American Council for University Planning and Academic Excellence, 1990. 136p. ISBN 0-939877-05-08.
Offers ratings of both traditional colleges and universities and non-traditional programs (independent study, non-resident, external degree, etc.) on academic quality and social prestige. Another section presents school rankings and ratings from other sources and discusses the pitfalls involved in using such evaluations. An explanation of accreditation and a listing of accrediting bodies are also included. Not indexed. Other titles by this author which appear to offer similar evaluations or ratings are:

   <u>Comprehensive Guide to the Best Academic Programs and Best Buys in College Education in the United States</u>. Washington, D.C.: Elite Associates Internat., 1990. 146p. ISBN 0-939893-05-3.

   <u>National Rating and Rank Order of Colleges and Universities in the United States</u>. Washington, D.C.: ACUPAE, 1990. 146p. ISBN 0-939877-09-0.

278. *Directory of Member Institutions, Institutional Representatives and Associates*. Washington, D.C.: Council of Graduate Schools, 1977- . Annual.
A guide to member institutions, institutional representatives, and associates. This source includes a geographical list of approximately four hundred graduate schools in the United States. Each entry includes the institution's name and address, and the name, title, discipline, and telephone number of institutional representatives.

279. *Directory of On-Campus Lodging for Tourists*. 4th ed. Indian River, Mich.: Jess Miller Publishing, 1987- . Annual.
Lists over 120 colleges and universities which offer dormitory rooms for tourist lodging. Information includes dates and total number of rooms

available, single and group rates, other campus facilities, local points
of interest, and the campus contact person.   Entries are arranged
geographically.

280. *Directory of Postsecondary Institutions.* Washington, D.C.: U.S.
      Dept. of Education, Office of Educational Research and Improve-
      ment, Center for Education Statistics, 1987- . 2 vols. Annu-
      al. ISSN 0898-2317.
First appearing as part of the <u>Education Directory</u> (1894/95-.), this work
lists all institutions in the United States and its outlying areas in two
volumes: Vol. 1 includes four-year and two-year institutions, and Vol.
2 the less-than-two-year institutions. Entries include name of institution, location, telephone number, unit identification (UNITID) code,
Federal Interagency Committee on Education (FICE) code, control, highest
level of degree awarded, programs offered, accreditation, and other
useful data. Institutions are arranged alphabetically by state.
Appendices include additions, reinstatements, deletions, mergers, and
other information. Includes both an index of institutions and a list of
tables.

281. *Directory of Public Vocational-Technical Schools and Institutes in
      the U.S.A.*   5th ed. DeKalb, Ill.: Media Marketing Group and
      Minnesota Scholarly Pr., 1990. 377p. Biennial. ISSN 0898-2686.
Drawing on state vocational education offices and individual schools'
catalogues, this directory lists post-secondary institutions that offer
occupational education.   Schools are grouped by state, and each entry
includes school name, address, phone number, director or president, and
programs or courses of study offered, with their duration and degree or
certificate awarded. Indexes by school and by program are included.

282. *Directory of United States Traditional and Alternative Colleges and
      Universities.* Washington, D.C.: National Assn. of State Approved
      Colleges and Universities and the American Council for Univ.
      Planning and Academic Excellence, 1984-   . Triennial.   ISSN
      0882-7745.
Grouped by type of program, some four thousand institutions are listed
here, including both conventional colleges and those which offer
alternatives such as external degree, correspondence and independent
study programs, evening or weekend courses, or instruction through mass
communications media.   State higher education offices, accrediting
organizations and scholarship sources are also listed. Entries provide
addresses, telephone numbers, contact persons and program descriptions.

283. *The Fiske Guide to Colleges 1992.*   New York: Times Books/Random
      House, 1991. 880p. ISBN 0-8129-1908-4. Annual. ISSN 1042-7368.
This selective guide profiles over three hundred U.S. colleges and
universities the compilers consider to be the "best and most
interesting." Besides providing basic facts and statistics on each
school, entries include a descriptive essay, averaging twelve hundred
words, that touches on academic quality, social life and campus environment. Geographic and price range indexes are provided.

284. *Guide to Background Investigations.*   Tulsa, Okla.: Source
      Publications, 1988-   . Semiannual. ISSN 0897-3156.
A listing of sources of background information on job applicants,
including government agencies and offices and some thirty-six hundred
postsecondary education institutions. Entries are grouped by type of
information available (e.g., driving record, educational history) and
include, for the colleges, contact information, accreditation, degrees

offered, and policies on confirming students' attendance and releasing transcripts.

285. *Index of College Majors: Profiles of American Colleges in a Convenient Chart Format.* 17th ed. Hauppauge, N.Y.: Barron's Educational Series, 1990. 366p. ISBN 0-8120-4349-9.
Uses a tabular format to indicate the major fields of study offered at the nearly fifteen hundred accredited institutions listed in Barron's Profiles of American Colleges. Entries are arranged by state and also include each school's address and telephone number, enrollment data, tuition and room and board charges, and a competitiveness rating. The volume has an index by school name and a "College Admissions Selector," which lists schools by degree of admissions competitiveness.

286. *Insider's Guide to the Colleges.* New York: St. Martin's Press, 1970- . Annual. ISSN 0093-5220.
Noteworthy for its reliance on descriptions and impressions gathered from students who have attended the schools, this guide covers about three hundred colleges and universities in the U.S. and Canada. The compilers include schools with superior academic programs, but also favor large and state-affiliated universities, while providing a representative sampling of smaller colleges. Entries provide some basic data on admissions criteria, enrollments, costs, etc., but consist mainly of two- to three-page descriptive essays on each school's salient characteristics, quality of life and ambience. Introductory matter includes commentary on selecting a college, the admission process, and current trends, a glossary, and a "College Finder" index to the schools by selected characteristics. An institution name index is also provided.

287. *Institutions of Higher Education: Index by State and Congressional District.* Washington, D.C.: U.S. Dept. of Education, 1974-75- . Biennial. ISSN 0145-7721.
This work lists all institutions that offer at least a one-year program leading to a degree and meet the department's accreditation standards. The list groups the schools by Congressional district in each state and indicates the current representative of each district. Location, ZIP code, control, institution type, enrollment and student costs are given for each institution. Puerto Rico, American Samoa and other "outlying areas" are also included.

288. *Jewish Student's Guide to American Colleges.* New York: Shapolsky Publishers, 1989. 221p. ISBN 0-933503-32-6.
Useful as a supplement to more general selection guides and directories, this work offers narrative descriptions of some ninety four-year institutions, focusing on those features of interest to prospective Jewish students. Entries sketch the general character of the school and campus and indicate the number of Jewish students enrolled; the presence of Hillels and other organizations, Jewish libraries, publications, residences, programs and activities; availability of synagogues, religious services, and Kosher dining. Names and addresses of Hillel directors and other contact persons are included, as well as the admissions office address and telephone number.

289. *List of School Openings and Other Dates.* Oberlin, Ohio: Nat. Assn. of College Stores, n.d. Annual.
Published since the 1980s, this source provides dates of class sessions, vacations, and commencements at some forty-three hundred universities, four-year colleges, and community colleges. Arrangement of institutions is geographical. Location and enrollment are also given for each school.

290. *Lovejoy's College Guide.* New York: Monarch Press, 1952-   . Biennial. ISSN 0076-132X.
This standard, authoritative source includes sections on financial aid, admissions procedures and standardized tests, a listing of accrediting bodies and associations, as well as indexes of majors and of intercollegiate sports. The largest section is a listing by state of twenty-five hundred two- and four-year institutions. For each four-year and residential two-year school, a detailed profile provides information on enrollments, costs, admission statistics and criteria, accreditation, academic program and resources, student life and athletics. Indexed by institution name.

291. *National Directory of Catholic Higher Education.* New Rochelle, N.Y. Catholic News Publishing Co., 1983-   . Irregular. ISSN 0736-9476.
More than two hundred Catholic colleges and universities are listed geographically with the following information: institution name, address, and telephone number. Entries also include enrollment, costs, programs offered, and admission requirements. Includes an index of major courses offered.

292. *National Directory of College Athletics.* Men's ed. Amarillo, Tex.: Ray Franks Publishing Ranch, 1969-   . Annual. ISSN 0547-616X.
Includes men's athletic departments at more than two thousand senior and junior colleges in the United States and Canada. Entries include school names, addresses, enrollments, colors, and team names. Also provided are the stadium or gym capacities; presidents; men's athletic directors, physical education directors, and coaches for each sport; athletic departments; telephone numbers; and association affiliations. Arrangement is alphabetical by institution name.

293. *National Directory of College Athletics.* Women's ed. Amarillo, Tex.: Ray Franks Publishing Ranch, 1977-   . Annual. ISSN 0739-1226.
Covers women's athletic departments at about two thousand senior and junior colleges. Each entry includes school name, address, enrollment, colors, stadium or gym capacity, and nickname. Also included are names of presidents, women's athletic directors and physical education directors, coaches for each sport, athletic departments' telephone numbers, and association affiliations. Arrangement is alphabetical by institution name.

294. *National Review College Guide: America's 50 Top Liberal Arts Schools.* New York: National Review, 1991. 211p. ISBN 1-56121-068-4.
This highly selective guide provides information on schools judged to offer top quality undergraduate education. The editors sought out institutions with curricula based on the Western tradition and American values, faculty who give high priority to classroom teaching, administrations that do not pursue educational fads, an atmosphere of true intellectual freedom, and an in loco parentis approach to student life.

295. Nemko, Martin. *How to Get an Ivy League Education at a State University.* New York: Avon Books, 1988. 774p. ISBN 0-380-75375-8.
The largest section of this timely work contains informative profiles of 115 high quality public institutions. Profiles are five to seven pages long and address areas such as student body, class size, extracurricular activities, housing, costs, situation for minorities, gays and handi-

capped. Introductory chapters offer information and advice on choosing, getting accepted by and getting the most from a state university.

296. Norman, Jay. *Peterson's Directory of College Accommodations: The Low-Cost Alternative for Travelers in the United States and Canada*. Princeton, N.J.: Peterson's Guides, 1989. 172p. ISBN 0-87866-869-1.
Lists lodgings available to travelers at 175 colleges and universities in the U.S. and Canada. While details may be dated, information about institutions offering such facilities remains useful.

297. Ohles, John F. and Ohles, Shirley M. *Private Colleges and Universities*. (The Greenwood Encyclopedia of American Institutions, v. 6) Westport, Conn.: Greenwood Pr., 1982. 2v. ISBN 0-313-23323-3, 0-313-23324-1.
A companion to the authors' *Public Colleges and Universities* (Greenwood Pr., 1986), this source covers 1,290 privately run educational instituions. Entries are arranged alphabetically by institution. Each entry provides an institutional profile and includes founding date, name origin, former administrators and alumni and other basic directory information, i.e., degrees offered, library collection size, etc.   Six appendices list institutions by founding date, state professional schools, religious orientation, important events in U.S. higher education, and sexually segregated institutions. There is a combined index of institutions, personal names, and geographic locations. The encyclopedia treatment renders this a unique source tracing the origin and establishment of private colleges and universities in the United States.

298. Ohles, John F. and Ohles, Shirley, M. *Public Colleges and Universities*. (The Greenwood Encyclopedia of American Institutions) Westport, Conn.: Greenwood Pr., 1986. 1,014p. ISBN 0-313-23257-1.
A major contribution of this source is the provision of hard-to-find historical background information about the founding and development of 578 public colleges and universities. The lengthy descriptions, arranged by school name and averaging two pages for each institution, also trace important events such as campus expansion, achievements and impacts of new college presidents, and establishment of new schools or programs of study. Reference to source materials consulted is given at the end of individual narratives. Four appendices identify institutions by years founded, state, land-grant, and specializations such as maritime, military, etc. There is one combined personal names and institutions index. This is a companion to <u>Private Colleges and Universities</u> of the same series.

299. *Patterson's American Education*. Mount Prospect, Ill.: Educational Directories, 1954/55-   . Annual. ISSN 0079-0230.
A continuation of Patterson's American Educational Directory, which began in 1904, this comprehensive work contains two major sections. Part 1, "Secondary Schools," is a geographic listing of state education departments and boards, over twelve thousand school districts, over thirty-four thousand public, private and parochial schools and more than seventy-three hundred postsecondary institutions of all types. In this section, only names and addresses of the postsecondary institutions are given. Part 2, "Post-Secondary Schools," is also updated and published separately as <u>Patterson's Schools Classified</u> (q.v.). Here, the postsecondary institutions are arranged by type (preparatory schools; vocational, technical and trade schools; junior colleges; graduate schools, etc.) and by fields of study. Entries include institution name, address and president

and/or admissions officer. Some schools provide lengthier descriptions
of their history, programs, enrollment, costs, etc. There are indexes
by type of school and school name.

300. *Patterson's Schools Classified*. Mount Prospect, Ill.: Educational
      Directories, 1951-   . Annual. ISSN 0553-4054.
This companion to Patterson's American Education (which covers secondary
education) includes more than sixty-five hundred colleges, universities,
junior colleges, and military, trade, vocational, technical, hospital,
and private preparatory schools. The following information is provided:
school name and address, name of administrator or admissions officer.
Many entries also include descriptive material supplied by the individual
schools. Listings are arranged by subjects offered. There are no
indexes.

301. *Peterson's Competitive Colleges*.   10th ed. Princeton, N.J.:
      Peterson's Guides, Inc., 1991-   . 382p. ISBN 1-56079-041-5.
Editors of this directory have identified over three hundred colleges as
having a selective admissions policy. The institutions are listed alphabetically (art and music schools are listed separately). The following
data are provided: institution name, address, telephone number, and the
name of contact personnel. Also included are data about faculty and
students, majors offered, tuition and room and board costs, financial
assistance available, athletic programs, and application information.
Includes a geographic area index.

302. *Peterson's Graduate Education Directory*.   Princeton, N.J.:
      Peterson's Guides, 1986-   . Annual.
Covers more than fourteen hundred institutions in the U.S. and Canada
which offer graduate and professional programs. Institutions are listed
alphabetically.   Entries provide the following: institution name and
address, telephone number, and contact person. Also included are administrators' and faculty heads' names and telephone numbers, description
of programs, campus facilities, enrollment, and tuition costs. Includes
geographical and name indexes.

303. *Peterson's Guide to Certificate Programs at American Colleges and
      Universities*. Princeton, N.J.: Peterson's Guides, 1988. 351p.
      ISBN 0-87866-741-5.
Lists four-year colleges and universities providing certificate programs
which are specialized fields of study developed and implemented by
faculties of the respective institutions. Institutions are arranged
geographically.   Entries include: names of institutions, certificate
program names, names and addresses of contact persons for each program,
programs' formats, evaluations, enrollment requirements, program costs,
housing information, and student services. More than fifteen hundred
programs are profiled.   Includes a classified guide to programs and an
index of institutions.

304. *Peterson's Guide to College Admissions*. 5th ed. Princeton, N.J.:
      Peterson's Guides, 1991. 579p. ISBN 1-56079-018-0.
More than seventeen hundred four-year colleges in the U.S. are arranged
geographically in this volume. The following information is provided:
school name, location, admissions contact name and phone number, campus
setting, enrollment, costs, difficulty of admission, application
deadlines for admission and financial aid. This source covers all the
steps that students encounter during the admissions process. No index.

305. *Peterson's Guide to Four-Year Colleges*.   Princeton, N.J.:

Peterson's Guides, 1983-   . Annual.
Originally published as <u>Peterson's Annual Guide to Undergraduate Study</u> (1970-1982), this work includes both directories and sections of advice for those seeking higher education. Blue pages contain information on financial aid and taking standardized tests, as well as three directories: an entrance difficulty directory, in which colleges are listed alphabetically within categories ranging from most difficulty to noncompetitive; a cost-ranges directory, in which colleges are listed alphabetically in categories ranging from least to most expensive; and, a majors directory. White pages present college profiles and special announcements for about seventeen hundred institutions (22nd ed., 1992). Entries, arranged alphabetically by institution name include: name and location; enrollment (both undergraduate and graduate, as well as percentage of each gender); application deadline; standardized test scores (percentages); tuition and fees; room and/or board, and ease of entrance. Included as well are undergraduate profiles, prior year's freshman data, enrollment patterns, freshman admissions, transfer admissions, graduation requirements, expenses, financial aid, special programs, housing, campus life/student services, athletics, majors, and contact persons with titles, address and telephone numbers. In-depth two-page descriptions of more than eight hundred colleges and universities, prepared exclusively by college officials, are arranged alphabetically by official name of the institution. Index of colleges and universities.

306. *Peterson's National College Databank: The College Book of Lists.* 5th ed. Princeton, N.J.: Peterson's Guides, 1990. 518p. ISBN 1-56079-020-2.
Nearly thirty-five hundred two-year and four-year colleges and universities are classified by their common traits (e.g., special courses required, housing guarantees, etc.). Entries are further arranged geographically. Each includes the following information: the institution's name, address, academic information, degrees offered, enrollment characteristics, admission information, expenses, financial aids, intercollegiate athletic programs, campus facilities, and majors. In this edition users can find such information as colleges having the lowest student-computer ratio. No index.

307. *Peterson's Register of Higher Education.* Princeton, N.J.: Peterson's Guides, 1989-   . Annual. ISSN 1046-2406.
Formerly <u>Peterson's Higher Education Directory</u>, this work covers almost thirty-six hundred accredited U.S. postsecondary degree-granting institutions and lists nearly seventy-five thousand administrative officers and academic unit heads. In the largest section, school "profiles" are arranged alphabetically and provide general information on each institution (contact information, FICE code, entity number, date of founding, control, academic calendar, degrees offered, enrollment, institutional and program accreditations, library and research resources) and listings of its administrators and academic officers with their titles and telephone numbers. An appendices section provides directories of U.S. Dept. of Education offices, state higher education agencies, general and specialized accrediting bodies, and higher education associations and consortia. There are also a personnel index and institution indexes by state and type of accreditation.

308. *Randax Education Guide to Colleges Seeking Students.* Randolph, Mass.: Education Guide, 1972-   . Annual.
Lists about two hundred, two-and four-year colleges, health care schools, and vocational schools that are actively recruiting students and advertise in this publication. Entries include: school name, address, and

telephone number; degrees and courses offered; date founded; type of control; enrollment costs; and, admission requirements. Entries are arranged geographically. Three indexes cover the major fields of study,
state and institution name.

309. *The Right College*. New York: Arco/Prentice Hall, 1988-   .
    Annual. ISSN 0899-588.
Covers more than fifteen hundred colleges and universities in the United
States and Canada. Entries include college name, telephone number,
costs, and the numbers of faculty and students. Also provided are admission requirements, name, title, and telephone number of admissions
contact staff, description of facilities, student life, programs of
study, athletics and financial aid available. Arrangement is geographical. Included are articles and tables covering aspects of college life,
numbers of graduates going on to graduate study, etc. Indexes by college
name, major, intercollegiate sports, and various comparisons (ranked by
competitiveness, average test scores, costs, etc.). The work is
published with cooperation of the College Research Group.

310. *Rugg's Recommendations on the Colleges*. Sarasota, Fla.: Rugg's
    Recommendations, 1980-   . Annual.
Appearing annually only since 1988, this source lists recommended undergraduate programs of study. Results are based on review of several hundred institutions. In the 1990-1991 issue, six hundred institutions were
examined for thirty-nine fields of study. Ratings categories for institutions are : most selective, very selective, and selective. The work
concludes with coverage of average Scholastic Aptitude Scores (both ver-
bal and mathematical) reported by cited institutions in the section on
recommended programs. Six appendices cover college categories and
planning aids (e.g., timetables, checklists, etc.). Found useful by
students and parents, but caution is advised regarding methodologies
employed by this and similar sources of program review.

311. *The 300 Most Selective Colleges*. New York: Arco Publishing, 1989.
    499p. ISBN 0-136-02913-2.
Provided by the College Research Group of Concord, Massachusetts, this
guide describes three hundred institutions with selective admission
requirements. Entries include such information as institution name,
address, contact person, programs of study, faculty and student size,
financial aid, computer facilities, and other services. Includes subject
and name indexes.

312. *Transfer Credit Practices of Designated Educational Institutions*.
    Washington, D.C.: American Assn. of Collegiate Registrars and
    Admissions Officers. 198 -   . Biennial.
Lists more than thirty-six hundred colleges and universities. The
geographically arranged entries include name, address, telephone number,
and title of selecting member. Those for other institutions include:
name, city, zip code, name changes, codes indicating general practices
regarding acceptance of academic credits from other institutions, highest
level of work offered; regional accreditation status; year of first accreditation or of first candidacy for accreditation; and accreditation
by other accrediting associations which are members of the Council of
Postsecondary Accreditation. Index of institution names.

313. *U.S. and Worldwide Travel Accommodations Guide*. Newport Beach,
    Calif.: Campus Travel Service, 1980-   . Annual. ISSN 0898-4247.
Lists more than six hundred colleges and universities in the United
States and twenty-six other countries which accept paying guests when

classes are not in session. Some of these institutions limit their guests to teachers, students, or alumni. Entries are arranged geographically and provide the following information: the institution's name, address, and phone number; rates; any restrictions; dates available; food service; and activities in the area. The volume includes a list of foreign tourist offices in the United States.

314. *World List of Universities.* New York: Stockton Pr., 1974- . Triennial. ISSN 0084-1889.
This English-French directory is designed to facilitate educational exchanges. The first part consists of a listing of universities and other institutions by country, providing the address of the institution and the year of its founding. For most countries listed, various departments of each institution are included. The second section of each chapter lists international and regional organizations concerned with higher education and includes descriptive notes. More detailed description in the second part of the work provides: history, aims, structure, and activities of each major group outlined. Academic associations and scholarly bodies concerned only with specific disciplines are excluded. Prior to 1985 the directory was published biennially. Includes an index.

Community, Vocational, and Technical Colleges

315. *AACJC Guide to Community, Technical, and Junior Colleges.* Washington, D.C.: American Assn. of Community and Junior Colleges, 1988- . Annual. ISSN 1041-3413.
Currently covers about fifteen hundred accredited institutions and their chief personnel in administrative and student services. Entries include the institution name, address, telephone number, and the names and titles of chief administrators. Arrangement of institutions is geographical. Separate indices cover college names, and names and titles of chief administrators.

316. *AACJC Membership Directory.* Washington, D.C.: American Assn. of Community and Junior Colleges, 1986- . Annual.
Currently includes the more than one thousand member institutions. Entries provide the institution name, address, and telephone number. Also included are the names of the chief executive officers, current enrollment, and year established. Member institutions are listed alphabetically by state. Appendices provide a list of state directories, the AACJC constitution and bylaws, State associations of community colleges, and a series of policy statements. Indexes for member colleges and chief executive officers.

317. *Chronicle Two-Year College Databook.* Moravia, N.Y.: Chronicle Guidance Publications, 1979-80- . Annual. ISSN 0191-3662.
Similar in purpose, organization and format to the <u>Chronicle Four-Year College Databook</u>, this work covers over twenty-three hundred institutions. The volume comprises two major sections: 1) a listing of schools by programs or major areas of study, with an indication of the level of degrees or other certification offered, and 2) basic information on the characteristics of the institutions, presented in tabular form and arranged by state. Entries in this "chart" section include name, address and telephone number, academic calendar, control, enrollment, admissions selectivity and requirements, costs and financial aid. Appendices provide additional information about individual schools, a listing of accrediting bodies and an index to the charts section by school name.

318. *A Directory of Public Vocational-Technical Schools and Institutes
      in the U.S.A., 1990-1992.* 5th ed. DeKalb, Ill.: Media Marketing
      Group, 1990. Biennial. ISBN 0-933474-47-4.
Describes public schools and institutes offering postsecondary occupational education. This work provides the following information about the
institutions: name and address, directors name and telephone number, and
complete program/course listings. Organized by State, entries are arranged alphabetically within each according to the school's name. There
is a brief paragraph at the head of each state section which provides a
description of the system and the address and telephone number of the
appropriate state agency. School index and program index.

319. Herbert, Tom and Coyne, John. *Getting Skilled: A Guide to Private
      Trade and Technical Schools.* 2d ed. Washington, D.C. Nat. Assn.
      of Trade and Technical Schools, 1989. 145p. ISBN 0-942426-00-2.
A step-by-step guide leading students through the process of identifying
their inclination for vocational technical training. In five chapters,
it begins by explaining the importance of getting skills and job prospects; then moving on to the reasons for technical schools as opposed to
community colleges. The next chapter teaches the technique for evaluating the schools and curriculum offered. The last two chapters explain
the admission procedures and provide tips on surviving academically.
There is a ten-page bibliography, but no index. It remains useful for
counselors in spite of the publication date.

320. *Peterson's Guide to Two-Year Colleges.*   Princeton, N.J.:
      Peterson's Guides, 1983-   . Annual.
Similar to Peterson's Guide to Four-Year Colleges (1983-   ). This
title evolved from Peterson's Annual Guide to Undergraduate Education
(1970-1982). The work includes only those institutions that recognize
federal laws prohibiting discrimination on the basis of sex, race, color,
handicap, or national or ethnic origin. Its arrangement (1992) is essentially the same as that of the four-year colleges guide, with the exception that the blue pages have two majors directories: one for associate
degree programs at two-year colleges and a separate one for associate
degree programs for four-year colleges. Its white pages include about
fifteen hundred institutions and provide college profiles covering such
topics as location information, enrollment data, application deadlines,
standardized test scores, tuition and fees, financial aid, special programs, student life and services, and a number of other items. In addition there is an "Open Forum" for colleges on a voluntary basis, which
includes about fifty institutions.

321. Ryan, G. Jeremiah. *Corporation and Foundation Giving to Community,
      Technical, and Junior Colleges.* Washington, D.C.: American Assn.
      of Community and Junior Colleges. 1989. 81p. ISBN 0-87117-195-
      3.
Compiled by the author during his tenure as an AACJC fellow, this source
identifies 190 of the largest corporations and foundations. They are
presented alphabetically by name, including the address, contact persons,
and whether they accept proposals from community colleges. Two separate
lists provide names of over 160 institutions that do not require matching
fund and 860 institutions that have matching-gift policies. Since no
addresses are provided, these lists must be used in conjunction with
other sources such as the Foundation Directory (The Foundation Center,
1992). The remaining twenty pages of this poorly typed source are
devoted to explaining fund raising activities among community colleges,
statistical tables, a description of the methodology employed, and

references consulted. While it fills a gap, its usefulness could be enhanced by a table of contents.

322. *Technical, Trade, and Business School Data Handbook.*   Concord, Mass.: Orchard House, 1985-   . Biennial.
Almost four thousand accredited public and proprietary postsecondary schools offering programs in technical, trade, or business fields are listed in a geographical arrangement. Each entry provides: the school name, address, and telephone number; accrediting body; admissions contact; course offerings; placement services; and a profile of the school. The work is available in a two-volume national edition or in two regional editions. There is a subject index.

323. *Who's Who in Community, Technical, and Junior Colleges.* Washington, D.C.: American Assn. of Community, and Junior Colleges, 1990-   . Annual.
Not so much a biographical dictionary, as a guide to key personnel listed under their respective institutions. Entries are alphabetical by state; under each, arrangement is alphabetical by institution, with top officials listed in hierarchical order by position. The major portion of the directory is devoted to United States institutions, while a second part covers American Samoa, Canada, Guam, Micronesia, Panama, and Puerto Rico. An appendix lists state directors. This is followed by indexes of administrators and institutions. Preliminary pages list AACJC officers and associate members.

Disabilities

324. *BOSC Directory, 1987 Supplement: Facilities for Learning Disabled People.* Congers, N.Y.: BOSC Publishers, 1987. 92p.
Supplements the original BOSC Directory (1985), which omitted schools lacking special programs for learning-disabled people, by listing those with special services for such students. Colleges and universities are listed alphabetically by state and location within each state. The following information is provided: name, address, telephone number, contact, fees, prerequisites, special courses, mainstreamed (required/ expected), certificate or degree, comments. There is also a listing of relevant agencies in eight states and Canada. Includes a cumulative index of schools.

325. *Directory of College Facilities and Services for People With Disabilities.* 3d ed. Phoenix, Ariz.: Oryx Pr., 1991. 361p. ISBN 0-89774-604-X.
A guide for individuals with disabilities, as well as a source for school and college counselors, providing information about more than sixteen hundred colleges and universities in the United States, its territories, and Canada.   Entries are arranged alphabetically by state, city, and territory and Canadian province and city. Entries are concise, including: institution name, location and description; campus facilities and services; names and addresses of clearing houses and databases; print sources; and grant programs. Separate indexes cover institutions, disabilities served and programs.

326. *Financial Aid for the Disabled and Their Families.* Redwood City, Calif.: 1988-   . Biennial. ISSN 0898-9222.
Comprehensive listing of financial aid programs primarily or exclusively for the disabled and members of their families. Fellowships, scholarships, loans, grants and internships are grouped by type of

disability. Also provided are a list of information sources for state aid and a list of more general financial aid directories. Program title, sponsoring organization, geographic, subject and deadline date indexes are provided.

327.   Lipkin, Midge. *Schoolsearch Guide to Colleges with Programs or Services for Students with Learning Disabilities*. Belmont, Mass.: Schoolsearch Press, 1990. 696p. ISBN 0-9620326-3-8.
This work covers some six hundred colleges and universities. The entry for each school includes application and admission information, enrollment, academic offerings, description of the campus and student activities, and the extent and unique features of its disabilities programs. Appended tables contain further information on institutions' test requirements, disabilities served, special services and aids, and academic accommodations that can be made.

328.   *Lovejoy's College Guide for the Learning Disabled*. 2d ed. New York: Monarch Press, 1988. 163p. ISBN 0-671-64717-2.
This guide includes a listing of over four hundred colleges and universities with services and programs for the learning disabled. Entries are arranged by state and include general information about each school, admission requirements, academic programs, support services available to the learning disabled, and the name of a contact person. An index of college names is provided.

329.   *National Directory of Four-Year Colleges, Two-Year Colleges, and Post High School Training Programs for Young People with Learning Disabilities*. Tulsa, Okla.: Partners in Publishing Co. Irregular.
About two hundred institutions with programs for learning-disabled students are arranged geographically. Information provided includes: school name, address, name of contact, description and type of program, admission policies, courses offered, curriculum modifications, enrollment, percentage of learning-disabled students completing the program, and remedial clinics.

330.   *Peterson's Guide to Colleges with Programs For Learning Disabled Students*. 2d ed. Princeton, N.J.: Peterson's Guides, 1988. 398p. ISBN 0-87866-689-3.
Covers two- and four-year U.S. colleges and universities which provide services and programs for students with learning disabilities, such as aphasia, dyslexia, and minimal brain dysfunction. More than nine hundred entries are listed in two sections which cover, respectively, institutions with comprehensive programs and those with programs with special services. Each entry provides the name of the institution, location, special services, admission procedure, tutoring and advising services offered, testing, housing, and staff information. Includes separate list of resource organizations and a geographical index.

Faculty

331.   *Directory of American Fulbright Scholars*. Washington, D.C.: Council for International Exchange of Scholars. 1983-   . Annual. ISSN 0883-0975.
Classified by field of study, this work identifies nearly one thousand American Fulbright Scholars for domestic assignment or abroad. Each entry includes name, title, address, award and duration of award. Access is by means of host country index, recipient name index, and an index by recipient's home address. Formerly published as the Directory of

American Fulbright Scholars University Lecturing and Advanced Research Abroad.

332. *Directory of ASHE Membership and Higher Education Program Faculty.*
College Station, Tex.: Assn. for the Study of Higher Education,
Texas A & M Univ., 1977-   . Biennial.
Identifies graduate level programs and member faculty involved in the
study of higher education. Apart from address information, faculty's
research interests are identified. The main section provides separate
lists of the programs and faculty. The work was formerly entitled Directory of Higher Education Programs and Faculty. Includes indexes by
organizations and personal names.

333. *Faculty White Pages.* Detroit: Gale Research Co., 1989-   .
Annual. ISSN 1040-1288.
A subject-classified directory listing names, addresses, and telephone
numbers of faculty at United States colleges and universities, and other
institutions of higher education. This source would be of special use
to those involved with job-recruiting, searching for consulting services,
arranging guest lectures, soliciting manuscripts and book reviews, or
seeking expert testimony. Entries are arranged into forty-one general
subject sections outlined in the table of contents. A guide to subject
sections arranges three hundred specific disciplines into the general
subjects. Entries within each subject section are arranged alphabetically by last name. A separate "Roster of Colleges and Universities"
provides contact information for each institution covered. Does not
include a separate name index.

334. *National Faculty Directory.* Detroit: Gale Research Co., 1970-
. Annual. ISSN 0077-4472.
The 1991 edition of this directory lists 597,000 faculty members at
approximately three thousand four hundred American colleges and universities, plus approximately 240 Canadian institutions. Only faculty
members with classroom teaching responsibilities are included since the
directory is designed for use by publishers for the sale of textbooks.
The names of faculty members are arranged alphabetically with the
following information included: name of academic department, name of
college or university, address. A roster of institutions arranged
geographically by state or province precedes the faculty listing.

Financial Assistance

335. *Better Late Than Never: Financial Aid for Re-Entry Women Seeking
Education and Training.* Washington, D.C.: Women's Equity Action
League, 1987. 59p.
Lists about forty programs which provide financial aid and counseling,
federal financial aid, and other sources of scholarships, fellowships,
grants, and loans of interest to non-traditional students. The programs
are classified by type. The following information is offered: program
title; organization or agency name, address, and telephone number; contact name; description of aid, services, and program requirements; and
application deadline. An alphabetical index and a subject index are
provided.

336. *CFAE Corporate Handbook of Aid-to-Education Programs.* New York:
Council for Aid to Education, 1984-   . Biennial. ISSN 1041-
455X.
Formerly published as CFAE Casebook: A Cross-Section of Corporate Aid-to-

Education Programs, this work supplies the following information about two hundred United States corporations and/or their corporate foundations which have aid-to-education programs: corporation or foundation name, address, and telephone number; name of administrator; Fortune 500 rank; annual sales; number of employees; purpose, policies, and total grants, descriptions of funded programs; expenditures; and recipients. Entries are arranged alphabetically. Four indexes: geographic, line of business, size of program, categories of giving.

337. _Chronicle Student Aid Annual_. Moravia, N.Y.: Chronicle Guidance
      Publications, 1978-   . Annual. ISSN 0190-339X.
This publication lists mainly non-collegiate organizations and both AFL-CIO-affiliated and independent labor unions. Also included are federal and state governments which offer financial aid programs for undergraduate and graduate study. Entries are arranged alphabetically and include the following information: name of the sponsoring organization, address, amount of aid, eligibility requirements, application, selection procedure. This work was formerly published under the title _Student Aid Annual_. Three indices provide access according to field of study/subject, organization name, and program name.

338. _College Check Mate: Innovative Tuition Plans That Make You a
      Winner_. 5th ed. Alexandria, Va., Octameron Associates, dist. by
      Dearborn Trade, 1991. 167p. ISBN 0-9459-8155-4.
The 1990 edition lists by state one thousand institutions which offer innovative assistance programs. Most entries provide a general description of each school's financial aid patterns as well as its noteworthy special plans. The volume's introductory section explains the various loans, payment options, tuition guarantees, discounts, shortened degree, work and scholarship programs that may be offered.

339. _The College Cost Book_. New York: Coll. Entrance Examination Board,
      1981-   . Annual. ISSN 0270-8493.
Designed to help students and their families deal with college costs. Introductory chapters cover everything from estimating and managing costs to determining need and eligibility for financial aid. The major part of the work is comprised of tables, arranged by state and institution, including data on tuition and fees, books and supplies, costs of campus residency, home costs, number of students receiving aid, need based aid, grants and scholarships, financial aid application deadlines, and documentation requirements. Includes an index of institutions, institutions offering tuition and/or fee waivers and special tuition payment plans, and sources of information about state grant programs and the Stafford Loan Program. A good source of step-by-step advice on getting financial aid.

340. _College Financial Aid Annual_. New York: Arco, dist. by Prentice-
      Hall, 1988-   . Annual. ISSN 1040-8282.
Written as a handbook as well as a directory, this work offers guidance and information on getting financial aid. It includes chapters which discuss such topics as trends in financial aid, public and private sources of aid, tax considerations, cooperative education programs, financing and aid-seeking strategies. There is also a glossary and a bibliography of other guides and directories. A major portion of this work is a listing of over twenty-three hundred selected scholarships and grants, arranged by fields of study and other eligibility criteria. Entries in this section provide the name of the award, contact information for the sponsoring organization, number and size of awards available, fields of study, eligibility criteria and application deadline. There

are also indexes of academic majors, award criteria and scholarship names.

341. *College Loans from Uncle Sam: The Borrower's Guide that Explains It All, from Locating Lenders to Loan Forgiveness.* 11th ed. Alexandria, Va.: Octameron Associates, 1992-1993. ISBN 0-9459-8151-1.
Formerly published as Scholarship Programs of the States (1980) and Help from the Governor and Locating Lenders: Two Contact Directories for Scholarships and Student Loans (1981), this directory lists federal student loan programs and state loan guarantee agencies. The material is arranged geographically and provides the agency's name, address, telephone number, and key personnel.

342. *Corporate Tuition Aid Programs: A Directory of College Financial Aid for Employees at America's Largest Corporations.* 2d ed. Princeton, N.J.: Peterson's Guides, 1986. 214p. ISBN 0-87866-482-3.
A listing of over seven hundred major companies which provide tuition support for their employees and their families. Entries are arranged alphabetically and include each company's eligibility requirements, level of support and any restrictions or limitations. Includes a bibliography on financial aid.

343. *Earn and Learn: Cooperative Education Opportunities Offered by the Federal Government.* Alexandria, Va.: Octameron Associates, 1985- . Annual.
This brief guide lists some 850 colleges and universities (including about fifty two-year schools) that have work-study arrangements with federal agencies. Entries provide basic contact information. The schools section is arranged geographically; the agencies section alphabetically.

344. *Financial Aid for Veterans, Military Personnel and Their Dependents 1990-1991.* San Carlos, Calif.: Reference Service Pr., 1990. 290p. Biennial. ISBN 0-918276-11-X.
One of five financial aid sources by the publisher, this one lists 1,120 funding agencies. Names of programs and institutions are grouped by type of funding: scholarships, fellowships, loans, grants, awards, and internships. Under each of the above are special categories for veterans, military personnel and dependents. Three other sections include a list of state sources, an annotated bibliography of related directories, and five indexes: program title, sponsoring organization, geographic, subject and calendar.

345. *Financial Aids for Higher Education.* Dubuque, Iowa: William C. Brown, 1974-1975- . Biennial. ISSN 0364-8877.
Intended for graduating high school seniors and college undergraduates, this work lists over twenty-five hundred scholarships and aid programs, with information on eligibility, value of award, application procedures and any restrictions for each one. A useful introductory section includes advice to aid-seekers and scholarship counselors and a list of other information sources. A general index and a special "program-finder" index are provided.

346. *Finding Financial Resources for Adult Learners: Profiles for Practice.* New York: College Entrance Examination Board, 1985. 56p. ISBN 0-87447-206-7.
Profiles some seventy financial aid programs for adult college students,

including for each a description, history, eligibility requirements, number participating, and the name and address of the school offering the aid. Profiles are grouped in two sections: those based on campus sources of aid (scholarships, loans, student employment, modified tuition plans, credit for prior learning) and those derived from community resources, such as banks, business and industry, unions, the military, and civic and non-profit organizations. This work is based on a survey of over one hundred college financial aid officers done in 1983, so some information may be outdated.

347. *Guide to Department of Education Programs.* Washington, D.C.: U.S. Dept. of Education, 1981-   . Annual.
Provides a listing, arranged by its sponsoring offices, of the Department's funding programs, many at the postsecondary level, available to state or local agencies, organizations, institutions, schools, groups or individuals. For each, the program's title and purpose, type of assistance, eligibility criteria and contact information are provided. Formerly a special issue of <u>American Education</u>.

348. *Guide to Federal Assistance.* Rock Hill, S.C.: Wellborn Associates, 1978-   . Looseleaf. Base volume and monthly updates. ISSN 0278-5064.
A substantial directory of over five hundred education-related federal assistance programs, providing program names and descriptions, authorizing legislation, contact information, requirements, deadlines and related programs. Entries are arranged by program type and indexed by topic, funding level, deadline, agency contact, public law and <u>Catalog of Federal Domestic Assistance </u>entry.

349. *Guide to Federal Funding for Education.* Arlington, Va.: Education Funding Research Council, 1981-   . Looseleaf. Annual with monthly supplements. ISSN 0275-8393.
Lists nearly two hundred financial aid programs for agencies and institutions at the elementary, secondary and postsecondary levels. Programs are grouped in sixteen sections by area of concern (e.g., adult educational, bilingual education, vocational education), and each entry includes program title and purpose, type of assistance, eligibility criteria, application procedure and contact information. Indexed by program title.

350. *Peterson's College Money Handbook [year]: The Only Complete Guide to Scholarships, Costs, and Financial Aid at U.S. Colleges.* Princeton, N.J.: Peterson's Guides, 1983-   . Annual. ISSN 0894-9395.
Data for the 1991 edition were collected through questionnaires sent to accredited institutions in the U.S. that offer four- or five-year baccalaureate degree programs. The sections on college cost and aid profiles constitute the major part of this handbook. Colleges are alphabetically listed showing the annual expenses to students, summary of undergraduate financial aid, money-saving options, awards, and names of contact persons. Five indexes identify institutions by type of scholarship, ROTC or co-op programs, tuition prepayment plans, and athletic grants. Its emphasis is on college costs. For a better understanding of the financial aid process, users might consider <u>Lovejoy's Guide to Financial Aid</u> (Monarch Pr., 1985-   .), which provides a step-by- step approach.

Grants and Scholarships

351. *The A's and B's of Academic Scholarships.* 13th ed. Alexandria, Va.: Octameron Associates, 1990. 131p. ISBN 0-945981-30-9.
This work lists in tabular format some twelve hundred colleges which award scholarships on the basis of merit or academic achievement. Each entry includes the number and value of awards available, award criteria, fields of study, application dates and any restrictions.

352. *AFL-CIO Guide to Union Sponsored Scholarships, Awards and Student Financial Aid.* Washington, D.C.: American Federation of Labor and Congress of Industrial Organizations, n.d. Annual.
Lists local, national and international unions, labor councils, federations and similar organizations that award scholarships and other financial aid. Entries are arranged by the nature of the union or aid program and include union name and address, type and amount of aid and eligibility criteria.

353. *Annual Register of Grant Support.* Wilmette, Ill.: Nat. Register Publishing, 1969-   . Annual. ISSN 0066-4049.
Guide to grant support programs of over three thousand public and private foundations, government agencies, corporations and associations in the U.S. and Canada. Arranged by broad subject areas, the entries include name and contact information of the grant-making organization, its areas of interest, the nature and size of grants available, qualifications and restrictions, application procedures and deadlines, principal personnel, officers and contact person(s). Subject, organization, geographic and personnel indexes are provided.

354. *Awards Almanac: An International Guide to Career, Research, and Education Funds.* Chicago: St. James Pr., 1990-   . Annual.
Currently provides information on twenty-five hundred grants, awards, fellowships, and other types of educational and research funding available for individuals in all disciplines, at the graduate level and beyond. Most organizations cited are located in the United States or England. Entries are listed alphabetically according to foundation name. Each includes pertinent information about the organization, area of study, requirements and application procedures, award amount, deadline for application, and the ratio of awards to applicants. Indexed according to subject, eligibility, and geographic location.

355. Bauer, David G. *Complete Grants Sourcebook: Higher Education.* 3d ed. Washington, D.C.: American Council on Education, 1991. 480p. ISBN 0-02-901952-4.
This work offers a detailed "how to" section on grant seeking as well as information on over four hundred sources -- foundations, corporations and government agencies -- selected for their record of support for higher education projects. Entries are grouped by type of granting source and include the organization's areas of interest, contact information, eligibility requirements and sample grants. Geographical and subject indexes are provided. (Based on examination of 2d ed.)

356. Blum, Laurie. *Free Money for College: A Guide to More Than 1000 Grants and Scholarships for Undergraduate Study.* New York: Facts on File, 1991. 272p. ISBN 0-8160-2313-1.
Intended for high school and college students, this work lists sources of financial aid geographically. Entries include address and telephone number of the granting organization, size of awards given, eligibility requirements and restrictions, and application deadline.

357. Blum, Laurie. *Free Money for Foreign Study: A Guide to More Than 1000 Grants and Scholarships for Study Abroad.* New York: Facts on File, 1991. 262p. ISBN 0-8160-2450-2.
Lists programs that support undergraduate or graduate study overseas. Information is arranged geographically and by field of study and includes the type and amount of aid offered as well as contact information and application procedures.

358. Blum, Laurie. *Free Money for Graduate School: A Directory of Private Grants.* New York: Henry Holt, 1990. 288p. ISBN 0-8050-1325-3.
Lists sources of aid by broad fields of study and for women, ethnic and international students.   Entries include contact information for the granting organizations as well as the size and number of awards given, eligibility requirements, restrictions and application deadlines.   Includes an index.

359. Cassidy, Daniel J. *The Graduate Scholarship Book: The Complete Guide to Scholarships, Fellowships, Grants, and Loans for Graduate and Professional Study.* 2d ed. Englewood Cliffs, N.J.: Prentice Hall, 1990. 441p. ISBN 0-13-362328-9.
One of three publications by the author (The International Scholarship Book, The Scholarship Book), this addresses the need of graduate students for financial aids from the private sector. A total of 1,974 organizations/foundations are identified, each with a description of the award, deadline dates and eligibility requirements. It follows the same format as the other two publications, allowing the users to browse by field of study, and to use the Quick Find Index to focus on grants based on such factors as ethnic background, religious affiliation, union membership, physical handicaps, etc. Information is also extracted from the National Scholarship Research Service (NSRS) database.

360. Cassidy, Daniel J. *The International Scholarship Book: The Complete Guide to Financial Aid for Study Abroad.* 2d ed. Englewood Cliffs, N.J.: Prentice Hall, 1990. 389p. ISBN 0-13-477589-9.
Primarily a source to identify organizations that provide scholarships for particular field and area of study. Unlike UNESCO's Study Abroad, it does not include educational institutions, nor allow browsing by country. The main section categorizes funding agencies under business, education, engineering, humanities, natural studies, science and social sciences. These are further subdivided into subjects such as computer science, foreign language, mathematics, chemistry, marine biology, history, etc. The "Quick Find" index allows access by ethnic background, foreign language, country of intended study, religious affiliation, physical handicaps, etc. It also has a list of helpful publications.

361. Cassidy, Daniel J. *The Scholarship Book: The Complete Guide to Private-Sector Scholarships, Grants, and Loans for Undergraduates.* 3d ed. Englewood Cliffs, N.J.: Prentice Hall, 1990. 400p. ISBN 0-13-792052-0.
A companion to the author's The International Scholarship Book, it follows the same format, listing 1,753 private foundations/corporations. Such information is compiled from the database of the National Scholarship Research Service (NSRS). As in the companion work, names of foundations are arranged to allow browsing by field of study. The "Quick Find" index helps to pinpoint grants for specific interests or groups, such as type of occupation, armed forces, ethnic background, family ancestries, etc. There is an alphabetical index of organizations.

362. *Chronicle Sports Guide: Intercollegiate Athletics and Scholarships.*
      Moravia, N.Y.: Chronicle Guidance Publications, 1987. 367p. ISBN
      1-55631-005-6.
Lists intercollegiate sports programs and athletic scholarships for men
and women at over twenty-one hundred U.S. colleges and universities. The
work is divided into sections for seventeen different sports. Within
each section entries are grouped by state and include the name, address
and telephone number of each institution. No indexes.

363. *Complete Grants Sourcebook for Higher Education.* 2d ed. New York:
      Amer. Council on Education/Macmillan Publishing Co., 1985.
Provides information on more than four hundred "best prospects" grant
sources. These include foundation, corporate, and government funding
sources, including their areas of interest, eligibility requirements and
sample grants. A detailed "how to" section on grant seeking is provided.
Access through geographical and subject indexes.

364. *Corporate 500: The Directory of Corporate Philanthropy.* San Fran-
      cisco: Public Management Institute, 1980-   . Annual.
With quarterly updates, this source lists and describes companies
(primarily United States) that engage in grant-making. Entries include
examples of grants awarded, eligibility requirements, and the application
process. Includes indexes by type of activities, along with listings by
geographic area of giving and grant recipients.

365. *Corporate Foundation Profiles.* New York: Foundation Center, 1988-
      . Irregular.
The latest edition of this directory lists more than 750 of the largest
company-sponsored foundations in the U.S. with assets of 100 million
dollars or more or awarding grants in a recent year of 100 thousand
dollars or more. The foundation name, the state, and financial data are
provided for each entry. Almost 250 of these foundations receive a more
detailed description: foundation name, address, phone number, contact
name, detailed information on the parent company, names of major donors,
purpose and activities, fields of interest, giving limitations, application guidelines, names of officers, trustees, and directors, publications
and financial data. The detailed entries are arranged alphabetically,
while the others are ranked according to the total amount of grants.
Three indexes provide access by means of geographical location, subject
interest, type of support.

366. *The Directory of Athletic Scholarships.* New York: Facts on File
      Publications, 1987. 343p. ISBN 0-8169-1549-X.
This source is intended for use by athletes with average and above-
average talents who need to seek out athletic recruiters. The chapter
on the recruiting process gives useful hints on the rules, suggestions
on applications with sample letters, and how to compare aid packages.
This source lists scholarships based on athletic ability available at
two- and four-year colleges. Entries are arranged by school and include
basic data on each institution as well as athletic department telephone
numbers. Includes a sport index, state index, and an index of major conferences. While the athletic directors may have changed, this remains
a useful source to identify which educational institutions provide
scholarships for particular sports.

367. *Directory of Building and Equipment Grants.* Loxahatchee, Fla.:
      Research Grants Guide, 1988-   . Biennial. ISSN 1062-6492.
Non-profit organizations seeking grants for building, renovation, and
equipment will find approximately 540 foundations and about thirty

government agencies which sponsored such programs in the 1988 edition of this directory. Listings provide the foundation or agency name, address, telephone number, name and title of contact, geographical area served, description of grant, type of recipient group or groups. Access is by means of separate name and subject indexes.

368. *Directory of Grants in the Humanities.* Phoenix, Ariz.: Oryx Pr., 1986- . Annual. ISSN 0887-0551.
Lists current funding programs in the traditional humanities fields, including history, anthropology, fine and performing arts, crafts, and folklore. This is a narrower version of the Directory of Research Grants and the Grants database, both published by Oryx Press.

369. *Directory of Research Grants.* Phoenix, Ariz.: Oryx Press, 1975- . Annual. ISSN 0146-7336.
The 1991 edition of this directory lists some fifty-eight hundred research-related grants, including scholarships, fellowships, internships and conferences, in its main section, arranged by grant title. Each entry includes a description of the grant program, application deadline, funding amounts, any restrictions or requirements, and sponsor contact name, address and phone number. Two indexes list grant programs by subject and by sponsoring organization. A third lists sponsors with their addresses by type of organization.

370. *The Federal Educational and Scholarship Funding Guide.* 3d ed. West Warwick, R.I.: Grayco Publishing, 1992. 120p.
Drawing upon the 1989 issue of the Catalog of Federal Domestic Assistance (U.S. Office of Management and Budget), this work describes over 130 programs supporting study in the field of education with forms of assistance such as fellowships, grants, property donations, loans, counseling and technical information. Program descriptions include funding agency, types of assistance and restrictions, eligibility, selection criteria, contact information and examples of proposals funded. Listings for similar programs are roughly grouped together, and only a brief program index is provided

371. *The Foundation Directory.* New York: Foundation Center, 1960- . Annual. ISSN 0011-8092.
A standard reference source for organizations seeking funding from non-profit private foundations with assets of at least $1 million or $100,000 in annual giving. The 1991 (13th) edition provides descriptions for 7,581 entries with 1,225 new entries. Arranged alphabetically by state, foundations included fall into one of four categories: independent, company-sponsored, endowment, or community. While information is culled from IRS returns and published media, thirty-six percent of the foundations verified the data. Various tables before the main work provide comparisons as well as rankings. Includes six indexes: donors, geographic area, type of support, subject, new foundations, and foundation name. The types of support index identifies thirty-four categories such as building funds, land acquisition, equipment, matching funds, lectureships, etc. Appendices list foundations that are excluded from the directory. This source is kept current between editions by supplements appearing in the Foundation Center Information Quarterly. The 1991 edition is the first to be updated on an annual basis.

372. *Foundation Grants Index.* New York: Foundation Center, 1970-1971- . Annual. ISSN 0090-1601.
A compilation of over thirty-six thousand grants of $5000 or more made by hundreds of private, community or company foundations. Entries are by

foundation name, grouped geographically, and also include the recipients, location, amount and description of grants. Remains useful, while not specifically related to higher education. Provides several indexes: subjects, geographical area, keywords, and recipient names and types.

373. *Foundation Grants to Individuals.* 7th ed. New York: The Foundation Center, 1991. ISBN 0-87954-387-6.
Focuses on private U.S. foundations that make grants to individuals. The over twelve hundred entries are grouped by the subject of the grants. Each includes the name, address and telephone number of the foundation, name of contact person, foundation's total assets and grants as well as those made specifically to individuals, description of the grant program and application information. This work includes geographical, foundation name, type of support, and subject indexes.

374. *Fulbright and Other Grants for Graduate Study Abroad.* New York: Institute of International Education, n.d. Annual.
A geographical listing of approximately one thousand Fulbright-Hays grants and grants for pre-doctoral students available in all fields of study. Funding sources are administered by the institute in over one hundred countries. Provides information on eligibility, field and level of study, language requirements and application procedures.

375. *Fulbright Scholar Program Grants for Faculty and Professionals.* Washington, D.C.: Council for International Exchange of Scholars, 1987-   . Annual.
Published previously under various similar titles, this work lists about one thousand grants available to U.S. citizens for post-doctoral teaching and research in over one hundred countries. The geographically arranged entries indicate number of grants and time periods for which they are available, subject fields, language and other requirements, stipends and housing arrangements.

376. *Funding For Research, Study, and Travel: Latin America and the Caribbean.* Phoenix, Ariz.: Oryx Pr., 1987-   . Irregular.
Describes nearly four hundred fellowship, grant, and scholarship programs. Sources are primarily for graduate and post-doctoral studies. Included are lists of sponsoring organizations and a six- page bibliography. Includes indexes by subject and sponsor type.

377. *GIS Guide to Four-Year Colleges.* Boston: Houghton Mifflin, 1989-   . Annual. ISSN 0897-8956.
Drawn from the Guidance Information System database, this work covers some 1,750 institutions. It provides basic contact information for each school, as well as accreditation. Entries also include information concerning enrollment, programs offered, costs, admission requirements, financial aid and application deadlines.

378. *Grants in the Humanities: A Scholar's Guide to Funding Sources.* 2d ed. New York: Neal-Schuman Publishers, 1984. 175p. ISBN 0-918212-80-4.
Alphabetical listing of over 150 foundations, government agencies and information centers, research centers, libraries and humanities committees which fund or otherwise support postdoctoral research. Entries include name, address and telephone number, and the organization type, areas of interest, requirements and deadlines of funding bodies. Dated but useful for those seeking funding sources in the associated fields.

379. *The Grants Register.* New York: St. Martin Pr., 1969-1970-   .

Biennial. ISSN 0072-5471.
The 1991-1993 edition of this source describes 1,056 United States and
international organizations providing funding for graduate and post-
graduate education. Entries are alphabetical without regard to country
of origin. The subject index, which precedes organization entries, is
arranged by twenty-nine broad fields of study such as art, cultural
studies, engineering, social sciences, etc. Individual disciplines, such
as sculpture, aerospace, anthropology, are lined up under the appropriate
fields of study with designation of the country of origin in italics and
country of eligibility in letter codes. There is an Index of Awards and
Awarding Bodies. Appendices list organizations which are no longer active, respond too late for inclusion, or never respond.

380. *Guide to Federal Grants*. Dubuque, Iowa: Kendall/Hunt, 1985. 624p.
      ISBN 0-8403-3664-0.
Lists nearly five hundred grants also found in the Catalog of Federal
Domestic Assistance. Grant descriptions are arranged by federal agency
and include information on purpose, type and amount of assistance, eligibility, requirements and application procedure. Indexed by subject.

381. *Matching Gift Details: Guidebook to Corporate Matching Gift
      Programs*. Washington, D.C.: Council for Advancement and Support
      of Education, 1986-   . Annual. ISSN 1052-9098.
Alphabetical listing of over a thousand companies that will match their
employees' contributions to schools, colleges, or other non- profit
organizations. Each firm's name, address, telephone number and contact
person are given, along with its gift-matching policies. There are separate lists of subsidiaries that participate in their parent company's
program, companies with programs overseas and companies that make
greater-than-matching contributions. A geographical index is also included.

382. *National Association of State Scholarship and Grant Programs Survey
      Report*. Harrisburg, Pa.: Nat. Assn. of State Scholarship and Grant
      Programs, 19 -   . Annual.
Includes entries for more than fifty state agencies which administer
scholarship and grant programs for undergraduate and graduate students
with financial need to attend public and private institutions of higher
education. Alphabetically arranged entries list the agency's name,
address, telephone number, and the names of key officials. The book's
largest portion provides reports and narrative summaries regarding the
administration of the aid programs. Also included are statistics on
state administered student aid for higher education.

383. *National Data Book of Foundations: A Comprehensive Guide to Grant-
      making Foundations*. 15th ed. New York: Foundation Center, 1991.
      1,914p. ISBN 0-87954-385-X.
This is the most complete listing of active foundations, with more than
twenty-five thousand source entries. This work is especially useful for
identifying small foundations. It is divided into five sections: private, company-sponsored and community foundations (arranged alphabetically by state), operating foundations (also arranged by state), an
appendix listing all terminated foundations (including those which have
merged with other entries), an index of all foundation names (alphabetically arranged), and a separate index of community foundations. The
brief entries include standard information (i.e., name, contact person,
etc.), along with fiscal information about the foundation (i.e., total
assets, asset type, total expenditures, etc.) and are based on foundations' reports to the U.S. Internal Revenue Service.

384. *National Directory of Arts and Education Support by Business Corporations.* (Arts Patronage Series, No. 14) Des Moines, Iowa: Washington International Arts Letter, 1982-   . Irregular.
Lists about fifteen hundred corporations and their twenty-nine hundred affiliates, divisions, and subsidiaries which provide some assistance to the arts and humanities in their budgets. Entries are arranged alphabetically and the following information is provided: corporation name, address, phone number, contact person for arts, names of officers, affiliates, divisions, and subsidiaries, size of corporation, annual sales, employee matching grants plan, description of corporate art collection. No index.

385. *Peterson's Grants for Graduate Students.* 3d ed. Princeton, N.J.: Peterson's Guides, 1991. 600p. ISBN 1-56079-052-0.
This compilation of over eight hundred sources of grant and fellowship support focuses on merit rather than need-based programs. Entries are arranged by sponsoring organization and include contact information, nature, purpose, size and number of awards; number of applicants; eligibility criteria; and application procedures and deadline. The work includes an annotated bibliography and keyword and subject indexes.

386. *Peterson's Grants for Post-Doctoral Students.* Princeton, N.J.: Peterson's Guides, 1991. 362p. ISBN 1-56079-053-9.
Similar in format to <u>Peterson's Grants for Graduate Students</u>, this work provides the same information for some 650 U.S. and overseas programs offering grants and fellowships for teaching, writing and research in a wide range of disciplines.

387. *Scholarships, Fellowships and Grants for Programs Abroad: A Handbook of Awards for U.S. Nationals for Study or Research Abroad.* Houston, Tex.: American Collegiate Service, 1989. 299p. ISBN 0-940937-02-6.
Designed for American Students from undergraduates to postdoctorates interested in pursuing their studies in a foreign country. Part 1 is a brief overview of matters of general interest to such students. Part 2 lists awards (only those above a minimum annual award of five hundred dollars). The 374 entries are listed alphabetically by the name of the awarding organization. The following information is provided: names; addresses; telephone numbers; names and quantities of awards offered; donations of awards; fields of study; requirements and eligibility; application procedures; and monetary values of awards. Part 3 provides brief profiles of 120 countries, with data on area, population, religion, languages spoken, linguistic skills required, and contact person. An appendix deals with Fulbright and other grants. Subject index included.

388. *Scholarships, Fellowships and Loans.* Vol. 8. Bethesda, Md.: Bellman Publishing, 1987. ISBN 87442-008-3.
Begun in 1949, this source provides information on fourteen hundred financial aid programs. This volume does not duplicate volume VII. These works should be consulted together. The key to use of Volume VIII is by way of the vocational goals index in the front. It presents, in a tabular format, funding institutions listed according to areas of study. Cross-tabulated with the institutions are requirements such as level of study, sex, type of award, residency, religious affiliation, ethnic group, and citizenship. This arrangement enables users to easily determine eligibility for funding. This source is updated by quarterly <u>Scholarships, Fellowships and Loans News Service and Counselors Information Services.</u>

389. *Scholarships for International Students: A Complete Guide to Colleges and Universities in the United States.* Alexandria, Va.: Octameron/Scholarship Research Group, 1986-1988. 276p.
Provides information on financial aid offered by individual institutions. The work also includes useful supplementary sections on United States education, applying to colleges, immigration regulations, maps, even a brief "customs and lifestyle" section. A useful source needing better organization.

390. *Selected List of Fellowship Opportunities and Aids to Advanced Education for United States Citizens and Foreign Nationals.* Washington, D.C.: National Science Foundation, 19 - . Irregular.
This volume was formerly published as two separate volumes: Selected List of Major Fellowship Opportunities and Aids to Advanced Education for United States Citizens; and Selected List of Major Fellowship Opportunities and Aids to Advanced Education for Foreign Nationals. About one hundred foundations, associations, state and federal agencies, corporations, and other organizations which offer fellowships, grants, and scholarships are listed. A separate directory of about forty-five publications lists other sources of grants and awards. Entries for organizations include: organization name and address, description of awards and the organization, academic level, number and duration of awards, fields supported, and application procedure. Entries for publications provide the title of the publication and the publisher's name and address. Entries are arranged alphabetically.

391. *The Student Guide: Five Federal Financial Aid Programs.* Washington, D.C.: U.S. Dept. of Education, Office of Educational Research and Improvement, n.d. Annual.
This brief but highly useful booklet informs users about federal student aid programs and how to apply for them. Programs covered are: Pell Grants, Supplemental Educational Opportunity Grants, College Work-Study, Perkins Loans (formerly National Direct Student Loans), and Guaranteed Student Loans (Parent Loans to Undergraduate Students and Supplemental Loans for Students). General information is provided on eligibility, making application, deadlines, etc. A chapter on debt management covers such topics as borrowing rights and responsibilities, and consolidating loans. Provided as well are a state-by-state list of state educational agencies, and a glossary. Access is through the table of contents.

392. *Where America's Large Foundations Make Their Grants.* 5th ed. Hartsdale, N.Y.: Public Service Materials Center, 1983. 253p. ISBN 1-486-37909-8.
A state-by-state account of 651 foundations and their total funding for the years 1980 or 1981. Names of organizations and institutions together with the amount received are collected from annual reports. These lists reflect only a small percentage of total funding where very large foundations are concerned. Where appropriate, grantees are further identified by the type of funding such as community programs, humanities, medical services, etc. An 'Additional Insights' feature for some entries provides information on the foundations' preferences and emphases, which may no longer hold true. It is still useful as a source to locate names and addresses of large foundations continuing to provide aid.

393. *Winning Money for College: The High School Student's Guide to Scholarship Contests.* 2d ed. Princeton, N.J.: Peterson's Guides, 1987. 207p. ISBN 0-87866-555-2.
This source directs students to privately funded scholarships won through

contests based on talents other than athletic abilities. This edition includes more than fifty contests, including the AT&T Engineering Subscription Program, Westinghouse Science Talent Search, Scholastic Photography Awards, and the Science Essay Awards Program. Entries include rules and procedures, strategies, samples of test questions, and excerpts of winning essays, making this a unique guide for highly motivated students. An interest-area index provides access to contests by broad subjects such as the humanities, science, journalism, arts, business and leadership.

International Study and Travel

394. *Academic Year Abroad.* New York: Institute of International Education, 1972-1973-   . Annual.
Provides information about study-abroad programs offered during the academic year, and that are at least one academic quarter in length (usually eight to ten weeks). A recent issue covers approximately eighteen hundred programs, with nearly seventy-five percent of them offered by accredited United States colleges and universities. Programs are organized into six geographic world regions. Each region is subdivided alphabetically by country and city. Entries include the institution name and location, program dates, eligibility, credit, instruction language and format, costs, housing, and other useful information. Appendices cover statistics on study abroad, survey form used to collect data for the yearbook, a list of sponsoring institutions, consortia, and an index of fields of study.

395. *Applying to Colleges and Universities in the United States, 1987: A Handbook for International Students.* 2d ed. Princeton, N.J.: Peterson's Guides, 1986. 389p. ISBN 0-87866-530-7.
Four-year colleges, with their addresses, are listed alphabetically under each state. A profile for each college describes it in the following terms: institutional control, institutional type, student body, founding date, degrees awarded, and institutional and program accreditation. Also covered are campus setting, enrollment, faculty, library holdings, major sports, applications, and a host of other category items. Similar information for two-year colleges is offered in tabular form. A directory of colleges with ESL programs lists them alphabetically with their locations. A majors directory groups colleges alphabetically under the title of the major. Information on applying to colleges and universities in the United States, a glossary, and a map are included. Includes an index to the colleges covered.

396. *College Handbook Foreign Student Supplement 1992.* New York: College Board, 1991. 267p. ISBN 0-87447-411-6 (pbk.).
Lists over two thousand United States colleges and universities that are open to foreign students. The following information is provided for each institution: name, location, degrees offered, numbers of American and foreign students enrolled, tests and other requirements, deadlines for application, fees, and financial aid available to foreign students. The volume includes maps. On the cover: the only guide to U.S. colleges and universities for students from other countries.

397. *Directory of Overseas Educational Advising Centers, 1989-90.* Washington, D.C.: College Board Office of International Education, 1989. 158p.
Provides names, addresses, and telex and cable addresses of centers that

collect information on educational opportunities overseas for Americans. Index of center directors.

398. *Financial Aid for Research, Study, Travel and Other Activities Abroad 1990-1991.* San Carlos, Calif.: Reference Service Press, 1990. 586p. ISBN 0-918276-12-8.
Intended to be a comprehensive listing of funding sources specifically for Americans pursuing international activities, this work provides descriptions of over seventeen hundred financial aid programs grouped by level (high school/undergraduate, graduate, post-doctorate, professional/other) and purpose (research, study, travel, other). Entries include program name, contact information, purpose, eligibility, duration, number of awards, application deadline and special features. An annotated bibliography of other financial aid directories is also provided, as are indexes by program title, sponsoring organization, geographic area, subject and application deadline.

399. *Financial Resources for International Study: A Definitive Guide to Organizations Offering Awards for Overseas Study.* Princeton, N.J.: Peterson's Guides, 1989. 252p. ISBN 0-87866-837-3.
Lists over six hundred awards of $500 or more available to U.S. citizens for study abroad at the undergraduate, graduate, post-graduate and professional levels. Entries are arranged by name of the granting organization and include information on the type, purpose and field of study of the award, the amount granted and expenses covered, yearly number of applicants and awards made, requirements and restrictions, and application procedures and deadline. Indexes by award name, discipline and academic level are provided.

400. *Funding for U.S. Study.* New York: Institute of International Education, 1989- . ISSN 1047-2541.
Intended for non-U.S. students seeking financial support for higher education in the United States. Included in the alphabetical list of more than six hundred entries are organizations, endowments, foundations that provide fellowships, internships, scholarships, travel grants, etc. Apart from the standard directory information of addresses, telephone numbers, etc., specific selection criteria such as eligibility, duration, nationality, restrictions are identified. Other useful features are the practical advice on planning and cost estimation, and several indexes by field of study, country, and educational level.

401. *Guide to Academic Travel.* Coral Gables, Fla.: Shaw Associates, 1990. 240p. ISBN 0-945834-07-1.
With increasing popularity of combining vacation and study, this guide fills the need with narratives of programs, cultural organizations, museums, and travel companies in alphabetical order. It enables users to estimate the cost of travel, learn of refund notices, and academic itinerary. There is a geographic index of sponsors, and a separate specialty index of research projects.

402. *Guide to International Education in the United States.* Detroit: Gale Research, Inc., 1991- . 589p. ISSN 1052-9586.
A broadly focused guide providing information about programs and resources covering: area studies, educational exchange, foreign language instruction, foreign students and visitors in the United States, global education, intercultural education, international affairs and studies, peace and conflict resolution studies, study and educational travel a-abroad, and world issues. Some thirty-eight hundred listings are arranged into three sections: topics in international, intercultural, and

global education; area studies by region; and area studies by country. Entries are concise, giving name and location information, degree/certificate offering, faculty, courses available, areas of emphasis, and publications. A confusing array of resources for studying and learning about other cultures, societies, and languages. Includes name and subject indexes.

403. *International Funding Guide: Resources and Funds for International Activities at Colleges and Universities.* Washington, D.C.: American Assn. of State Colleges and Universities, 1985. 40p. ISBN 0-88044-109-7.
Lists resources and public and private funds for college and university international activities. Included are programs of the United States and foreign governments, service organizations, and foundations. The guide is arranged in four chapters: federal agencies, private and service agencies, foundations, and national governments and multinational organizations. Entries provide information about the association or organization and include such other information as deadlines, contact, telephone numbers and materials to be ordered. Indexes list program titles, type of support, geographical region, and subject area supported.

404. *Study Abroad.* 28th ed. Paris, France: UNESCO, 1991. 1,275p. Biennial. ISBN 92-3-002715-4.
In three languages (English, French, and Spanish) this work serves as a guide to 2,846 funding sources worldwide. In Part I, international organizations providing scholarships are identified in alphabetical order, specifying the subject areas and amounts funded. Part 2, which constitutes the major portion, lists national scholarships and institutions by country. Description for each country begins with information on academic year, language and currency of the country. This is followed by institutions that offer scholarships with details on eligibility, deadline date, grant value, etc. Finally, individual academic institutions with campuses open to foreign students are included. Three indexes cover international organizations, national organizations, and subjects of study. This is a very handy source to funding for study abroad when the country of destination is a first priority.

Minority Groups and Women

405. *Black Student's Guide to Colleges.* 2d ed. Providence, R.I.: Beckham House Publishers, 1984. 495p. ISBN 0-931761-00-X.
This selective guide covers 158 colleges, including historically black institutions, but also selective residential colleges, colleges with significant African-American enrollments, generally "popular" institutions and schools representing diverse geographic areas. Information is drawn from survey responses from college administrators and narrative comments of students, both black and white. Entries on individual schools are arranged alphabetically and run two to three pages. The include African-American and total figures on enrollments, graduates and faculty, as well as costs, financial aid and percent of blacks receiving financial aid. The narrative part of each entry addresses African-American studies and other academic programs of interest, support services, organizations, social activities, relations with African American administrators and faculty, and the general campus climate. Introductory sections include a glossary and discussions of such topics as choosing a college, applying for admission, financial aid, study skills and managing stress. Some information may be out of date, but this is the most recent edition.

406. Bowman, J. Wilson. *America's Black Colleges.* South Pasadena, Calif.: Sandcastle Publishing, 1992. 242p. ISBN 0-9627756-1-4. Lists one hundred historically or predominantly black institutions by state. Each entry includes contact information, historical background, enrollment figures, degrees offered, tuition, and other charges, and a list of notable alumni. The following lists appear as appendices: schools alphabetically with their addresses, schools by state with their athletic association memberships, schools receiving United Negro College Fund support, church-affiliated schools by denomination, and doctorate-granting institutions.

407. *Directory of Financial Aids for Women.* San Carlos, Calif.: Reference Service Pr., 1978- . Biennial. ISSN 0732-5215. A comprehensive, international listing compiled for Americans and intended primarily or exclusively for women. It is arranged according to the following: 1) a listing of scholarships, fellowships, loans, grants, awards, and internships; 2) sources of information on education benefits of individual states; 3) a bibliography of general financial aid directories; 4) a section of indexes to program titles, sponsors, geographic areas, subjects, and filing dates. A unique and useful work.

408. *Directory of Special Programs for Minority Group Members.* Garrett Park, Md.: Garrett Park Pr., 1974- . Irregular. ISSN 0093-9501. The fifth edition (1990) of this work lists four thousand education, training, internship, business development, employment, exchange and other programs offered by nearly three thousand organizations and institutions and available to African American, Asian, Hispanic or Native American minorities. Well over a quarter of the programs are related to postsecondary study or financial aid. Entries are arranged alphabetically and provide a brief description of each program and the name and address of the sponsoring body. Also included are a glossary, bibliography and index.

409. *Higher Education Opportunities for Minorities and Women: Annotated Selections.* Washington, D.C.: U.S. Dept. of Education, Office of Postsecondary Education, 1983- . Irregular. For students and parents seeking sources of financial assistance for postsecondary education. The latest edition updates and adds to earlier versions. While designed for minorities and women, a number of opportunities described are for all students. Included as well is information on how and where to find help in preparing for college and beyond. In the 1989 edition, sources are arranged in parts dealing with general information, opportunities at the undergraduate and graduate levels arranged according to field of study, and postdoctoral opportunities. Items are arranged alphabetically by source name within each part, along with a brief explanation of the source program. Access is provided through the table of contents. The work was formerly titled Selected List of Postsecondary Education Opportunities for Minorities and Women.

410. *National Association for Women Deans, Administrators, and Counselors Member Handbook.* Washington, D.C.: Nat. Assn. for Women Deans, Administrators, and Counselors, 19 - . Annual. Lists approximately two thousand American and foreign administrators. Entries, arranged geographically, provide the following: name, institution, office and home address and telephone number; education; position; and committee memberships. Includes an index.

Personnel

411. *American Association of Collegiate Registrars and Admissions Officers: Membership Guide.* Washington, D.C.: The Association, n.d. Irregular.
Covers more than twenty-three hundred member institutions and eighty four hundred college and university registrars, financial aid officers, admissions officers, and officials of international education and institutional research organizations. Arrangement is geographical. Includes a personal-name index.

412. *Association for School, College, and University Staffing Membership Directory and Subject Field Index.* Addison, Ill.: Assn. for School, Coll., and Univ. Staffing, 1987-   . Annual.
Covers institutional members, and the names, addresses, and telephone numbers of those on college campuses responsible for career planning and placement options. Also included are associate members having responsibility for recruitment and selection of personnel for school districts and professional organizations. Entries, arranged alphabetically by state, include institution names, addresses, telephone numbers, and contact personnel. Appendices contain additional information about the association. Includes a personal name index and a guide to subject fields of teacher-training institutions.

413. *Association of College and University Housing Officers-International: Directory.* Bloomington, Ind.: The Association, n.d. Annual.
Provides information about nine hundred member institutions. Entries include the institution name, address, and telephone number; data on enrollment, number of rooms available for families and individuals; and names, titles, and telephone numbers of housing officers. Arrangement of institutions is geographical. Indexes cover personal names, institutions lacking state or province names in their titles, and committee membership (including institution name).

414. *Catholic Campus Ministry Directory.* Dayton, Ohio: Catholic Campus Ministry Assn., 19 -   . Annual.
Lists nearly two hundred directors of Catholic campus and young adult ministry programs. Entries include: member name, address, and telephone number; and name of diocese. Arrangement is alphabetical by diocese. Former title: Directory of Diocesan Directors of Campus Ministries.

415. *College Entrance Examination Board: Membership Directory.* New York: College Board Publications, n.d. Annual.
Geographical listing of the Board's more than twenty-seven hundred member colleges, secondary schools, school systems and associations. This work includes names of committee and board members.

416. *College Media Advisers Directory.* Memphis: College Media Advisers, n.d. Annual.
An alphabetical listing of the approximately six hundred members of the College Media Advisers organization. Advisers, directors and board chairs of student print and broadcast media are included, as well as others, such as journalism school or department heads. Entries consist of each individual's name, address, telephone number and affiliation.

417. *College/University Food Service Who's Who Directory.* Wilhoit, Ariz.: Informational Central, n.d. Triennial.
A geographical listing of food service programs at over 1,750

institutions. For each, the school's name, contact information and enrollment are given, along with total yearly food purchases, meals served daily, name of food service director or manager and name of management company. An alphabetical index is included. This work is also available on compu-ter-readable diskette.

418. *Council for Advancement and Support of Education: Membership Directory*. Washington, D.C.: Council for Advancement and Support of Education, n.d. Annual. ISSN 1044-5579.

Arranged geographically, this work lists the names, addresses of institution, and council representatives. It is primarily for use by public relations officers to identify fund raisers, government relation offices, and publications officials at colleges, universities, community colleges, and private institutions. Includes an institution index.

419. *CUPA Membership Directory [year]*. Washington, D.C.: Coll. and Univ. Personnel Assn., n.d. Annual. ISSN 1046-221X.

A recent issue of this membership directory, which has been published over the past decade, contains lists of some forty-five hundred individuals and thirteen hundred institutions. Entries for individuals are arranged alphabetically and provide name, title and telephone number. Institutions are arranged geographically with their addresses and the names of their CUPA representatives.

420. *Directory of Faculty Contracts and Bargaining Agents in Institutions of Higher Education*. New York: Nat. Centers for the Study of Collective Bargaining in Higher Education and the Pro-fessions, Baruch College, City University of New York, 1976-   . Annual. ISSN 0276-7805.

Lists U.S. and Canadian institutions of higher education with bargaining agents. Arrangement is by state. Information includes unit size, date of contract, type of college, and contract expiration date, etc. Since 1985, contracts for adjunct faculty are listed separately. Introductory pages provide detailed description of union activities during the year. Statistical tables summarize geographic distribution of agents, status of legislation on collective bargaining, etc. Includes an institution index.

421. *Directory of Ministries in Higher Education*. Nashville, Tenn.: Board of Higher Education and Ministry, United Methodist Church, n.d. Annual.

Published over the past decade, this directory lists approximately fourteen hundred campus ministers and college chaplains, representing some fifteen denominations. Entries are grouped geographically and include name, address, telephone number and denomination. Includes a name index.

422. Douglas, Joel M. *Directory of Non-Faculty Bargaining Agents in Institutions of Higher Education*. New York: Nat. Center for the Study of Collective Bargaining in Higher Education and the Professions, Baruch College, City University of New York, 1991. 59p. ISSN 1054-7568.

Information from 345 institutions is arranged by state in a tabular format. Entries include type of school, classes of employees unionized, size of bargaining units and abbreviated bargaining agent names. Supplementary tables give full names of bargaining agents, list states that permit public employee collective bargaining, and show the geographic distribution of non-faculty represented by unions.

423. *International Association of Campus Law Enforcement Administrators Membership Directory.*   Hartford, Conn.: The Association, n.d. Annual.
Contains names, addresses and positions of Association representatives at eleven hundred institutions. This body was formerly the International Association of College and University Security Directors.

424. *National Association of College Admissions Counselors - Directory.* Alexandria, Va.: Nat. Assn. of Coll. Admissions Counselors, 19 - . Annual.
Lists about four thousand member high schools, school districts, colleges, universities, professional associations, and individuals. Arranged geographically, entries provide institution or organization name, address, telephone number, and other staff members' names and titles. Includes a personal name index.

425. *National Association of College and University Attorneys - Directory.*   Washington, D.C.: Nat. Assn. of Coll. and Univ. Attorneys, 19 - . Annual.
Includes approximately twenty-three hundred attorneys representing United States colleges and universities. Entries are arranged alphabetically, providing the name, address, and telephone number of the institution, and the local legal officer.

426. *National Association of College and University Business Officers - Directory.*   Washington, D.C.: Nat. Assn. of Coll. and Univ. Business Officers, 19 - . Annual.
Lists more than two thousand college and university business officers. Entries, arranged geographically, include the name and address of the institution and the local business officer.

427. *National Association of College and University Food Services - Directory.* East Lansing, Mich.: Nat. Assn. of Coll. and Univ. Food Services. 19 - . Annual.
Lists about twenty-five hundred persons affiliated with six hundred colleges or university food services, residence halls, and student centers. Entries are arranged alphabetically and include name, title, affiliation, and address. A geographic index and an index of institution names are included.

428. *National Association of College Deans, Registrars and Admissions Officers - Directory.* Albany, Ga.: Nat. Assn. of Coll. Deans, Registrars and Admissions Officers, 19 - . Annual.
Lists more than three hundred member deans, registrars and admissions officers at nearly ninety predominantly black schools. Arranged alphabetically, the entries include: institution name, address, and telephone number; names and titles of key personnel; enrollment; and institutional control type (i.e., public or private).

429. *National Association of Educational Buyers - Directory.* Woodburg, N.Y.: Nat. Assn. of Educational Buyers, 19 - . Biennial.
Lists more than two thousand purchasing officials at colleges, universities, and health-care institutions. Arranged alphabetically by last name, entries include title, affiliation, address, and telephone number.

430. *National Association of Student Financial Aid Administrators - National Membership Directory.* Washington, D.C.: Nat. Assn. of Student Financial Aid Administrators, 19 - . Annual. ISSN 0196-3279.

Arranged geographically, entries for more than thirty-five hundred institutions of postsecondary education and their financial aid administrators provide the institution's name, the names of key personnel, address, and phone numbers.

431. *State Higher Education Executive Officers - Directory of Professional Personnel.* Denver, Colo.: State Higher Education Executive Officers, 19 - . Annual.
Includes state coordinating and governing boards in the United States and Canada. Entries include the agency name, address, telephone number, and names and titles of key personnel. Entries are arranged geographically. Includes an index.

Programs and Courses

432. *Barron's Index of College Majors.* New York: Barron's Educational Series, 1976- . Biennial.
Provides "profiles of American Colleges in a convenient chart format." Approximately fifteen hundred institutions are arranged alphabetically by state, including the college name, address, telephone number, tuition, application deadline, enrollment by level, sex and full- or part-time status. Two important features are the ranking of institution's competitiveness, and the provision of ACT scores and SAT verbal/mathematics scores. Institutions are then cross-tabulated against programs organized in nine major groups from agriculture, biological sciences to engineering and social sciences. Includes an index of institutions. The 1990 edition continues in part Barron's Profiles of American Colleges.

433. Bear, John. *College Degrees by Mail.* Berkeley, Calif.: Ten Speed Pr., 1991. 212p. ISBN 0-89815-379-4.
Provides one-page descriptions of programs at one hundred selected institutions that offer bachelor's, master's, doctoral and law degrees on a purely home study basis. Also includes sections on credit for life experience, equivalency examinations, accrediting bodies and bogus "diploma mills."

434. *Campus-Free College Degrees.* 4th ed. Tulsa, Okla.: Thorson Guides, 1989. 136p. ISBN 0-916277-04-6.
This is a detailed but useful guide to earning bachelor's, master's, doctoral, and professional development degrees through accredited off-campus study. The programs listed require either no or limited residency. Thorson discusses gaining college credit through correspondence study, learning from life experience, credit through examination, military service, work-study, and certificates and diplomas. A full page of information for each college or university cited in the early chapters includes contact information, accreditation, degree offered, and tuition fees.

435. *Directory of Graduate Programs. Vol. A: Agriculture, Biological Sciences, Psychology, Health Sciences, Home Economics. Vol. B: Arts, Humanities. Vol. C: Physical Sciences, Mathematics, Engineering. Vol. D: Social Sciences, Education.* Princeton, N.J.: Educational Testing Service, 1983- . 4 vols. Biennial. ISSN 0743-0566.
Intended to be a comprehensive starting point for information about graduate study, this set covers accredited institutions that offer Master's or higher degrees. Professional programs, such as law, medicine, and dentistry, are excluded. Each of the four volumes has an index

to the programs covered by the entire set and is divided into the following major sections: 1) Program/discipline table listing institutions that offer each one and the school's enrollment, faculty, degrees awarded, program prerequisites and financial aid; 2) A similar tabular section for "Special and Interdisciplinary Programs;" 3) Institution table indicating programs offered at each, tuition, fees, financial aid deadline; 4) "Narratives" section for further general information on each institution; 5) "Addresses" section with institutions' addresses and phone numbers for general information, applications, financial aid and housing.

436. *Directory of Higher Education Programs and Faculty.* 4th ed. Washington, D.C.: Association for the Study of Higher Education and ERIC Clearinghouse on Higher Education, 1984. 47p.
The first of this work's three sections is an alphabetical listing of nearly one hundred U.S. and Canadian graduate-level higher education programs and research centers, with addresses, telephone numbers and names of directors/chairs. The remaining sections list, respectively, full-time and part-time faculty in these programs, including their institutional affiliations, addresses, telephone numbers and areas of specialization.

437. *The Gourman Report: A Rating of Graduate and Professional Programs in American and International Universities.* Los Angeles: National Education Standards, 1980-   . Biennial. ISSN 1049-717X.
Includes college and university graduate programs in various academic disciplines as well as law, medicine, pharmacy, dentistry and optometry. The professional schools are grouped by country, academic programs by subject fields, with each entry providing institution's name and address and a description and evaluation by the author. While there have been questions about the author's methodology for establishing rankings, students continue to find this work useful.

438. *The Gourman Report: A Rating of Undergraduate Programs in American and International Universities.* Los Angeles: National Education Standards, 1980-   . Biennial. ISSN 1049-7188.
Describes and evaluates college and university undergraduate programs in some one hundred subject areas. U.S. schools are arranged by discipline, foreign schools by country. In the recent past, questions have arisen concerning the methodology for establishing rankings, although students continue to find the work useful.

439. *Guide to American Graduate Schools.* 6th ed. New York: Viking Penguin, 1990. 608p. ISBN 0-14-046856-0.
Covers over two thousand accredited U.S. institutions that offer graduate or professional programs. Arranged alphabetically by school name, entries include location, type of control, programs of study offered, enrollment, faculty, academic calendar, research facilities, admission requirements, costs and housing. Indexed by state and field of study.

440. *Index of Majors.* New York: The College Board, 1977-   . Annual. ISSN 0192-3242.
An alphabetical listing of some six hundred major fields of study offered by accredited two-year, four-year and graduate institutions. Under each major, the schools that offer it are grouped by state with codes indicating the levels (certificate, associate, bachelor's, etc.) at which the major is available at each institution. Special types of academic programs, such as accelerated study, cooperative education, external degree and study abroad, appear in another section with the schools that offer

them. Two additional sections provide a listing of schools by state and type and an alphabetical index of the majors.

441. *Innovative Graduate Programs Directory, 1989-1990.* 5th ed. Saratoga Springs, N.Y.: State Univ. of N.Y., Empire State College, Coordinating Center, 1989. 139p.
Covers over a hundred institutions which offer non-traditional graduate or post-graduate programs. For each of the more than three hundred programs, this work provides institution name and contact information, description of the program, degree offered and accreditation status. A subject index to the programs is provided.

442. *Interdisciplinary Undergraduate Programs: A Directory.* Oxford, Ohio: Association for Integrative Studies, 1986. 277p. ISBN 0-9615764-0-5.
Provides listings of over two hundred thirty programs with contact information for each one and a one-page description that usually addresses its history, size, administration and curricular offerings. Arranged alphabetically by institution with indexes by state and by organization type (institution, department, major, etc.) and/or thematic emphasis.

443. *Internships: 50,000 On-the-Job Training Opportunities for College Students and Adults.* Princeton, N.J.: Peterson's Guides, 1991- . Annual. ISSN 0272-5460.
Intended for people preparing for a career, changing careers or re-entering the labor market, this work lists a wide range of internship programs. Arranged by broad career fields, the entries include the employer and a contact person, a description of the position, qualifications sought and salary. Geographic, industry and sponsor organization indexes are included.

444. *Macmillan Guide to Correspondence Study.* 3d ed. New York: Macmillan, 1988. 676p. ISBN 0-29-921641-9.
Listing of some 240 institutions, including proprietary, non-profit and government-operated schools as well as colleges and universities, that offer course work on a correspondence basis. Listings are grouped by type of institution and include school description and contact information, accreditation, faculty, costs, academic policies and admission requirements, along with the home study courses available. Indexed by institution name and subject of study.

445. *Peterson's Accounting to Zoology.* Princeton, N.J.:   Peterson's Guides, 1987. 390p. ISBN 0-87866-537-4.
Provides definitions and descriptions of about three hundred graduate and professional fields of study categorized systematically under Humanities and Social Sciences; Biological, Agricultural and Health Sciences; Physical Sciences and Mathematics; and Engineering and Applied Sciences. The entries are written and signed by graduate educators from the appropriate fields for inclusion in this work and in the publisher's <u>Annual Guides to Graduate Study</u> (q.v.). The descriptions not only define the field in question but also discuss the types of graduate programs and degrees, current research, applications and trends, and the employment outlook. Access is through the detailed table of contents and an alphabetical index of fields.

446. *Peterson's Annual Guides to Graduate Study, Book 1: An Overview; Book 2: Humanities and Social Sciences; Book 3: Biological and Agricultural Sciences; Book 4: Physical Sciences and Mathematics;*

Book 5: Engineering and Applied Sciences; Book 6: Business, Education, Health and Law. Princeton, N.J.: Peterson's guides, 1983-   . Annual. ISSN 0163-6111.
This comprehensive set provides current information on graduate and professional programs at nearly fifteen hundred accredited U.S. and Canadian institutions. Books 2 through 6 consist primarily of brief profiles of programs, arranged by discipline. The profiles, based on the publisher's annual survey of institutions, include name of program or administrative unit, accreditation, academic offerings, current faculty research, admissions, enrollment, degrees awarded, entrance and degree requirements, expenses, financial aid, and program head or contact person. Long program descriptions or "announcements" appear if provided by the school or department. Each of these volumes also includes a list of institutions with programs offered and discipline indexes for the volume and for the entire set. Book 1, the Overview, provides information on each institution as a whole and lists institutions by the 309 disciplinary fields covered in the other volumes as well as the fields offered at each institution.

447.   *Vacation Study Abroad: The Most Complete Guide to Planning Study Abroad.* New York: Institute of International Ed., 1950-   . Annual.   ISSN 0898-4727.
A recent edition (1989) provides information on over thirteen hundred study programs and short courses, representing all levels of higher education. Programs listed are offered by U.S. colleges and universities, foreign universities and language schools, and by non-profit and proprietary educational organizations. Programs are arranged by geographical regions of the world. Each is subdivided alphabetically by country, city, province, etc. Within each city sub-section, names of sponsoring institutions are arranged alphabetically. Entries include location information, as well as subjects offered, credit, eligibility, costs, housing, deadlines, and contacts. Includes indexes for sponsoring institutions and fields of study. An introductory chapter outlines the planning process.

Publishers and Publishing

448.   Albanese, Sandy. *Directory of Software in Higher Education.* Dublin, Ohio: OCLC Online Computer Library Center, 1987. 85p. ISBN 1-55653-033-1.
Presents information compiled from "Computer Software for Higher Education" columns in the Chronicle of Higher Education for the two academic years 1985-87. Over five hundred entries are arranged by software title and include a brief description of each package, along with its application, disciplinary field, hardware requirements, price, vendor contact information and citation to the original Chronicle article. There is an index of software titles by discipline and another by application, which also shows which processors can run each package.

449.   *Association of American University Presses: Directory.* New York: Assn. of American Univ. Presses, 1947-   . Annual. ISSN 0739-3024.
A timely guide to more than one hundred scholarly presses with membership in the Association of American University Presses. Entries, which are arranged alphabetically by member press, include addresses, telephone and fax numbers, key personnel by title, and editorial programs. Included as well are: year established, year admitted to AAUP membership, title output, and titles currently in print. A handy subject area grid links

subject areas in which individual presses have a strong interest. Concluding sections list press personnel by function, and include the association by-laws and membership guidelines.   Presses are listed by membership category in the table of contents. A most valuable source for scholars, librarians, and others.

450. *College Alumni and Military Publications*. New York: Larimi Media
      Communications, n.d. Annual. ISSN 1046-7602.
This work combines College Alumni Publications and Military Publications, formerly published by Public Relations, New York. More than five hundred publications of colleges and universities, written by alumni, are included.   There are separate geographical sections for alumni and military publications. Entries include the publication name, sponsor or publisher name and address, a brief description of the audience or scope, circulation, advertising rates, frequency, page size, number of pages. Records indicate this source ceased with the 1989 edition.   Includes a title index.

451. *College Alumni Publications*. New York: Public Relations Publishing
      Co., 1980. 173p. ISBN 0-913046-124.
The largest of the various sections of this work is a directory of U.S. college and university alumni publications, arranged by state and institution.   Each directory entry includes the name of the publication, publisher, address and phone number, circulation, frequency, size and advertising information. The authors also provide a list of the forty-five highest-circulating titles and a useful index by publication name. Introductory essays survey this publishing field generally and describe in detail some of the foremost individual titles. A useful supplement to more recent sources.

452. *The College Media Directory*. New York: Oxbridge Communications,
      1967-1968-   . Annual. ISSN 1046-4255.
Formerly the Directory of the College Student Press in America, this work lists the student print and broadcast media at nearly thirty-seven hundred campuses in the U.S. and Canada. Entries are grouped by state or province and include brief information about each institution as well as the nature, format, frequency, circulation, advertising rates, etc. of its publications. Also included are a college name index and indexes to law journals, publications that take advertising, alumni publications that take advertising and alumni associations.

453. *College Newspaper Directory and Rate Book*. Seattle: American Passage Media, 1982-   . Annual.
A geographically arranged listing of some fourteen hundred college newspapers. Each entry gives the name of the publication, the college, its enrollment and location, and the paper's publisher, format, frequency and rates.

454. *Directory of Software Sources for Higher Education: A Resource
      Guide for Instructional Applications*. Princeton, N.J.: Peterson's
      Guides, 1987. 173p. ISBN 0-87866-679-6.
The six sections of this work cover commercial and non-commercial sources of software, listings and catalogs of vendors, journals that either review software or regularly cover computing, and organizations such as consortia and professional associations concerned with applications of software in higher education. Information given includes addresses of organizations and companies, descriptions of software available, machines on which it runs, licensing terms and prices. Indexed by title, subject and name of organization.

455. *Newsletters in Print.* 5th ed.   Detroit: Gale Research, 1990.
    1,354p. ISBN 0-8103-6865X.
A classified guide to more than ten thousand subscription, membership and
free newsletters, bulletins, digests, updates, and similar serial publications published in the United States and Canada. Sources are arranged
in thirty-three subject chapters. Entries include complete publication
information, descriptions, editorial policies, intended audiences, where
indexed, and other data. More than sixty entries are listed under "Universities and Colleges." Other entries are found under such subjects as
"College Publications," "Sports," "Black Colleges," "Community and Junior
Colleges," etc. Title has varied: <u>Newsletters Directory</u>, <u>National Directory of Newsletters and Reporting Services</u>. Includes indexes for publishers, subjects, and title keywords.

4.

HANDBOOKS, MANUALS, AND OTHER COMPENDIUMS

INTRODUCTION

This chapter brings together more than one hundred handbooks and manuals. Among them are sources which provide rules for guiding the user in performing tasks or giving direction to a process. Other works are designed for quick location of facts. Among the titles are guides to academic heraldry and protocol, the settlement of contractual negotiations, and decision making in the academic department. Faculty members will find handbooks for improving teaching skills, while administrators will receive directions for improving fund-raising results.

To facilitate access, sources are arranged in fifteen subject sections. Beginning with a section of sources dealing with higher education in general, topics covered include Academic Degrees and Ceremony, Administration, Collective Bargaining, Community Colleges, Disabilities, Economic Factors, Faculty, Financial Assistance, Higher Education and Government, Institutional Advancement, Law, Minority Groups and Women, Personnel, Students, and Teaching and Learning. Individual works may also be identified through the author, title and subject indexes.

While we sought to include the largest number and widest range of publications, we particularly emphasized works that would have current application and value. Some sources will be found useful to the novice, while others are designed for the experienced administrator. They will serve the needs of the teacher/researcher, the trustee, and food-service employee. Others will be of assistance to students, the institutional advancement officer, and the physical plant manager.

Regarding currency of coverage, while only a few titles include a publication date in the 1990s, nearly one-half were published in the 1980s. The earliest date of publication was 1951, with the largest number of pre-1980s publications representing the 1970s.

Although seeking to be comprehensive in coverage, we did not include shorter works such as articles in journals, pamphlets and other

ephemera, and documents available in the Educational Resources Information Center (ERIC) publication series.

GENERAL WORKS

456. Carnegie Commission on Higher Education. *Digest of Reports of the*
      Carnegie Commission on Higher Education. New York: McGraw-Hill
      Publishing Co., 1974. 399p.
Part 1 of this three-part work presents a digest of twenty-one reports
of the Commission issued from 1970 through 1973. A second part includes
all the Commission's recommendations arranged according to the persons,
agencies, and institutions most directly affected by them and most likely
to be able to take steps to implement them. A third and final part provides an index to recommendations arranged alphabetically by topic.

457. Carnegie Commission on Higher Education. *Sponsored Research of the*
      Carnegie Commission on Higher Education. New York: McGraw- Hill
      Publishing Co., 1975. 397p.
One of three works (First volume: Priorities For Action(1973); Second
volume: A Digest of Reports(1974)), which comprise the summary report of
the Carnegie Commission on Higher Education at the conclusion of its
endeavors (from 1967 to 1973). This source provides summary statements
of the more than eighty research projects sponsored, in whole or in part,
by the Commission. Reports are arranged in seven major divisions: Look-
ing at the System, Diversity, Increasing Options, Social Justice, Service
to Society, Quality, and Strengthening the Institutions. Includes a topic index to the studies.

458. Carnegie Council on Policy Studies in Higher Education. *Carnegie*
      Council on Policy Studies in Higher Education: A Summary of Reports
      and Recommendations. San Francisco: Jossey-Bass, 1980. 489p. ISBN
      0-87589-474-7.
Provides digests of fifteen Policy Reports and thirty-eight Sponsored Research and Technical Reports of the Carnegie Council, which began its
work in 1974 and concluded it in January 1980. The book is in four
parts, with Parts 2 and 3 treating policy reports and sponsored reports
individually. Part 1 covers the reports generally, while a final part
provides various membership lists, dates and locations of meetings, and
publications of the Commission and the Council. A detailed index
concludes the work.

459. Franks, Ray. *What's in a Nickname?* Amarillo, Tex.: Ray Franks
      Publishing Ranch, 1982. ISBN 0-943976-00-6.
What is the most popular of all nicknames in college athletics? For the
answer to this and a number of related questions, this is the source.
It covers more than two thousand nicknames of U.S. colleges, universities, junior colleges, and a number of Canadian institutions of higher
education. Entries in this delightful and readable work include origins
of nicknames, mascots, school colors, along with logos and other bits of
information. The work begins with a series of brief, illustrated essays
of "Interesting Facts About College Nicknames and Mascots." The main
portion of the book arranges entries in three sections: senior colleges,
junior colleges, and Canadian colleges. Within the sections institutions
are arranged alphabetically by name. No index.

460. Freed, Melvyn N., Hess, Robert K. and Ryan, Joseph M. *The Educa-*
      tion Desk Reference (EDR): A Sourcebook of Educational Information
      and Research. New York: American Council on Education/Macmillan

Publishing Co., 1989. 536p. ISBN 0-02-910- 740-7.
Provides selected, basic information of use primarily to the beginning
researcher in education. The main sections cover such topics as information sources, journal, book and software publishers, and their guidelines
for authors. Also covered are microcomputer software for educational
research; standardized tests and inventories; a synopsis of research
processes, including design and sampling methods; and national and regional organizations. Information in the directory sections is arranged
both by name and by type or subject. This and the detailed table of contents compensate somewhat for the sketchy organization/title/topic index.
Though all educational levels are covered much here is relevant to higher
education.

461. Goodman, Steven E. *Handbook on Contemporary Education.* New York:
      Bowker, 1976. 622p. ISBN 0-8352-0690-8.
The 118 brief essays (average length, about five pages) gathered here are
intended to provide information on a wide range of topics and issues in
education. The lists of references, often quite lengthy, that accompany
the papers point the way to additional research sources. Papers are
grouped in eight sections covering broad areas such as Administration and
Management, Students and Parents, and Teaching and Learning Strategies.
Brief keyword and author indexes are provided. No more recent edition
is in print, so the original currency of this work has been lost, but it
does retain some historical value as many of the topics dealt with are
perennial issues. About a quarter of the papers deal directly with higher education.

462. Lessiter, Mike. *The College Names of the Games: The Stories Behind
      the Nicknames of 293 College Sports.* Chicago: Contemporary Books,
      1989. 342p. ISBN 0-8092-4476-4.
A handy source of information covering the background and origins of mascots and nicknames associated with college sports. The work's main portion is arranged under thirty-two major athletic conferences. A final
section covers independent institutions separately. Page-length entries
of United States and Canadian colleges and universities include the institution name and nickname, address, school colors, year founded, and
information about the institution's arena or stadium. Each entry also
includes discussion about the nickname's origins. Many entries provide
a replica of the team mascot or logo. Includes an index.

463. O'Brien, Robert F. *School Songs of America's Colleges and Univer-
      sities: A Directory.* New York: Greenwood, Pr., 1991. 197p. ISBN
      0-313-27890-3.
Lists approximately eighteen hundred songs (alma maters, fight songs,
other songs) of nearly nine hundred American colleges and universities.
Entries are arranged alphabetically by state, and within each state,
alphabetically by institution. Each entry includes the name of the alma
mater, fight song, or other major song or songs associated with the institution. Where possible information is provided about the composer,
the tune and publisher or copyright status. Extensive use of abbreviations for frequently used terms keeps the entries brief and to the point.
Separate listings include references to song sources, school names, reference works consulted, publishers, and a song index.

464. Smart, John C. *Higher Education: Handbook of Theory and Research.*
      New York: Agathon Pr., 1985-   . Annual. ISSN 0882-4126.
This work brings together and synthesizes an ever-growing and fragmented
body of research findings and policy matters. The handbook is organized
around twelve major subject areas, ranging from faculty and organization-

al theory and behavior, to legal issues, governance and planning. Contributing authors are instructed to provide an integrative review, critique the research in terms of its conceptual and methodological rigor, and set the agenda for future research. The plan is to have one chapter per major subject area in each volume. This is a major work, with a distinguished group of associate editors, for the scholar, student, and administrator. Each chapter report includes a substantial bibliography. Indexes provided for cited authors and general subjects.

465. Wickremasinghe, Walter. *Handbook of World Education: A Comprehensive Guide to Higher Education and Educational Systems of the World.* Houston, Tex.: American Collegiate Service, 1991.   898p. ISBN 0-940937-03-4.
A concise source of current information covering major aspects of educational systems in countries of the world, with focus on higher education. Arrangement is alphabetical by country name. Each country chapter is organized in four sections: background, primary and secondary systems, higher education systems, and issues and trends. The higher education unit covers such topics as governance, study programs, research, costs, faculty, and other topics. Each chapter is written by a scholar native to the country, and includes a brief bibliography. Access is by means of the table of contents.

SPECIAL WORKS

Academic Degrees and Ceremony

466. Eells, Walter Crosby. *Degrees in Higher Education.* New York: Center for Center for Applied Research in Education, 1963.   118p.
While not strictly a reference work, this volume does supplement Eells and Haswell's Academic Degrees(1960) and provides a concise account of the origins, history and current status of the degrees in use in American higher education.   The range from Associate to doctorate is covered, along with the professional and honorary variants at each level, and some less frequently seen types, such as specialist and occupational degrees. There is a detailed table of contents, an institution/organization index and a brief bibliography.

467. Eells, Walter Crosby and Haswell, Harold A. *Academic Degrees: Earned and Honorary Degrees Conferred by Institutions of Higher Education in the United States.* (Bulletin 1960, no. 28) Washington, D.C.: U.S. Department of Health, Education and Welfare, Office in Education, 1960. 324p.
Compiled from survey and historical sources as a catalog or dictionary of the twenty-four hundred degrees formerly or currently in use, this work first briefly examines the development and types of degrees, types of institutions, degrees for women, honorary and spurious degrees, and the confusion and inconsistency in degree abbreviations. Graphs and tables supplement this part of the text. The last three chapters, the bulk of the volume, provide listings of degrees classified by field, degree names arranged alphabetically, and degree abbreviations arranged alphabetically. Brief historical discussions precede each subject field list, and, for each degree currently in use, the number of institutions conferring it is shown. A subject index is also provided. Unique and useful despite its age.

468. Gunn, Mary Kemper. *A Guide to Academic Protocol.* New York: Columbia Univ. Pr., 1969. 112p.

Unabashedly opinionated advice to persons charged with planning and managing campus public events from one who performed this function at Columbia for a number of years. Matters of academic protocol are certainly dealt with, but much of the work is devoted to the practicalities of making arrangements (schedules, checklists and even recipes are provided) and to considerations more accurately termed academic etiquette. Separate chapters deal with the major types of campus events: receptions, teas, lectures, dinners, convocations, etc. A checklist for estimating expenses is appended. No indexes. Much that is valuable here, but dated by changing social sensibilities and the advent of photocopiers and microcomputers.

469. Haycraft, Frank W. *The Degrees and Hoods of the World's Colleges and Universities.* 5th ed. Lewes, Sussex: W. E. Baxter, 1972. 162p.
Includes about forty pages describing the Intercollegiate Code and the hoods in use at U.S. institutions, but dated and marred by the editorial and design flaws to which privately published works are susceptible.

470. Keiser, Albert. *College Names, Their Origins and Significance.* New York: Bookman Associates, 1952. 184p.
Elucidates the names of more than seven hundred American institutions of higher education. The work is divided into two sections, with the second devoted to black institutions. Arrangement in both sections is alphabetical by the name of the institution. Entries include the name, religious affiliation (where appropriate), level (junior colleges are included), control type, and whether co-educational. Entries range from a single sentence to several paragraphs, giving information about founders, sums raised, and educational mission. Includes cross references. No index.

471. Lockmiller, David A. *Scholars on Parade: Colleges, Universities, Costumes and Degrees.* New York: Macmillan Publishing, 1969. 290p.
Presents a brief history of higher education in the United States, including some consideration of its European roots, with the particular emphasis indicated by the subtitle. Two of the eleven chapters deal with degrees, another with academic costumes and emblems. Many illustrations and photographs depict academic ceremonies and costumes. Four appendices contain a list of degrees and their abbreviations, colors and designs of selected institutions' hoods, color and trim of doctoral regalia by discipline and, finally, a costume code and ceremony guide. A bibliography and index are also provided.

472. Paget, R. L. *Cap and Gown: Third Series.* (Granger Poetry Library) Great Neck, N.Y.: Roth Publishing, 1979. 331p. ISBN 0-89609-144-9.
Anthology of poetry selected from publications of forty-one colleges and universities, covering a broad array of subjects, from humor and love to nature. This is a reprint of an earlier edition (Page, 1903). Includes a list of college publications represented in the volume, a table of contents, and an index of contributors.

473. Schweitzer, George K. *The Doctorate: A Handbook.* Springfield, Ill.: Charles C. Thomas, 1965. 106p.
Surveys in its four chapters the history, current status, etiquette and ceremony of the degree. Appendices present such related information as abbreviations of degrees, names and hood colors of doctorate-granting institutions, forms of address for clergy, a short bibliography, and a proposal for reform of degree designations, colors and regalia. Brief index.

474. Sheard, Kevin. *Academic Heraldry in America*. Marquette: Northern
      Michigan Coll. Pr., 1962. 78p.
Essentially a series of lists showing: faculty colors; various hood
designs; hood color(s) by institution; single-color hood linings, by
color along with institutions; chevron(s), by color along with
institutions; and a list of non-code hoods (e.g., Art Institute of Chicago, Ohio College of Chiropody, etc.). The work concludes with brief essays on academic processions, ceremony, seals, and flags. Also included
are color plates of faculty hood colors and a short bibliography. No
index.

475. Smith, Hugh. *Academic Dress and Insignia of the World: Gowns,
      Hats, Chains of Office, Hoods, Rings, Medals and Other Degree In-
      signia of Universities and Other Institutions of Learning*. 3 vols.
      Cape Town, South Africa: A. A. Balkema, 1970.
A "simple reference work containing a record of academic dress and insignia," encompassing most of the institutions of higher education of the
world and non-university bodies that use academic dress. Omitted are
countries which have not finalized their codes of academic costume, those
which do not prescribe such costume, and those which did not reply to the
author. The first volume covers the British Commonwealth, the Irish Republic, and the Republic of South Africa; the second deals with Europe,
Africa, Asia, the United States, and Central and South America. The
third volume contains a glossary and definitions, hood identification
tables, the U.S.A. Intercollegiate Code, abbreviations, and an index.
Well illustrated with labeled line drawings.

476. Sparks, Linda and Emerton, Bruce. *American College Regalia: A
      Handbook*. Westport, Conn.: Greenwood Pr., 1988. 392p. ISBN 0-
      313-26266-7.
An easy to use source providing information about alma mater and fight
songs, newspapers and yearbooks, nicknames, school colors and mascots of
469 colleges and universities with enrollments of twenty-five hundred or
more. Arrangement of entries is alphabetical by state and by institution
name under the appropriate state. Includes separate indexes by school
name, school colors, and mascot.

477. UNESCO. *World Guide to Higher Education: A Comparative Survey of
      Systems, Degrees, and Qualifications*. Paris, France: Unipub, 1976.
      302p. ISBN 0-85935-043-6.
This work facilitates comparison between systems of higher education, degrees, and diplomas throughout the world. The book's major portion, the
section dealing with individual countries, is arranged alphabetically and
divided into complementary parts: a description of each nation's system
of higher education (with emphasis on fundamental stages) and a glossary
of its principal degrees and diplomas.

Administration

478. *College and University Business Administration*. 4th ed. Washing-
      ton, D.C.: Nat. Assn. of Coll. and Univ. Business Officers, 1982.
      527p. ISBN 0-915164-12-4.
The product of numerous contributors and a broad professional consensus,
this volume is the Association's authoritative compendium of management
principles. The thirty chapters cover the general areas of administrative management, business management, fiscal management, and financial
reporting and accounting. Includes a twenty-three page bibliography and
an index.

479. Coughin, Caroline M. and Gretzog, Alice. *Lyle's Administration of the College Library*. 5th ed. Metuchen, N.J.: Scarecrow Pr., 1992. 603p. ISBN 0-8108-2552-X.

An updated version of Guy Lyle's classic work of the same title. The authors state their purpose as providing a simple, logical and self-contained introduction to all aspects of library administration as they apply to college libraries. Twenty chapters cover such topics as Business Financial Affairs, Collection Management, Educating the Library User, Human Resource Management, Organization of the Library, and Technology and Integrated Library Systems. Chapters include notes and suggested reading. An appendix offers the Association of College and Research Libraries 1986 Standards for College Libraries. Includes an index.

480. Creswell, John W. *Academic Chairperson's Handbook*. Lincoln: Univ. of Nebraska Pr., 1990. 128p. ISBN 0-8032-1450-2.

A highly useful and practical guide, based on interviews with two hundred chairpersons nominated as "excellent" at seventy U.S. campuses. The first of two parts offers fifteen strategies for building a positive environment, developing leadership skills and establishing positive communication. In Part 2 strategies are applied in such areas as hiring, teaching performance, improving scholarship and other personnel issues. Suggested readings are included along with a topical index to strategies.

481. Dressel, Paul L. *Handbook of Academic Evaluation*. San Francisco: Jossey-Bass, 1976. 518p. ISBN 0-87589-276-0.

A review of thinking about evaluation, with eighteen chapters in four parts: Basic Considerations, Evaluation of Student Experience and Educational Progress, and Evaluation of Programs and Personnel. Each chapter can be consulted independently of the others. The book covers the concepts, approaches, processes, tests, and instruments used in evaluation. Extensive bibliography and subject index included.

482. Dressel, Paul L. *Institutional Research in the University: A Handbook*. San Francisco: Jossey-Bass, 1971. 347p. ISBN 0-87589-099-7.

Includes thirteen chapters by nine leading practitioners. It discusses major problems, nature of institutional research, planning studies, evaluation, long range planning, and the future. Bibliographies are included at the end of each chapter, citing sources from the American Council on Education, government documents, the Association for Institutional Research, as well as journals. One of the purposes of the handbook is to "show pathways to vitally needed reform" through institutional research. Includes a subject index.

483. Fairbrook, Paul. *College and University Food Service Manual*. Stockton, Calif.: Colman Publishers, 1979. 438p. ISBN 0-9602456-0-X.

The author draws on his own considerable experience in the field, as well as that of others, to produce this survey and reference manual for food service directors and management personnel. Nineteen chapters deal with such topics as organization, purchasing, budgets, cash operations, sanitation, special events and public relations, and are generously illustrated with charts, tables and sample forms and documents. Additional illustrative material is presented in a series of appendices. Includes an index.

484. Fairbrook, Paul. *Public Relations and Merchandising: A Handbook for College and University Food Services*. Stockton, Calif.: Colman

Publishers, 1984. 352p. ISBN 0-9602456-1-8.
Similar in style and approach to the author's College and University Food Service Manual (1979), this work focuses on the promotional aspects of food service, offering guidance to the inexperienced manager and new ideas to the veteran. Topics covered include public relations techniques, marketing campaigns, press releases, merchandising in cash operations and residence halls, nutrition education, and communicating with the campus community. Numerous forms, posters, press releases, menus, announcements and the like are reproduced as illustrations to the text and as samples in the generous appendix. An index is also provided.

485. Flawn, Peter T. *A Primer for University Presidents: Managing the Modern University.* Austin: Univ. of Texas Pr., 1990. 210p. ISBN 0-292-76522-3.
The author, an experienced university president and administrator, intends this work to be a "practical guide" for actual and prospective university presidents. While lacking the detailed information and data of lengthier handbooks, this work does offer clear, often trenchant, advice and guidance on the full range of issues that arise in the management of the university. The sixteen chapters bear titles such as "Governance and Management," "The Faculty," "Budget and Planning," "Development," "Academic Ceremonies and Official Occasions," and, finally, "Exiting the Presidency." Includes a subject index.

486. Hefferlin, JB Lon and Phillips, Ellis L. *Information Services for Academic Administration.* (Jossey-Bass Series in Higher Education) San Francisco: Jossey-Bass, 1971. 160p. ISBN 0-87589-096-2.
After establishing both the problems of and the need for administrative information, the authors devote separate chapters to an examination and critique of each major information channel: intra- and interinstitutional communication, institutes and workshops, publications, consultants, and information centers. Each chapter concludes with proposals and lists of resources available (specific programs, organizations, publications) for improving each information medium. An index and a directory of agencies and organizations are provided.

487. Hughes, Raymond M. *Manual for Trustees of Colleges and Universities.* 3d ed. Ames: Iowa State Coll. Pr., 1951. 178p.
Written as a guide for board members, particularly the inexperienced, this work addresses the specific responsibilities of trustees, their place in the governance structure and their role as representatives of the institution. The author examines the background, circumstances and structures peculiar to academic institutions, explaining matters such as enrollments and admissions, campus and buildings, the faculty, the library, daily chapel, athletics, and student life. Though some advice here may still be sound, much of the work is outdated and mainly of historical value. No references or bibliography; brief index.

488. Ingram, Richard T., and others. *Handbook of College and University Trusteeship: A Practical Guide for Trustees, Chief Executives, and Other Leaders Responsible for Developing Effective Governing Boards.* (Jossey-Bass Series in Higher Education) San Francisco: Jossey-Bass, 1980. 514p. ISBN 0-87589-450-X.
The twenty chapters of this substantial work, contributed by nineteen experienced college trustees or administrators, are grouped into five major sections dealing with 1) the evolution, responsibilities and current outlook of governing boards; 2) board organization and management; 3) the institutional oversight function; 4) developing and managing resources; and 5) evaluation of board, president and institutional perform-

ance.   A sixth section offers supplementary sample policies and
assessment materials and an annotated list of recommended readings for
each chapter.   A twenty-page reference list and an index are also included.

489.   Jedamus, Paul and Peterson, Marvin W.   *Improving Academic Manage-
       ment: A Handbook of Planning and Institutional Research.* (Jossey-
       Bass Series in Higher Education)   San Francisco: Jossey- Bass,
       1980.   679p.   ISBN 0-87589-477-1.
Intended to be a definitive guide for the 1980s and still of significant
value, this comprehensive work presents thirty-one chapters contributed
by thirty-six authorities and practitioners.   Chapters are grouped in
seven broad topical sections: the planning and research environment,
strategic planning and research, academic planning and research, allocat-
ing resources, assessing performance, increasing campus involvement, and
current practice.   Each chapter concludes with a brief bibliographic essay and a list of references. The volume is provided with both name and
subject indexes.

490.   Jones, Dennis P. and Drews, Theodore H.   *A Manual for Budgeting and
       Accounting for Manpower Resources in Postsecondary Education.* Wash-
       ington, D.C.: National Center for Education Statistics, 1977. 66p.
       (Also distributed as NCHEMS Technical Report, No. 84)
A revised version of W. John Minter's Manual for Manpower Accounting in
Higher Education (NCHEMS, 1972), this work describes a standardized information system, based on the NCHEMS Program Classification Structure,
for use in managing institutional human resources.   Major sections discuss definitions, data and procedures required for: classification and
measurement, allocation and utilization, and the description of assign-
ments and activities.   Charts, tables and sample forms illustrate the
text.   Appendices provide a glossary of terms, further personnel classifications and the NCHEMS Structure.   No index or bibliography.

491.   Kieft, Raymond N., Armijo, Frank and Bucklew, Neil S.   *A Handbook
       for Institutional Academic and Program Planning: From Idea to Im-
       plementation.*   Boulder, Colo.: Nat. Center for Higher Education
       Management Systems, 1978.   67p.
Intended to be a basic guide to implementing or improving centralized
planning processes at institutions not deeply involved in research activities.   The authors describe in detail the major steps and procedures
in a planning cycle based on conclusions drawn from case studies by
NCHEMS.   Numerous charts and tables and a selected bibliography are included.   No index.

492.   Knowles, Asa S.   *Handbook of College and University Administra-
       tion.*   2 vols.   New York: McGraw-Hill Publishing Co., 1970.
This massive work, representing the efforts of over 160 contributors,
attempts to cover the full range of activities, issues, procedures and
areas of concern for administrators at all types of institutions.   One
volume is devoted to General Administration and includes sections on
planning, public relations, physical plant, business and finance and the
like.   The other volume, on Academic Administration, covers such areas
as admissions, learning resources, student personnel administration,
health programs, athletics and religion.   In each volume these sections
are further subdivided into a total of two hundred topical chapters.
Emphasis throughout is on practical information and readily applicable
principles.   Profusely illustrated with real and hypothetical examples,
sample forms and documents,   tables, charts and outlines.   Bibliographic

references accompany many of the chapters, and each volume has its own
index. An aging landmark work.

493. Mason, Henry Lloyd. *College and University Government: A Handbook
     of Principle and Practice.* (Tulane Studies in Political Science,
     Vol. 14) New Orleans: Tulane Univ. 1972. 235p.
The author, a professor of Political Science and member of AAUP's Committee T on College and University Government, writes for those who are
creating or implementing a system of government in their own institutions. In the first of three chapters, he surveys the contemporary
literature on the major principles, components and issues involved, and
in the remaining two examines actual and model constitutional provisions.
Relevant AAUP documents appear in appendix sections. Bibliography, name
and subject indexes. Dated, but remains useful.

494. McCabe, Gerard B. *Academic Libraries in Urban and Metropolitan
     Areas: A Management Handbook.* Westport, Ct.: Greenwood Pr., 1992.
     261p. ISBN 0-313-27536-X.
Comprised of practical and useful information by a number of knowledge-
able library administrators, educators, and practitioners. A leadoff
article provides a bibliographic essay covering more than one hundred
source citations. Six following sections cover: Services to External
Population Groups; Service to Internal Population Groups; Extended Campus
Considerations; Security, Safety, and Preservation; and Managerial Perspectives. Topics include policies for private citizens and high school
students, reference and information service, bibliographic instruction,
personnel management, and a wide range of other topics related to academic libraries in the urban setting. Includes an index.

495. McCarthy, Jane, Ladimer, Jane and Sirefman, Josef P. *Managing Fac-
     ulty Disputes: A Guide to Issues, Procedures, and Practices.* San
     Francisco: Jossey-Bass, 1984. 270p. ISBN 0-87589-623-5.
A practical source for trustees, presidents, deans, division and department heads, and others who participate in governance. According to the
authors, emphasis is on the process of dispute management, not on substantive solutions to specific problems. Nine chapters are divided into
three sections covering recurring disputes (e.g., tenure, discipline,
collective bargaining), procedures for resolving recurring disputes, and
disputes that occur infrequently, yet have major impact (disputes over
institutional policies, and financial problems). A concluding section
provides a checklist for assessing grievance systems, model procedures
for resolving faculty disputes, components of grievance, procedures, and
grievance procedures of three institutions. Includes a list of readings,
a detailed table of contents, and a general index.

496. Miller, Richard I. *Assessment of College Performance: A Handbook
     of Techniques and Measures for Institutional Self-Evaluation.* San
     Francisco: Jossey-Bass, 1979. 374p. ISBN 0-87589-406-2.
Elements, criteria and procedures involved in self-evaluation are presented in a series of chapters that consider the major components of the
institution in turn. Chapters cover objectives, student learning, faculty, programs, support staff and facilities, administrative leadership,
the governing board, etc. Other chapters consider the planning and implementing of the self-evaluation process. Specific institution - wide
studies and comparative studies of graduate and professional schools are
described in two appendices. Includes an annotated bibliography, extensive list of references, and an index.

497. Millett, John D. *Planning in Higher Education: A Manual for Col-*

leges and Universities. Washington, D.C.: Academy for Educational Development, 1977. 526p.
Examines major components of a comprehensive planning process, devoting separate chapters to such topics as: the external environment, mission, programs, instruction, enrollment, organization, budgets and, finally, evaluation of results. Illustrated with tables and charts; no index or bibliography.

498.   National Association of Educational Buyers. *Purchasing for Educational Institutions.* New York: Teachers College, Columbia Univ., 1961. 282p.
A comprehensive guide to procurement practice in the higher education setting. Twenty chapters describe and explain such areas as organization, negotiation for purchase, legal problems, suppliers, research and ethics. Bibliography and index are provided.

499.   National Association of Private, Nontraditional Schools and Colleges. Commission on Postsecondary Education. *Handbook on Accreditation: Guidelines for Accreditation by Contract.* 2d rev. ed. Grand Junction, Colo.: The Association, 1980. 188p.
Institutions in which academic requirements can be met outside the conventional campus instruction model can use this guide in seeking or maintaining accreditation with the Association. The opening sections define and discuss the concept of nontraditional education and the nature and goals of the Association. The standards and procedures of the "accreditation by contract" process are then presented, including eligibility criteria, on-site visits, development of an action plan, required reports, dues and fees. Additional policies, guidelines and a glossary appear in appendices. Bibliography, no index.

500.   Petersen, Dorothy G. *A Current Profile: Accrediting Standards and Guidelines: A Study of the Evaluative Standards and Guidelines of 52 Accrediting Agencies Recognized by the Council on Postsecondary Accreditation.* Washington, D. C.: Council on Postsecondary Accreditation, 1979. 168p. ISBN 0-318-13851-4.
The opening section of this work presents an objective, comparative analysis of differences and commonalities in the evaluative standards and guidelines of institutions using a voluntary system of peer accreditation. A second and third part, respectively, cover institutional accreditation and specialized and professional education. A fourth part includes a summary, conclusions, and recommendations. A list of tables follows the table of contents. Includes a selected bibliography and an appendix listing the accrediting agencies recognized by the Council.

501.   Quann, C. James. *Admissions, Academic Records, and Registrar Services: A Handbook of Policies and Procedures.* San Francisco: Jossey-Bass, 1979. 481p. ISBN 0-87589-419-4.
Various authors detail the role, function and responsibilities of registrars and admissions officers and the interpretation and enforcement of academic policies and standards. The table of contents lists thirteen chapters with sub-topics and further reading for each chapter. A separate listing of tables, figures, and exhibits follows the table of contents. Seven appendices and a general index are included.

502.   Rogers, Rutherford D. and Weber, David C. *University Library Administration.* New York: H.W. Wilson Co., 1971. 454p. ISBN 0-8242-0417-4.
A standard work designed to provide librarians, library students, and other academic personnel with treatment of important issues in university

library administration. The book's eleven chapters cover all major areas
of administration, from program planning, personnel policies, and budget
and fiscal matters, to collections, technical and readers services,
automation, and building planning. Chapters include photographs, charts,
and tables.   Each concludes with a list of selected references.
Appendices provide sample forms, policies, and other useful reports and
guidelines.   While some facts may be dated, especially a chapter on
automation, this remains a highly useful guide to library administration.
Access is by means of the table of contents and a general index.

503. Romney, Leonard C. *Facilities Inventory and Classification Manual*.
      (DHEW Publication No. (OE) 74-11424) Washington, D.C.: U.S. Dept.
      of Health, Education, and Welfare, 1974. 152p.
Provides procedures and standard terminology for collecting and classify-
ing data on buildings and rooms only. Following an introduction, four
sections deal with the inventory process, the reporting process, uses of
the data, and treatment of special problems. Twelve appendices provide,
among other things, definitions of codes, a glossary, and comparisons
between the first edition and the present one.   Various figures
throughout the volume show sample floor plans and data-recording forms.
Room-use categories and program classification structure for facilities
inventory data are found on the inside front and back covers,
respectively. Subject index is provided.

504. Russell, John Dale and Doi, James I. *Manual for Study of Space
      Utilization in Colleges and Universities*. Athens, Ohio: American
      Assoc. of Collegiate Registrars and Admissions Officers, 1957.
      130p.
Prepared in anticipation of increased enrollments, this 1957 manual was
designed to aid college and university administrators in making a study
of space utilization in their institutions for the purpose of improving
utilization. Six chapters deal with the following topics: functions and
limitations of a college space utilization study; correct status of such
studies; definition of terms; forms and procedure for collection of data;
forms for the analysis and interpretation of data; and normative data for
space utilization. List of tables and a subject index.

505. Seldin, Peter. *Evaluating and Developing Administrative Perform-
      ance: A Practical Guide for Academic Leaders*. (The Jossey-Bass
      Higher Education Series) San Francisco: Jossey-Bass, 1988. 242p.
      ISBN 1-55542-119-9.
Attempts a practical approach to administrative performance, by discussing, among other things, the ethical legal considerations involved, the
practices, strategies, and forms used around the country, and the numerous development opportunities available. In addition, the author "provides readers with a distillation of the relevant research literature,"
the intended audience being college and university administrators. In
eight chapters, the following topics are covered: expectations and roles
of administrators; purpose of assessment of administrative performance;
evaluating administrative performance; planning, implementing, and managing a successful evaluation program; ensuring a sound legal basis for
evaluation activities; strategies for developing and improving administrative performance; providing opportunities for professional development
on and off campus; and evaluating and developing the president (a role
model for the process). An appendix provides chapter-by-chapter lists
of benchmarks for evaluating and developing administrative performance.
There are numerous exhibits of forms used in the procedures discussed.
A sixteen page bibliography and a subject/author index.

506. Simerly, Robert G. *Handbook of Marketing for Continuing Education.*
      (Jossey-Bass Higher Education Series) San Francisco: Jossey-Bass,
      1989. 521p. ISBN 1-55542-142-3.
Practical advice for continuing education professionals who are responsible for marketing their programs at four-year colleges, universities, and
community colleges. In addition to case studies, guidelines, suggestions, and advice, the book covers basic concepts of marketing, position
of the user's organization in the market, direct-mail marketing, effective public relations, advertising and personal sales, making marketing
work in the user's organization, strategies for ongoing success, and a
list of resources. Many figures, tables, exhibits, a fifteen-page bibliography, and a general index.

507. Sprunger, Benjamin E. and Bergquist, William H. *Handbook for Col-
      lege Administration.* Washington, D.C.: Council for the Advancement
      of Small Colleges, 1978. 340p.
For students of higher education and new and experienced college
administrators.   Seven chapters deal with the past and potential of
college administration, planning, organizing, staffing, leading, evaluating, and developing. The last two sections of each chapter provide
notes and documents, respectively; the latter section consists of practical resources in the form of actual techniques and forms used by various
colleges and universities. The table of contents lists the sections of
each chapter. A list of figures is provided. No index.

508. Wolotkiewicz, Rita J. *College Administrator's Handbook.* Boston:
      Allyn and Bacon, 1980. 265p. ISBN 0-205-06873-1.
Provides an overview for those entering the field of administration in
community colleges, four-year colleges, and colleges in a university system.   Ten chapters range in coverage from administrative roles, and
selection and evaluation of administrators, to faculty collective bargaining, planning, programming, and budgeting. Each chapter provides a
summary and list of readings cited. Practical advice is offered, including search committee procedures, steps for implementing equal opportunity
goals, and ways to develop informational programs. Includes charts, diagrams, sample forms, and other illustrative matter. Concludes with a
selected bibliography, author index, and subject index.

Collective Bargaining

509. Angell, George W. and others. *Handbook of Faculty Bargaining.* San
      Francisco: Jossey-Bass, 1977. 593p. ISBN 0-87589-320-1.
The intent is to help those involved to "maximize the opportunity for
peaceful settlement of contractual negotiations and grievance disputes."
The work is in five parts: Part 1 sets the tone with an overview of general opportunities and problems. Part 2 offers thoughts of ten eminent
practitioners (scholars, attorneys, and administrators) who review strategies and tactics "of negotiating viable working agreements and of avoiding violent confrontations". Part 3 focuses on administering the
contract, while Part 4 discusses statewide bargaining. The final part
includes suggestions "as to how university leadership can manage the impact of unions on budgets and traditional faculty-administrative relationships." Includes a list of references and an index.

510. Douglas, Joel M. and Garfin, Molly. *Contract Development in Higher
      Education Faculty Collective Bargaining: A Guide to Provisions,
      Clauses, Terms, and Counterproposals.* New York: National Center
      for the Study of Collective Bargaining in Higher Education, Baruch

Coll., City Univ. of New York, 1980. 363p.
Provides summaries or extracts, illustrating various approaches and word-
ings, derived from a review of more than three hundred collective bargaining agreements.   A unique feature is the provision of contract
clauses coded to the .type of institutions from which clauses are
extracted. The work is in four parts: components of bargaining
agreements, contract provisions and counterproposals (from bargaining
agent recognition to management rights), contract clauses (major portion
of the book), and a glossary. Includes tables, sample forms, and a
subject index.

511. Means, Howard B. and Semas, Philip W. *Faculty Collective Bargain-
      ing.* (A Chronicle of Higher Education Handbook) Washington, D.C.:
      Editorial Projects for Education, 1976. 124p.
This work makes essential material available in a truly convenient handbook format. Basic information on collective bargaining is provided in
a glossary of terms and in brief descriptions of the steps in bargaining,
the typical provisions of contracts and the strategies available to faculty and to management. Additional sections survey current legislation,
NLRB decisions, issues, trends, statistics and notable events at various
campuses. A bibliography and index are provided. Much of the basic information is still useful as an introduction to the topic, but the current survey sections are badly dated.   Unfortunately no more recent
edition is in print.

Community Colleges

512. Harper, William A. *Community, Junior, and Technical Colleges: A
      Public Relations Sourcebook.* Washington, D.C.: Hemisphere Publish-
      ing, 1977. 212p. ISBN 0-39116-043-4.
Written to guide the practitioner and increase the understanding and
awareness of faculty, administrators and trustees, this work discusses
the public relations function in the two-year college environment. Planning, organization and staffing, internal and external constituencies,
and special problems and tasks are among the topics addressed. Brief
chapter summaries and an index add to this work's reference value and
ease of use.

513. Monroe, Charles R. *Profile of the Community College: A Handbook.*
      (Jossey-Bass Series in Higher Education) San Francisco: Jossey-
      Bass, 1972. 435p. ISBN 0-87589-124-1.
Drawing upon both the literature and his own substantial experience, the
author presents an extensive examination of the public community college,
its unique nature and role and the issues and problems it faces. Individual chapters deal with topics such as the community college's historical development, objectives and functions, general and occupational
education, students, governance, organization and future prospects. A
bibliography and separate name and subject indexes are provided.

514. Potter, George E. *Trusteeship: Handbook for Community College and
      Technical Institute Trustees.* 2d ed. Washington, D.C.: Assn. of
      Community Coll. Trustees, 1979. 177p.
Covers skills required of trustees for governance and in their dealings
with administrators. Seven chapters cover such subjects as law, collective bargaining, and trustees' responsibilities. Includes a glossary of
terms, a list of acronyms, and a guide to recommended readings.

Disabilities

515. Cotler, Stephen R. and DeGraff, Alfred H. *Architectural Accessibility for the Disabled of College Campuses.* Albany, N.Y.: State
University Construction Fund, 1976. 133p.
Presents essential information for planning for the diversity of physically handicapped. The authors provide design and construction standards
for a wide range of campus facilities, brought together into thirty subject chapters. These range from alarm systems and hallways to parking
facilities and walkways. Included are a number of diagrams and
illustrations, with dimensions given in both feet and inches and in the
metric system. A brief bibliography concludes the handbook. While dated,
much of the information remains useful.

516. Milner, Margaret. *Planning for Accessibility: A Guide to Developing and Implementing Campus Transition Plans.* Washington, D.C.:
Assn. of Physical Plant Administrators of Universities and Colleges, 1977. 86p.
In accordance with the mandates of Section 504 of the Rehabilitation Act
of 1973, this work presents guidelines and recommendations for making
facilities accessible to the physically handicapped. The final chapter
offers four brief case histories, and appendices contain sample documents
and survey instruments and lists of resource publications and organizations. No index.

517. Scheiber, Barbara and Talpers, Jeanne. *Unlocking Potential College
and Other Choices for Learning Disabled People.* Bethesda, Md.: Adler and Adler, 1987. 199p. ISBN 0-917561-29-5.
A step-by-step guide to help learning disabled students achieve access
to college campuses and to help campuses become accessible to the handicapped. The book's first two chapters define and explain learning disabilities and describe diagnostic processes. Following chapters range
in coverage from college options and choosing courses to developing study
skills and offering innovative approaches to teaching. The last chapter
provides suggestions for starting postsecondary programs for the learning
disabled. Chapters also include suggested readings, checklists, organizations and other illustrative materials. Includes a general index.

518. Sclafani, Annette Joy and Lynch, Michael J. *College Guide for Students with Learning Disabilities.* Miller Place, N.Y.: SPEDCO
Associates, 1990. 210p. ISBN 0-9615856-5-9.
This handbook provides information and guidance on comparing and selecting colleges, the application and admissions processes, and standardized
admission tests. Additional practical help is given in the form of timetables, calendars, worksheets and checklists. A separate section lists
and describes two and four-year colleges with formal specialist-staffed
programs for the learning disabled, while another lists schools that offer significant services for this group. An index of colleges is included.

Economic Factors

519. Bossert, Philip J. *Strategic Planning and Budgeting for Colleges.*
Washington, D.C.: Nat. Assn. of Coll. and Univ. Business Officers,
1989. 79p. ISBN 0-915164-46-9.
Intended as a guide to implementing a strategic planning and budgeting
process. This work first examines the environment and conceptual framework of planning, then covers the other activities with which planning

interacts (and which are dealt with in related NACUBO manuals: Financial Self-Assessment, Operational Planning and Budgeting, and Management Reporting and Accounting). Finally, the integration of all of these into a single process is described. Text is illustrated with numerous charts as well as sample documents, tables and balance sheets. No bibliography or index.

520. Dickmeyer, Nathan, and Hughes, Scott K. *Financial Self-Assessment: A Workbook for Colleges and Universities.* 2d ed. Washington, D.C.: Nat. Assn. of Coll. and Univ. Business Officers, 1987. 90p. ISBN 0-915164-35-3.
A practical guide to using readily available data to assess an institution's financial condition. The work provides clearly structured directions and explanation, worksheets, charts and a diskette for use with Lotus 1-2-3 on IBM-compatible p.c.'s. Appendices include a glossary, hypothetical institutional example and a list of organizations and publications that can provide comparative data. A chapter on using and presenting the results of financial assessment also relates it to the budgeting and decision-making processes covered by NACUBO's other manuals: Management Reporting and Accounting, Operational Planning and Budgeting and Strategic Planning and Budgeting.

521. Dozier, John and others. *Operational Planning and Budgeting for Colleges.* 2d ed., rev. by Philip J. Bossert. Washington, D.C.: Nat. Assn. of Coll. and Univ. Business Officers, 1988. 78p. ISBN 0-915164-39-6.
Written to coordinate with the Association's other planning and management manuals (Strategic Planning and Budgeting, Management Reporting and Accounting and Financial Self-Assessment), this work describes in detail a model annual planning and budgeting process, specifying participants, tasks, schedule, and data required. The text is heavily illustrated with flowcharts, checklists, tables and sample forms. The final chapter contains case studies of four institutions which adapted this model to their own situations. No index or bibliography.

522. *Financial Responsibilities of Governing Boards of Colleges and Universities.* 2d ed. Washington, D.C.: Assn. of Governing Boards of Universities and Colleges and National Assn. of Coll. and Univ. Business Officers, 1985. 114p. ISBN 0-915164-17-5.
This work describes in basic, concise terms the part trustees play in generating, spending, managing and protecting financial resources and recommends methods of using financial accounting information that will enable them to readily grasp the financial requirements and consequences of the policies and priorities they set. "Suggested Questions" sections highlight areas of particular concern. Numerous illustrative tables, charts and forms appear in the text and in an appendix. A glossary and two-page bibliography are also included.

523. Forrester, Robert T. *A Handbook on Debt Management for Colleges and Universities.* Washington, D.C.: Nat. Assn. of Coll. and Univ. Business Officers, 1988. 114p. ISBN 0-915164-38-8.
Intended as a manual for both institutional treasurers and controllers, this work addresses topics such as debt, choice of funding sources, credit support, the effect of the 1986 Tax Reform Act, and accounting issues over the life of a debt. Appendices, which account for nearly half the volume, provide examples and answers to specific questions about debt accounting. Notes and a briefly annotated six-page bibliography offer access to additional sources of information. No index.

524. Hughes, K. Scott, Leonard, Jerry H. and Williams, M. J. *Management Reporting and Accounting for Colleges*. 2d ed., revised by Philip J. Bossert. Washington, D.C.: Nat. Assn. of Coll. and Univ. Business Officers, 1988. 84p. ISBN 0-915164-40- X.
Actually the fourth and most recent version of a handbook on financial management from NACUBO, this work is coordinated with the Association's other planning and management manuals: Strategic Planning and Budgeting, Operational Planning and Budgeting and Financial Self-Assessment. Its first section goes beyond basic balance sheets and fund statements to propose other reports and techniques that will improve management decision-making. The second section describes a fund accounting system to support these methods. Sample forms and fund definitions are given in appendices. Illustrated with flowcharts, tables, and sample reports. No index or bibliography.

525. Meeth, L. Richard. *Quality Education for Less Money: A Sourcebook for Improving Cost Effectiveness*. (Jossey-Bass Series in Higher Education) San Francisco: Jossey-Bass, 1974. 206p. ISBN 0-87589-211-6.
Reports and analyzes the results of a cost effectiveness study sponsored by the Council for the Advancement of Small Colleges in which sixty-six private liberal arts colleges participated. The author describes a planning approach other colleges can take in creating a cost-effectiveness program and recommends specific actions to increase efficiency. Numerous tables as well as sample forms for collecting and organizing data illustrate the text. A general bibliography, annotated bibliography and brief index are provided.

526. *Tough Choices: A Guide to Administrative Cost Management in Colleges and Universities*. Washington, D.C.: U.S. Dept. of Education, Office of Planning, Budget, and Evaluation, 1990. 47p.
Presents "practical, step-by-step advice on how to perform an administrative cost study." This handbook takes the user through seven basic components of a comprehensive cost-management study. Each component discussion provides a sample case. A brief, clearly presented work that includes charts and diagrams.

Faculty

527. Joughin, Louis. *Academic Freedom and Tenure: A Handbook of the American Association of University Professors*. Madison: Univ. of Wisconsin Pr., 1969. 374p. ISBN 0-299-05454-3.
Brings together the Association's various formal statements on the topic, resolutions adopted at its annual meetings, pertinent advisory letters selected and reprinted from its Bulletin, and a selection of articles and addresses from other sources. An introductory section describes the procedures the Association follows in dealing with complaints of infringement of tenure or academic freedom. Another section provides lists, updated through 1968, of institutions censured by the Association or upon which committee reports were issued. Of value for historical background purposes. Brief index included.

528. Kronk, Annie K. and Shipka, Thomas A. *Evaluation of Faculty in Higher Education: A Handbook for Faculty Leaders*. Washington, D.C.: Nat. Education Assn., c1980. 31p.
Briefly surveys major issues in evaluation, addressing rationale, methodologies, due process concerns, activities to be evaluated, and the uses and politics of evaluation. Brief selected bibliography.

529. Luey, Beth. *Handbook for Academic Authors*. Rev. ed. Cambridge, England: Cambridge Univ. Pr., 1990.
A highly useful source for the neophyte, and a good refresher for the more experienced writer. Users will find chapters on such topics as revising the dissertation for publication, writing journal articles, finding publishers for scholarly books, guidance in manuscript preparation, as well as information on dealing with publishers. Includes a bibliography and an index.

530. Miller, Richard I. *Developing Programs for Faculty Evaluation: A Sourcebook for Higher Education*. (The Jossey-Bass series in Higher Education) San Francisco: Jossey-Bass, 1974. 248p. ISBN 0-87589-203-6.
A sourcebook for the development and maintenance of faculty evaluation systems. It covers evaluative criteria, evaluation of faculty and administrators, and use of student evaluations. The second half of the book provides an annotated bibliography of some 350 articles and monographs, includes sample evaluation questionnaires and rating scales. The program developed at Texas Christian University is discussed. Includes author and subject indexes.

531. Miller, Richard I. *Evaluating Faculty for Promotion and Tenure*. (Jossey-Bass Higher Education Series) San Francisco: Jossey-Bass, 1987. 257p. ISBN 1-55542-069-9.
Written for adaptation to a variety of academic settings, this work deals first with evaluation procedures, which the author believes to be crucial to good promotion and tenure systems. A second section covers the various aspects of promotion and tenure systems, including purposes, advantages and disadvantages, decision-making procedures, legal questions, and the roles of the various administrators involved. Appendices include sample rating forms updated from the author's earlier Evaluating Faculty Performance, a listing of selected student rating instruments, and a twenty-seven-page annotated bibliography. Twenty-five pages of references and an index conclude the work.

532. Miller, Richard I. *Evaluating Faculty Performance*. (Jossey-Bass Series in Higher Education) San Francisco: Jossey-Bass, 1972. 145p. ISBN 0-87589-123-3.
An approach to evaluation of faculty is presented in four chapters. The first focuses on defining basic assumptions and procedures, and the second is devoted entirely to a consideration of classroom teaching. Other performance areas, such as research, publication, student advising, professional and administrative activities, are dealt with in chapter three. The process of arriving at an overall performance rating is the subject of the final chapter. Sample appraisal forms for each evaluation area are included, plus a forty-three-page annotated bibliography and a brief index.

533. Seldin, Peter. *Successful Faculty Evaluation Programs: A Practical Guide to Improve Faculty Performance and Promotion-Tenure Decisions*. Crugers, N.Y.: Coventry Pr., 1980. 182p.
Provides insight into the subject of a faculty evaluation in order to improve faculty performance. The book encompasses guidelines, forms, and strategies which have been field-tested and adjusted for workability as a practical resource in developing and upgrading programs for instructor evaluation. Includes a thirty-page bibliography, and an appendix containing five forms for evaluation. Lacks an index.

Financial Assistance

534. *Barron's Complete College Financing Guide.* New York: Barron's, 1992. 256p. ISBN 0-8120-4950-0.
Formerly titled Dollars for Scholars: Barron's Complete College Financing Guide. The first of this work's three sections describes the financial aid application process and how aid is determined and discusses financial planning options, alternative funding sources, tax considerations, loans and debt. Section 2 lists financial aid programs grouped by source (federal, state, school-sponsored, military, etc.) and by particular recipient groups (minorities, women, graduate students, international students, etc.). The final section includes a listing of federal and state assistance program offices and higher education associations. There is also a list of U.S. two and four-year schools giving their tuition and other charges and financial aid office telephone number. An index of organizations and aid programs is provided.

535. Bear, John. *Bear's Guide to Finding Money for College.* Berkeley, Calif.: Ten Speed Press, 1984. 157p. ISBN 0-89815-126-0.
Groups the various approaches to paying for college in major sections on getting money and saving money. Individual chapters examine such sources and strategies as foundations, the military, corporations, loans, employment, federal and state government programs, non-traditional colleges and advanced placement programs. In addition to advice and discussion, many chapters include brief directory-style listings of specific programs and organizations. The author also provides a checklist, flow-chart and selected bibliography.

536. Betterton, Don M. *How the Military Will Help You Pay for College.* 2d ed. Princeton, N.J.: Peterson's Guides, 1990. 181p. ISBN 0-87866-996-5.
A guide to military sources of student financial aid, including scholarships for college bound high school graduates, appointments to the service academics and support for those who enter the armed forces out of high school. The work also examines and compares ROTC programs.

537. *Federal Student Financial Aid Handbook.* Washington, D.C.: U.S. Dept. of Education, Office of Student Financial Assistance, 1982- . Annual. ISSN 0730-8922.
Intended primarily for college financial aid officers, this work is a guide to the rules and regulations governing all the major federal student aid programs, including National Direct Student Loans, Guaranteed Student Loans, State Student Incentive Grants, Pell Grants, Supplemental Education Opportunity Grants and College Work Study.

538. Fenske, Robert H., Huff, Robert P. and others. *Handbook of Student Financial Aid: Programs, Procedures and Policies.* (Jossey-Bass Higher Education Series) San Francisco: Jossey-Bass, 1983. 508p. ISBN 0-87589-571-9.
The eighteen chapters of this work, written by the authors and seventeen other contributors, address various aspects of the topic in four main sections: Development, Scope and Purposes of Student Aid; Delivering Aid to Students on Campus; Ensuring Effectiveness in Administering Aid Programs; and Importance of Aid in Meeting Student Needs and Institutional Goals. Individual chapters cover such topics as historical background, determining financial need, managing aid funds, organizing the financial aid office, and legal considerations. In addition to an index, there are also an annotated selective guide to the literature and a twenty-page bibliography.

539. Krefetz, Gerald. *How to Pay for your Children's College Education.*
New York: College Entrance Examination Board, 1988. 158p. ISBN
0-87447-248-2.
Explores and explains the various financial strategies available to
families anticipating the need to meet college costs. Saving, gifts,
trusts and borrowing are considered, as well as the importance of planning and the impact of tax laws. The variety of approaches that may be
appropriate is illustrated in a series of six case studies. Includes a
glossary and index.

540. Lawliss, Chuck and McCarty, Barry. *How to Pay for your Child's
College Education.* (Real Life, Real Answers Series) Boston:
Houghton Mifflin, 1990. 87p. ISBN 0-395-51107-0.
Covers many of the same topics as Krefetz (see above) but with greater
emphasis on obtaining and maximizing various forms of financial aid,
pursuing scholarships and taking advantage of programs that may reduce
costs, such as advanced placement, external degree and cooperative
education.

541. Leider, Robert and Leider, Anna. *Don't Miss Out: The Ambitious
Student's Guide to Financial Aid.* 16th ed. Alexandria, Va.: Octameron Associates, 1991. 119p. ISBN 0-945981-48-1.
Lists sources of college financial aid and scholarships. Arranged by
type of sponsor, the entries include sponsor name and address, description of the aid program, and eligibility requirements.

542. Leider, Robert and Leider, Anna. *Lovejoy's Guide to Financial Aid.*
3d ed. New York: Simon and Schuster, 1989. 263p. ISBN 0-671-
68814-6.
Aims to help users assemble a plan of action to finance a college education. The work advises on issues such as setting up a trust, determining
needs, borrowing, and investing in rental property. In each instance a
concise question or heading is used to introduce the explanations. Examples are given to illustrate the pros and cons of certain courses of
action. A list of major academic scholarships, arranged by state and
college, is included. This is essentially a workbook to help parents or
students arrive at a clear picture of their financial situation. Appendices provided actual forms used to determine parents' or independent
students' contribution to financial aid. A usable and helpful source.

543. Margolin, Judith B. *Financing a College Education: The Essential
Guide for the 90s.* New York: Plenum Press, 1989. 307p. ISBN 0-
306-40371-1.
Intended particularly for a middle income audience, this work offers information and guidance for coping with college education costs. Its
eight chapters deal with such topics as private and government sources
of aid, personal investment and savings strategies, loans, student employment and cooperative education, "bargain" institutions, and creative
financing plans. An index and five page bibliography are included.

Higher Education and Government

544. *Catalog of Federal Domestic Assistance.* Washington, D.C.: United
States General Services Administration, 1965-   . Annual.
A government-wide compendium of more than one thousand federal financial
and non-financial assistance programs, projects, services, and activities. There are fifteen assistance categories including formula and
project grants, direct payment for specified and unrestricted uses, spe-

cialized or advisory services, training, etc. Entries are classified and include such information as program objectives, eligibility, application process, etc. A number of indexes cover agencies, specific programs, applicant eligibility, and deadlines (according to program classification code, functions, and subjects). Under "higher education" are listed more than sixty programs, and nearly twenty related subject categories. Appendices cover review and authorization requirements, financial information, agency addresses, additional information, etc. A well designed, valuable source to federal assistance across agency lines.

545. Halstead, D. Kent. *Statewide Planning in Higher Education.* Washington, D.C.: U.S. Dept. of Health, Education and Welfare, Office of Education, 1974. 812p.
A comprehensive work that examines the important components, issues, problems and solutions in all major areas of planners' concern. The fourteen chapters deal with such topics as statewide organization, staffing, financial aid, assessment and projection of needs, facilities planning, and budgeting. Numerous tables, diagrams, charts and graphs provide both examples and real-world data to accompany the text. Each chapter concludes with a lengthily annotated bibliography. Appendices offer data on finances by institution type and on student migration by state, as well as information on price indexes. A short index and detailed table of contents are provided. A significant work in need of updating.

546. McGuinness, Aims C. *State Postsecondary Education Structures Handbook: 1988.* Denver, Colo.: Education Commission of the States, 1987. 179p.
Comparative tables, plus individual profiles of each jurisdiction, describe the organization, authority, responsibilities and membership of the governing and coordinating bodies of the states and the District of Columbia. The work is introduced by an essay surveying the current status, trends and issues in state-level governance.

547. Scurlock, Gargan. *Government Contracts and Grants for Research: Guide for Colleges and Universities.* Washington, D.C.: Nat. Assn. of Coll. and Univ. Business Officers, 1975. 415p.
Although the author notes in his introduction implications concerning the relationship between government and academia, and attempts to provide "the background required to understand the nature of the relationship created and the consequences [emphasis added] for the institution," there is no reference to questions of academic freedom or intellectual probity in the material presented. The user might be encouraged to consider these questions by the presence of the brief section on military security requirements. Part 1 deals with grant-contract analysis, while Part 2 covers contract-clause analysis. Part 3 provides supplementary reference materials. A thirty-five-page revision is appended updating the guide with changes in various regulations. Includes a glossary and subject index.

Institutional Advancement

548. *Management Reporting Standards for Educational Institutions: Fund Raising and Related Activities.* Washington, D.C.: Council for Advancement and Support of Education and the Nat. Assn. of Coll. and Univ. Business Officers, 1982. 18p.
A brief but useful source of definitions and instructions. This work is designed for higher education and independent secondary school develop-

ment officers and business officers who compile, report, and compare results of fund-raising activities in the standard formats required by
NACUBO and the American Institute of Certified Public Accountants. Information is organized in the order needed to complete these standard
forms. Blank forms are used to illustrate the text. Does not include an
index.

549. Pray, Francis C. *A Handbook for Educational Fund Raising: A Guide
      to Successful Principles and Practices for Colleges, Universities
      and Schools.* (The Jossey-Bass Series in Higher Education) San
      Francisco: Jossey-Bass, 1981. 442p. ISBN 0-87589-501-8.
Provides "how to" information on fund raising, covering as well the
broader issues of educational fund raising. Various marketing aspects,
from donor programs to institutional uniqueness, are covered. The text
is followed by four groups of resources, offering sample maxims, audit
reports, case statements, and a selected readings list. General bibliography and general index provided.

550. Rowland, A. Westley. *Handbook of Institutional Advancement.* 2d
      ed. San Francisco: Jossey-Bass, 1986. 796p. ISBN 0-87589-689-8.
A basic reference work for the beginner as well as the seasoned professional. This book "is designed as a practical, functional resource, for
the wide variety of professionals who write and edit news releases, design and prepare publications, edit periodicals, raise funds, work with
alumni, coordinate relationships with government, recruit students, work
with community groups, write and give speeches, arrange special events,
take photographs, do research, or manage the advancement function." This
is a collaborative effort, with contributions from experts in all major
areas of institutional advancement. It is loaded with practical advice
from paring prices with printers, and cutting mailing and postage costs,
to planning meaningful reunions. Includes indexes to names and subjects.

551. Strand, Bobbie J. and Hunt, Susan. *Prospect Research: A How-to
      Guide.* Washington, D.C.: Council for Advancement and Support of
      Education, 1986. 150p. ISBN 0-89964-244-6.
A guide for fund raisers investigating the backgrounds of possible donors
to their institutions. The volume covers many techniques and sources of
information for such research. Many figures and tables enhance the usefulness of the book.

552. Willmer, Wesley Kenneth. *Friends, Funds, and Freshmen for Chris-
      tian Colleges: A Manager's Guide to Advancing Resource Develop-
      ment.* Washington, D.C.: Christian College Coalition, 1987. 91p.
A summary of data collected from Coalition members sharing their experience in the successful development of external funding sources. Six
chapters cover the methods of the survey, executive management, fund
raising, alumni affairs, recruitment and admissions, and public relations. A table of contents, list of tables, and four appendices are
included.

Law

553. Alexander, Kern and Solomon, Erwin S. *College and University Law.*
      Charlottesville, Va.: 1972. 776p.
A handbook for students and administrators, discussing the law governing
colleges and universities. Twelve chapters focus on legal precedents of
"cases forming the parameters of the law of higher education." They
cover such topics as the legal structure of higher education, religion,

taxes, private support, fees and tuition, faculty, constitutional rights
of students, racial issues, tort liability, and government and charitable
immunity. A pocket supplement (Michie Co., 1976) extends coverage of
most chapters of the original text. Access is by means of the topical
table of contents, table of cases, and a subject index.

554. *Am I Liable?: Faculty, Staff and Institutional Liability in the
      College and University Setting.* Washington, D.C.: Nat. Assn. of
      Coll. and Univ. Attorneys, 1989. 101p.
How should I handle a request for a letter of reference? Am I liable for
my academic counseling? These and a number of other questions are discussed in a clear, concise style. An introductory chapter provides an
overview of tort law concepts. Six following chapters discuss issues
involving criminal intruders on campus, student groups and alcohol, academic advising, workers compensation, liability releases, and an overview of risk management and insurance procurement. This work is useful
to administrators, faculty and students. Footnotes provide case law
citations. Includes a table of contents and a brief list of suggested
readings. Lacks an index.

555. Chambers, Merritt Madison. *College and the Courts, 1962-1966.*
      Danville, Ill.: Interstate Printers and Publishers, Inc., 1967.
      326p.
Continuing work begun in 1936, this source examines about three hundred
decisions of state and federal courts affecting higher education in the
United States. The 1936 title covers the century and a quarter following
the Dartmouth College decision of 1819. The next two editions cover the
periods 1936 to 1940 and 1941-1945 respectively. All three were published by the Carnegie Foundation for the Advancement of Teaching. A
fourth volume, covering 1946-1950 was published in 1952 by the Columbia
University Press. A fifth work, covering about four hundred decisions
since 1950, was published in 1964 by Interstate Printers and Publishers.
A supplement was published in 1976 by Illinois State University. The
works consist of summary discussions grouped by general subject covering
faculty, staff and students, government and charity, and private sources
of support. Later editions conclude with a selective bibliography, table
of cases, and an index. Access is also facilitated by a detailed table
of contents.

556. Cole, Elsa Kircher. *Sexual Harassment on Campus: A Legal Com-
      pendium.* 2d ed. Washington, D.C.: Nat. Assn. of Coll. and Univ.
      Attorneys, 1990. 265p.
A compilation of articles, policy guidelines, and sample sexual harassment policy statements assembled by the noted General Counsel of the
University of Michigan. The work is divided into five chapters: Chapter
1 includes four essays including a general report entitled "Recent Developments in Sexual Harassment" (Cole) and a more narrowly focused paper
entitled "Consensual Amorous Relationships Between Faculty and Students"
(Elisabeth Keller). Included are sample policy statements of several
major universities, the American Council on Education, and the American
Association of University Professors. Among papers in Chapter 4 is one
providing guidelines for handling the investigation of sexual harassment
claims. According to the editor, this work serves as a companion to the
first edition (1988). The final chapter is comprised of a brief list of
additional resources. A cumulative list of cited cases and statutes
would have been helpful. Access to this highly important work is by
means of the table of contents. Lacks an index.

557. Edwards, Harry T. and Nordin, Virginia Davis. *Higher Education and*

the Law. Cambridge, Mass: Institute for Educational Management, Harvard Univ., 1979. 844p. ISBN 0-934222-00-2.
Uses some six hundred law cases to clarify various legal issues in four major sections: college as a legal entity, faculty rights, student rights, and federal regulation of higher education. This is a handy source for the study of law cases in higher education. Subject index included.

558. Hollander, Patricia A. *Legal Handbook for Educators.* Boulder, Colo.: Westview Pr., 1978. 287p. ISBN 0-89158-420-X.
Begins by surveying currently significant legal issues and concepts in their historical contexts, then focuses on areas such as personal liability, admissions, students, hiring and collective bargaining. Each chapter examines relevant statutes, cases and regulations and recommends ways to avoid legal difficulties. Summaries of twenty-four key federal statutes and statements of administrator and faculty professional standards appear in appendices. Access is through the detailed table of contents and an index of cases.

559. Hollander, Patricia A., Young, D. Parker and Gehring, Donald D. *A Practical Guide to Legal Issues Affecting College Teachers.* (Higher Education Administration Series) Asheville, N.C.: College Administration Publications, 1985. 41p. ISBN 0-912557-02-8.
This concise survey for the nonspecialist covers the faculty member's legal relationship to students and the institution, academic matters, student rights and responsibilities, employment, liability situations and minimizing risks. No specific cases are cited, but a concluding section provides brief summaries of relevant Federal laws.

560. Hustoles, Thomas P. and Connolly, Walter B. *Regulating Racial Harassment on Campus: A Legal Compendium.* Nat. Assn. of Coll. and Univ. Attorneys, 1990. 328p.
The authors aim to provide tools or guidelines for college and university councils and administrators to use when considering "approaches their institutions will take in balancing First Amendment and academic freedom values against racial incidents and the harm they cause." The work is in three sections: the first treats the University of Michigan policy development as a case study. Section 2 includes sample policies adopted or proposed by colleges and universities. Section 3 offers several articles and papers, followed by outlines on drafting policies. A final section includes a selected bibliography on the First Amendment and campus racial harassment, a brief list of article citations, and a table of cases. Includes a table of contents, but lacks an index.

561. Kaplin, William A. *The Law of Higher Education: A Comprehensive Guide to Legal Implications of Administrative Decision Making.* 2d ed. (Jossey-Bass Higher Education Series) San Francisco: Jossey-Bass, 1985. 621p. ISBN 0-87589-619-7.
The author, a recognized authority and practitioner in higher education law, writes for administrators and legal counsel as well as for students and researchers in the field. He provides first an overview, then detailed examinations of the legal principles and issues involved in institutions' relationships with administrators, faculty, students, local, state and federal governments, and accrediting agencies. Footnotes and selected annotated bibliographies in each chapter provide access to further material. Subject and case indexes included.

562. Kaplin, William A. and Lee, Barbara A. *1988 Update to W. A. Kaplin, The Law of Higher Education: A Comprehensive Guide to Legal*

Implications of Administrative Decision Making (2d ed., Jossey-Bass Inc., 1985). Distributed by the authors under sponsorship of Jossey-Bass, 1988. 60p.
Covers new developments and cites additional resources. Its organization is the same as the 1985 edition cited above, and its contents are keyed to that edition's corresponding sections.

563. Kaplin, William A. and Lee, Barbara A. *The Law of Higher Education, 1985-1990 Update.* Washington, D.C.: Nat. Assn. of Coll. and Univ. Attorneys, 1990. 364p.
A practical guide and ready reference for administrators, counsels, and others interested in higher education and the law. This source covers all levels and types of institutions, providing discussions of court opinions, statutes, and regulations, as well as citing selected law journal articles, books, and other sources. Chapter 1 provides an overview; three following chapters examine the relationship between the college and its staff, faculty and students. The remaining four chapters examine the college in relation to the community, state and federal government, and accrediting agencies. Chapters and sections are identical for purposes of cross referencing an earlier edition of the work of the same title (Jossey-Bass, 1985). An earlier version is also available (Jossey-Bass, 1978). Access to the update is by means of a detailed table of contents and separate tables of cases and statutes.

564. Metzger, Walter P. *The Constitutional Status of Academic Freedom.* New York: Arno Pr., 1977. 358p. ISBN 0-405-10038-8.
Includes reprints of articles and court decisions published from 1923 through 1972. Covered are eighteen court decisions along with reprints of six essays. Among the essays included are William P. Murphy's "Academic Freedom-An Emerging Constitutional Right," and William Van Alstyne's "The Specific Theory of Academic Freedom and the General Issue of Civil Liberty." Cases reported are listed in the table of contents.

565. Metzger, Walter P. *The Constitutional Status of Academic Tenure.* New York: Arno Pr., 1977. 231p. ISBN 0-405-09982-7.
Included are reports of seven court decisions, spanning the years 1887 to 1973, and reprints of five essays. Among essays covered are William Van Alstyne's "The Supreme Court Speaks to the Untenured" and Clark Byse's "Academic Freedom, Tenure, and the Law." Cases included are listed in the table of contents.

566. Miles, Albert S. *College Law.* Tuscaloosa, Ala.: Sevgo Pr., 1987. 121p. ISBN 0-943487-01-3.
A survey of the structure and basic concepts of the law and their application to higher education issues and situations. Because its organization is mainly by broad legal topics -- case law, the constitution, torts, contracts, agency, etc. -- and there is no subject index or glossary, this work is at best difficult for the untrained. An index of cases cited and a bibliography are provided.

567. Student Press Law Center. *Law of the Student Press.* Washington, D.C.: Student Law Center, 1985. 101p.
A concise survey of the legal environment of high school and college publications and media. Cases peculiar to student press issues are cited and analyzed, and their application to particular situations and relevant cases are also noted. Suggested procedures are discussed. Nine chapters cover such topics as freedom of expression, First Amendment protections, varieties of unprotected speech, prior review and publications guidelines, and the role of the adviser. Despite the copyright date, a

lengthy addendum on the impact of the 1988 Hazelwood decision is included. Two appendices provide respectively model guidelines for student
publications and the code of ethics of the Society of Professional Jour-
nalists. Case and statute citations are provided, but no further bibliography or index.

568. Van Tol, Jean E. *College and University Student Records: A Legal
Compendium.* Washington, D.C.: Nat. Assn. of Coll. and Univ.
Attorneys, 1989. 257p.
Focuses on the legal issues related to the acceptance, maintenance, retention, and release of academic records. The work is designed for use
of registrars and their campus legal advisors. Three sections cover
Fraudulent Academic Credentials, with reports on diploma mills and fals-
ification of applications; Academic Records, with sample forms and policies; and Resources, including a selected bibliography. Found here are
several law journal articles, some NACUA outlines, sample policies, and
selected state and federal laws. Includes a table of contents, but lacks
an index.

569. Weeks, Kent M. *Legal Deskbook for Administrators of Independent
Colleges and Universities 1987.* Macon, Ga.: Center for Constitutional Studies, Mercer Univ., 1987. 422p. ISBN 0-86554-180-9.
This work is the third supplement to the original edition (Univ. of Notre
Dame Pr., 1981) and updates and reprints all of that edition's text, except the appendices. It is divided into ten chapters covering broad
areas such as governance, employment, liability and taxation. Each chapter has its own detailed table of contents. Chapter subsections include,
in addition to concise analysis and discussion of each topic, comments
on state law and very useful lists of court decisions, bibliographic
references and model documents. No index.

570. Yudof, Mark G. *Legal Deskbook for Administrators of Independent
Colleges and Universities.* rev. ed. Macon, Ga.: Center for Constitutional Studies, Mercer Univ., 1988-   . Loose-leaf. ISBN
0-86554-180-9.
Examines legal issues affecting church-related and other independent
colleges and universities. With current updates, this source is intended
for campus administrators and legal counsels. Based on review of the
1982 edition (South Bend, Ind.: Notre Dame Univ.), this source is divided
into subject chapters with focus on such topics as employment practices,
students, taxation, liability, and physical facilities, and includes discussion of laws and planning procedures to facilitate compliance. Includes bibliographies and an index.

Minority Groups and Women

571. Bianchi, Anne. *Smart Choices: A Woman's Guide to Returning to
School.* Princeton, N.J.: Peterson's Guides, 1990. 174p. ISBN 0-
87866-989-2.
The author draws on the expertise of professionals in counseling and
adult education and on the experience of women who have themselves re-
turned to college as adults. The advice offered covers such topics as
choosing a program of study, getting financial aid, getting credit for
life experience, and coping with the impact returning to school has on
one's family.

572. Franklin, Phyllis and others. *Sexual and Gender Harassment in the
Academy: A Guide for Faculty, Students, and Administrators.* New

York: Modern Language Assn., 1981. 74p. ISBN 0-87352-333-4.
Brief chapters define terminology, survey legal background and Equal
Employment Opportunity Commision guidelines, and suggest individual and
institutional responses to harassment. A brief annotated bibliography,
a list of additional references and a list of organizations concerned
with the issue are also included. Codes of conduct and grievance
procedures from seven universities appear in an appendix. No indexes.

573. Green, Madeline F. *Minorities on Campus: A Handbook for Enhancing
      Diversity*. Washington, D.C.: American Council on Education, 1989.
      181p.
Those seeking not merely diversity but true pluralism on campus will find
here clearly organized information and practical advice. Chapters deal
with conducting an institutional audit, undergraduate and graduate
students, faculty, administrators, campus climate and the curriculum.
Each begins with a survey of current national trends, then offers strategies and suggestions for the individual campus and a listing of pertinent organizations and ongoing programs with addresses and contact
persons. Some chapters provide bibliographic references as well. A
final chapter describes the efforts and accomplishments of three
different institutions. Illustrated with tables, graphs and forms; no
index.

574. Schmitz, Betty. *Integrating Women's Studies into the Curriculum:
      A Guide and Bibliography*. Old Westbury, N.Y.: Feminist Pr., 1985.
      ISBN 0-935312-36-6. 192p.
A very useful guide to integrating women's studies into the liberal arts
curriculum, and securing local (internal) resources without sizeable external grants. The work is divided into three parts: Part 1 describes
implementing a project, and dealing with such matters as institutional
climate and resistance to change; Part 2 describes ten projects, along
with information on their goals, plans for action, and impact; and Part
3 provides an annotated bibliography of 178 items, including general
works, sources dealing with assessment methods and instruments, published essays and syllabi for courses developed to integrate women's
studies into the curriculum, recommended periodicals, and bibliographies.
Includes both author and subject indexes and a detailed table of contents.

      Personnel

575. Fortunato, Ray T. *A Handbook for Developing Higher Education Per-
      sonnel Policies*. Washington, D.C.: Coll. and Univ. Personnel
      Assn., 1988. 399p. ISBN 0-910402-79-5.
This highly practical work presents guidelines for developing policies
for forty-eight different personnel matters, ranging from the perennial
(Academic Freedom, Access to and Maintenance of Personnel Files, Educational Benefits for Dependents, Performance Evaluation) to the more
recent (AIDS, Child Care Leave, Sexual Harassment). After a brief introductory section, each guideline lists the important policy points that
should be considered for inclusion and provides examples of policy
language for each point. Sources of specific examples are not
identified, but a list of all contributing institutions appears in the
introduction. No bibliography or indexes; access is through the table
of contents.

576. Fortunato, Ray T. and Waddell, D. Geneva. *Personnel Administration
      in Higher Education: Handbook of Faculty and Staff Personnel*

Practices. (Jossey-Bass Series in Higher Education) San Francisco: Jossey-Bass, 1981. 384p. ISBN 0-87589- 506-9.
Written as a practical guide for academic personnel administrators, this work supplements straightforward advice and discussion with numerous checklists, charts, tables, scales, questionnaires and samples of policies, forms and documents. Chapters are grouped around three major areas: positions, people, and processes. An index and detailed table of contents are provided, as well as an eight-page bibliography.

577. Higgins, John M. and Hollander, Patricia A. *A Guide to Successful Searches for College Personnel: Policies, Procedures and Legal Issues.* (The Higher Education Administration Series) Asheville, N.C.: College Administration Publications, 1987. 89p. ISBN 0-912557-07-9.
A clear, concise and sensible treatment of every step of the search process, from organizing the search committee to advertising the position, conducting interviews and offering the position. Special attention is paid throughout to legal concerns. Charts, checklists, forms and sample documents supplement the text. Detailed table of contents; no index or bibliography.

578. Kauffman, Joseph F. *The Selection of College and University Presidents.* Washington, D.C.: Assn. of American Colleges, 1974. 82p.
The author, a professor of educational administration and former college president, writes primarily for those involved in selecting chief executives of four-year single-campus institutions. He presents not a detailed prescription, but rather a series of discussions of the important elements in the process that are to be considered in creating and implementing selection policies. An appendix provides descriptions of the approaches taken at five different institutions. A brief bibliography is included. No indexes.

579. Marchese, Theodore J. *The Search Committee Handbook: A Guide to Recruiting Administrators.* Washington, D.C.: American Assn. for Higher Education, 1987. 56p.
Concerned with administrator searches below the level of president. This work provides campus officers, as well as search committees, with practical information and guidance drawn from the literature on executive searching and from surveys, interviews, campus visits and correspondence. The seven chapters cover the entire search process from the occurrence of the vacancy through making the new appointment. Brief list of further readings.

580. Minter, W. John. *A Manual for Manpower Accounting in Higher Education.* Preliminary Edition. Washington, D.C.: Nat. Center for Educational Statistics, 1972. 122p.
Primarily a listing and definition of the Occupational Activity and Program Function categories to be used in the National Center for Higher Education Management Systems (NCHEMS). The NCHEMS system itself, which is used in Higher Education General Information Surveys (HEGIS), is also briefly described, as well as its relationship to other organizations' (NCES, CUPA, AAUP, etc.) survey categories and classification systems. Appendices contain a glossary, sample classifications and reports. Index included.

581. Munitz, Barry. *Leadership in Colleges and Universities: Assessment and Search.* Oak Brook, Ill.: Johnson Associates, 1977. 53p.
A practical guide to evaluating presidents and the relationships between

them and their governing boards. Illustrated with charts, checklists and sample documents; no bibliography or index.

582. Nason, John W. *Presidential Search: A Guide to the Process of Selecting and Appointing College and University Presidents.* Washington, D.C.: Assn. of Governing Boards of Universities and Colleges, 1980. 91p.

A clearly organized step-by-step guide which draws on survey responses from 326 institutions that had recently appointed new presidents, plus in-depth study and interviews at twenty-two selected institutions. The author breaks the selection process down into nine major steps, devoting a separate chapter to each. Numerous checklists, charts, timetables and sample letters enhance the clarity and usefulness of the presentation. Relevant sources of additional information are listed in the introduction and in most of the individual chapters.

Students

583. Baird, William Raimond. *Baird's Manual of American College Fraternities.* 20th ed. Jack L. Anson and Robert F. Marchesani, eds. Indianapolis, Ind.: Baird's Manual Foundation, 1991. Approx. 900p.

This standard authoritative guide, first published in 1879, includes men's and women's social and professional fraternities, honor societies and recognition societies. The detailed entries are grouped by type and include each society's history, government, traditions and insignia, publications, funds and philanthropies, headquarters address, membership figures and list of chapters with locations and founding dates. A separate section covers defunct fraternities, and there is also a listing of fraternity chapters by college. An introductory section describes the nature, origins, evolution and types of fraternities, inter-greek relationships and the national inter-greek organizations. A fraternity index and brief subject index are provided. (Based on examination of the 19th ed.).

584. Barnes, Gregory A. *The American University: A World Guide.* Philadelphia: ISI Pr., 1984. ISBN 0-89495-030-4.

Designed to aid the foreign student in understanding the "what" and "how" of the American university. This volume deals with such practical problems as credits, multiple-choice examinations, the structure of the faculty and administration, and other matters which might confuse newcomers. Problems of academic standards, grade inflation, learning styles, are all addressed. A glossary provides definitions of such phrases as "publish or perish," "work-study," and "extracurricular activities." One appendix offers useful addresses (e.g., the Immigration and Naturalization Service); another has a few sample forms. Bibliography and index included.

585. Barr, Margaret J. and Associates. *Student Services and the Law: A Handbook for Practitioners.* (The Jossey-Bass Higher Education Series) San Francisco: Jossey-Bass, 1988. 409p. ISBN 1-55542-079-6.

The author, together with fifteen administrators and attorneys, provides a broad overview of the legal issues in student affairs practice. Part 1 explores the legal foundation, and Part 2 legal responsibility and liability. Subjects include constitutional law, contract law, civil rights and discipline, etc. Part 3 addresses applications to student service activities such as residence life, counseling, and student press. Includes a list of case cited, case index and subject index.

586. Budzinski, Karrie and Guarnieri, Paul. *Guidebook for Non-*
      traditional Student Governments. Rev. ed. Needham, Mass.: U.S.
      Assn. of Evening Students, [c1985]. 48p.
Intended to provide concise general guidelines for part-time, evening and
adult student associations. Chapter topics include purpose, structure,
finances, communications, and activities. A model constitution and by-
laws are provided, as well as organization charts, a brief glossary, and
list of suggested readings. No index.

587. Cahn, Victor L. *A Thinking Student's Guide to Colleges*. Norwell,
      Mass.: Christopher Pub. House, 1988. 122p. ISBN 0-81580-445-8.
Useful in helping freshmen as well as prospective students and their
parents prepare for campus life. Topical chapters take students from
their acceptance letters to exploring college extracurricular activities.
Chapter titles include: You're Accepted, Why are you Going?, Ready to Go,
An Overview of the Curriculum, The Faculty, Creating a Program, Carrying
Out Your Program, Working with the Faculty, Beyond the Classroom, and A
Final Word.

588. *College Entrance Guide for American Students Overseas*. New York:
      College Entrance Examination Board, 1987. 82p.
Addresses the needs of overseas Americans seeking to attend U.S. institutions. The work includes descriptions of the types of colleges and campus life as well as advice on choosing a college. There is also
information on the admission and financial aid application processes, admission tests, and establishing state residency. A list of state agencies and a glossary are also included.

589. Council for the Advancement of Standards and Guidelines for Student
      Services/Development Programs. *CAS Standards and Guidelines for*
      Student Services/Development Programs. Iowa City, Iowa: The Coun-
      cil, 1988. 558p.
In loose-leaf binder format are guides for seventeen self-assessment
areas. These range from academic advisement and career programs to college unions and housing and residential life programs. Each area section
introduces the CAS Standards and Guidelines, provides a thirteen-part
worksheet for self-assessment, and states CAS Standards and Guidelines
for the particular area. By following the area guides, "an institution
can gain an informed perspective on its strengths and deficiencies and
then plan for program improvement." Does not include either a contents
listing or index.

590. Delworth, Ursula. *Student Services: A Handbook for the Profession*.
      2d ed. (The Jossey-Bass Higher Education Series) San Francisco:
      Jossey-Bass, 1989. 647p. ISBN 1-55542-148-2.
A comprehensive guide to the history, ethics, legal issues, theory, models of practice, competencies, and administrative techniques and strategies of student services. The work is designed for the professional.
Chapters cover everything from explicit delineation of professional role
models and new ways to organize and manage programs and services, to outcomes assessment. Some chapters include rather lengthy lists of
references. A detailed table of contents, including contributing
authors, a name index and a subject index, are included.

591. El-Khawas, Elaine. *Management of Student Aid: A Guide for Presi-*
      dents. Washington, D.C.: American Council on Education, 1979. 27p.
      ISBN 0-8268-1329-1.
This companion volume to the National Association of College and University Business Officers detailed <u>Management of Student Aid</u> (1979) provides

top administrators and board members with a concise review of the role and significance of financial aid and the president's responsibilities in administering it. It also makes general recommendations for planning and implementing an aid policy and assessing its effectiveness. Text is supplemented with checklists, sidebars, charts and graphs. No bibliography or index.

592. Farrar, Ronald T. *Peterson's College 101: Making the Most of Your Freshman Year.* Rev. ed. Princeton, N.J.: Peterson's Guides, 1989. 185p. ISBN 0-87866-730-X.
Covers academic, social, financial and other aspects of adapting to campus life, including such timely topics as AIDS, substance abuse, eating disorders, living arrangements, academic honesty and minority concerns.

593. Figler, Stephen and Figler, Howard. *Going the Distance: The College Athlete's Guide to Excellence on the Field and in the Classroom.* Princeton, N.J.: Peterson's Guides, 1990. 220p. ISBN 0-87866-952-3.
Written and illustrated to appeal to student-athletes, this work offers advice and guidance on deriving maximum benefit from all aspects of their college experience. It covers topics such as meeting the demands of both athletic and academic performance, avoiding substance abuse, evaluating potential for a professional sports career, and relating sports skills to other employment areas. Black and female athletes' concerns are given particular attention.

594. Fireside, Bryna J. *Choices: A Student Survival Guide for the 1990s.* Garrett Park, Md.: Garrett Park Pr., 1989. 112p. ISBN 0-912048-66-2.
Drawing on the experiences of the numerous young people the author interviewed, this work examines various options for students nearing the completion of high school. College attendance and early college admission are considered, as well as the possibility of delaying college or "stopping out" at some point and ways to use the time gained thereby: employment, career exploration, internships and the military. Many organizations and publications are cited in the text as sources of further information. An appendix lists college guides and directories. Not indexed.

595. Fischgrund, Tom, ed. *Insider's Guide to the Top 25 Colleges.* Atlanta: Platinum Press; Marietta, Ga.: dist. by Longstreet Press, 1989. 618p. ISBN 0-929264-64-9.
The institutions included here were selected on the basis of their percentages of applicants accepted out of acceptees who enroll, SAT scores and a U.S. News & World Report survey ranking by college presidents. While this guide does offer advice on selecting, applying for admission to, financing, and succeeding at a "top 25" college , it is mainly concerned with relating "what it is really like" to attend each of these institutions. It draws heavily on the experiences and comments of recent graduates, often in lengthy direct quotations. The approximately twenty pages on each school address its philosophy and distinctive characteristics, selectivity, composition of student body, financial aid, academic environment and programs, social life, extracurricular activities, and its graduates' prospects. Of use and interest to anyone seeking the "feel" of one of these elite institutions.

596. Fiske, Edward B. and Steinbrecher, Phyllis. *Get Organized! Fiske's Unbeatable System for Applying to College.* Princeton, N.J.: Peterson's Guides, 1989. 84p. ISBN 0-87866-995-7.

Offers step-by-step advice and guidance to those seeking college admission. The work includes a checklist and timetable for the application and selection process, and explanations of the terminology used by admissions officers.

597. Hayden, Thomas C. *Peterson's Handbook for College Admissions: A Family Guide.* 3d ed. Princeton, N.J.: Peterson's Guides, 1989. 218p. ISBN 0-87866-799-7.
Derives advice and guidance for those applying to college from an examination of how schools typically review and evaluate applications for admission.

598. Kaye, Evelyn and Gardner, Janet. *College Bound: The Student's Handbook for Getting Ready, Moving In, and Succeeding on Campus.* New York: College Entrance Examination Board, 1988. 159p. ISBN 0-87447-304-7.
Written to provide practical advice for making the transition to college life, this work is addressed to the "traditional" college student just out of high school. It covers preparations, money, getting oriented and settled in, and coping with the social and academic environment. Numerous checklists. No index or bibliography.

599. Lawhead, Alice and Lawhead, Steve. *The Ultimate College Student Handbook.* Wheaton, Ill.: Harold Shaw Publishers, 1989. 227p. ISBN 0-87788-864-7.
Numerous brief sections, ranging from a paragraph to a few pages, offer advice and information on adjusting to and coping with a wide variety of personal, social and academic facets of college life. The style is informal and often humorous. The text is generously interspersed with lists, cartoons, quotations and graphics. Access only through table of contents.

600. Linstrum, Helen. *Taking Your Show on the Road: A Guide for New Student Recruiters.* Washington, D.C.: Council for Advancement and Support of Education, 1990. 55p. ISBN 0-89964-274-8.
The author draws upon her extensive recruitment and admissions experience to provide concise, practical advice on such topics as the recruiter's role and image, campus presentations, college fairs, problem situations, follow-up, and travel arrangements. No index or bibliography.

601. *Management of Student Aid.* Washington, D.C.: Nat. Assn. of Coll. and Univ. Business Officers, 1979. 276p. ISBN 0-915164-07-8.
A guide to recommended practice which examines the implications, sources, and planning of financial aid, as well as major administrative responsibilities and procedures. Text is illustrated with charts and tables. Lengthy appendices present sample letters, procedures and forms, including some now dated HEW materials. Includes a glossary and brief bibliography. No index.

602. Moll, Richard. *The Public Ivys: A Guide to America's Best Public Undergraduate Colleges and Universities.* New York: Viking-Penguin Books, 1986. 304p. ISBN 0-14-009384-2.
Formerly published under the title The Public Ivys: A Guide to America's Best State Colleges and Universities, this work examines about ten public undergraduate institutions selected by the author using the following criteria: admission selectivity; the quality of the liberal arts program; funding; and amount of visibility and prestige. Entries include: institution name and address; and detailed descriptions of facilities, faculty, available programs, curriculum, etc.

603. Price, Janet R., Levine, Alan H. and Carey, Eve. *The Rights of Students: The Basic ACLU Guide to a Student's Rights.* 3d ed. (American Civil Liberties Union Handbook Series) Carbondale: Southern Illinois Univ. Pr., 1988. 181p. ISBN 0-8903-1423-1.
Defines "the scope of school officials' power to regulate students' lives, and their responsibilities to provide services and protections to students." Thirteen chapters cover such topics as the right to a free education, corporal punishment, tracking, sex discrimination and private schools. Each chapter addresses a specific question in its area, followed by notes citing relevant cases. Three appendices provide information on the use of the book and details of two significant cases. A selected bibliography, but no index.

604. Rowe, Bruce M. *The College Survival Guide: Hints and References to Aid College Students.* St. Paul, Minn.: West Publishing Co., 1989. 90p. ISBN 031452357X.
For all types of students in their first year of college. The volume contains three chapters, covering the topics of "starting out" (attitudes, choosing classes and teachers, etiquette, etc.), "developing study skills" (reading and library skills, writing reports, etc.), and "outside the college walls" (grades, education and travel). The guide concludes with three appendices dealing respectively with choosing a school, vocabulary building, and additional sources of information. Subdivisions of chapters in the table of contents provide easy access to advice on specific concerns. No index.

605. Schoenberg, B. Mark. *A Handbook and Guide for the College and University Counseling Center.* Westport, Ct.: Greenwood Pr., 1978. 305p. ISBN 0-313-20050-5.
Provides practical guidance, as well as offering background or historical matter related to the profession and its place in higher education. The reader finds everything from a discussion of the growth of counseling centers as an institution to setting up the office and selecting the staff. Each chapter concludes with a list of selected references. Access is through the table of contents. Includes a list of names represented. Remains a useful work, but in need of updating.

606. Sheldon, Henry D. *Student Life and Customs.* (American Education: Its Men, Institutions and Ideas, Series 1) Salem, N.H.: Ayer Co. Pubs., 1969. 366p. ISBN 0-405-01470-8.
Reprint of a general introduction to the subject (Appleton, 1901). The work ranges from medieval Europe through late nineteenth century United States, including a chapter on student societies in secondary schools. It includes a brief annotated bibliography. Access is by means of a detailed table of contents and a general index.

607. Shishkoff, Muriel M. *Transferring Made Easy: A Guide to Successfully Changing Colleges.* Princeton, N.J.: Peterson's Guides, 1991. 100p. ISBN 1-56079-04704.
Written by a specialist in transfer guidance, this work is intended particularly for the community or junior college student transferring to a four-year institution. It addresses such topics as policies and procedures, financial aid, and adjusting to life on a new campus. Special attention is given to the problems of adult students, minorities, military personnel and student athletes.

608. Silny, Josef. *Peterson's Handbook on Establishing an International Recruitment Program.* Princeton, N.J.: Peterson's Guides, 1988. 118p. ISBN 0-87866-707-5.

An aid for institutions in deciding upon and developing international recruitment programs at the graduate and undergraduate levels. A brief
discussion of support provisions and inducements for international re-
cruits precedes two chapters on recruitment planning and getting started.
The remainder of the volume is devoted to addresses of organizations,
associations, embassies, and overseas educational advisement centers,
arranged alphabetically by country. Lacks an index.

609. Smith, Michael Clay and Smith, Margaret D. *Wide Awake: A Guide to
      Safe Campus Living in the 90s.* Princeton, N.J.: Peterson's Guides,
      1990. 106p. ISBN 0-87866-973-6.
The authors, both lawyers involved in higher education, have written a
guide to campus survival in a more literal than usual sense. They offer
advice on protecting oneself from such dangers as theft, vandalism, substance abuse, sexual assault and date rape, hazing, and "white collar"
crimes. Safety checklists are included, as well as discussion of students' legal rights.

610. Van Raalte, Susan Drachman. *Apply Yourself: Writing College Appli-
      cations That Get Results.* New York: Fawcett Columbine, 1985. 111p.
      ISBN 0-449-90131-9.
Provides guidance for success in college application. Ten chapters deal
with such things as organizing oneself, the personal inventory, essay
writing, and overcoming fears. Two appendices deal respectively with analyzing questions and an analysis of three good essays.

Teaching and Learning

611. Basto, Nicholas. *Major Options: The Students Guide to Linking Col-
      lege Majors and Career Opportunities During and After College.* New
      York: Harper Collins, 1991. 328p. ISBN 0-06-271506-2.
This two-part career planning guide first examines frequently-chosen college majors, then turns to various career choices and their relationships
to fields of college study. Each chapter in the latter section includes
listings of professional associations for further information.

612. Blumenthal, Richard A. and Despres, Joseph A. *Major Decisions:
      A Guide to College Majors.* Concord, Mass.: Orchard House, 1990.
      155p. ISBN 0-944510-95-2.
Useful primarily to high school students and counselors, this work would
also be of some value to undergraduates. It covers 155 college majors
in one-page descriptions that include the courses commonly required for
each one, as well as high school subjects recommended to prepare for it,
career options it can lead to, and useful cross references to related
majors.

613. Chickering, Arthur W. and others. *Developing the College
      Curriculum: A Handbook for Faculty and Administrators.* Washington,
      D.C.: Council for the Advancement of Small Colleges, 1977. 313p.
The first part of the handbook deals with curriculum rationale, design,
practice and implementation. Especially useful are the appendices which
comprise the second half of the book. Included are eight curricular models, description of twenty-two innovative college curricula, and four
curriculum planning tools such as the Delphi technique and the educational environment scale. Lacks an index.

614. Gessner, Quentin H., ed. *Handbook on Continuing Higher Education.*
      New York: American Council on Education/Macmillan Publishing Co.,

1987. 261p. ISBN 0-02-911620-1.
A comprehensive survey of the field is provided by thirteen well-quali-
fied contributors in chapters dealing with such topics as: historical
perspective, organization, finances and funding, planning, marketing,
research and evaluation, and prospects for the future. Chapter references
and lists of suggested readings point to sources of further information.
Indexed.

615. Knowles, Asa S. and others. *Handbook of Cooperative Education.*
(Jossey-Bass Series in Higher Education) San Francisco: Jossey-
Bass, 1971. 386p. ISBN 0-87509-112-8.
This thorough examination of cooperative education is presented in twenty-one chapters and an epilogue, each written by one or more of twenty-
one authorities in the field. Chapters are grouped in six major sections
headed: History and Philosophy, Description of Programs, Conduct of Programs, Administration, Relevancy to Special Groups, and Development of
New Programs. While emphasis is primarily on the U.S., two of the authors offer perspectives from Canada and England. The text is supplemented with charts, tables and forms. Appendices contain a list of
institutions offering co-op programs, fields of study available, and examples of calendars and a co-op agreement. An eight-page bibliography
and index are also provided.

616. Lederman, Ellen. *College Majors: A Complete Guide from Accounting
to Zoology.* Jefferson, N.C.: McFarland, 1990. ISBN 0-89950-462-0.
Designed to complement College Board's Index of Majors (1979/80-   ),
this volume lists more than four hundred college majors that lead to a
degree, (associate through the doctorate). The following are provided:
brief description of the major, degree levels offered, a sampling of
typical courses required, related or complementary majors, needed
abilities (e.g. analytical abilities, interpersonal skills), and a brief
listing of career possibilities. Three appendices provide: major fields
of study by discipline; cross-referencing of majors; and correlation of
occupations and majors.

617. Levine, Arthur. *Handbook on Undergraduate Curriculum.* (Carnegie
Council Series) San Francisco: Jossey-Bass, 1978. 662p. ISBN 0-
87589-376-7.
Issued by the Carnegie Council on Policy Studies in Higher Education as
a resource for anyone involved in undergraduate education. The first of
its two parts, "Undergraduate Curriculum Today," surveys in nine chapters
the current state of such areas as general education, tests and grades,
and instruction methods. The second part provides "A Comparative and
Historical Perspective" in seven chapters which survey modern philosophies of education, historical and recent landmarks in the development
of the curriculum (supplemented by a documentary history in an appendix),
proposals for curriculum change and the undergraduate curricula in seven
other countries. Substantial reference lists follow each chapter. The
author has provided a glossary and an index. A valuable source in need
of updating.

618. McBeath, Ron J. *Instructing and Evaluating in Higher Education:
A Guide for Planning Learning Outcomes.* Englewood Cliffs, N.J.:
Educational Technology Publications, 1992. 355p. ISBN 0-87778-
242-3.
Includes eleven "self-instructional" modules covering such topics as preparing lectures, conducting discussions, and constructing multiple-
choice, essay questions and other tests. To assist users, this guide
includes exercises to reinforce concepts introduced in the text. The

book is designed for college instructors and teaching assistants.   It
includes an index and a brief bibliography.

619. McCabe, Gerard B., ed. *The Smaller Academic Library: A Management
      Handbook.* (The Greenwood Library Management Collection) New York:
      Greenwood Pr., 1988. 380p. ISBN 0-313-25027-8.
Thirty chapters, most contributed by practitioners in this type of library, cover administration, personnel, finance, collections, user services, technical services and physical plant.   Reference lists are
provided in each chapter; a bibliographic essay and an index conclude the
volume.

620. McKeachie, Wilbert J. *Teaching Tips: A Guidebook for the Beginning
      College Teacher.* 8th ed. Lexington, Mass.: D.C. Heath, 1986.
      353p. ISBN 0-669-06752-0.
This thorough and substantial work covers the full range of teachers'
concerns, from course preparation and classroom techniques to ethics and
improvement of teaching. The author also discusses the theory and research behind his suggestions. A detailed table of contents, index and
thirty-page bibliography are included.

621. Milton, Ohmer and Associates. *On College Teaching: A Guide To Con-
      temporary Practices.* San Francisco: Jossey-Bass, 1978.   404p.
      ISBN 0-87589-377-5.
Attempts to improve college teaching by encouraging all instructors in
all disciplines to consider new approaches and improve old ones. Fifteen
authors provide discussions of the following topics in fourteen chapters:
Clarifying Objectives; Lecturing; Leading Discussions; Classroom Testing;
Feedback for Learning; Using the Personalized System of Instruction; Com-
puters in the Classroom; Creating Contract Learning; Specifying and
Achieving Competencies; Being There Vicariously by Case Studies; Applying
Simulation/Gaming; Learning Through Field Experience; Working with Older
Students; and Evaluating Teachers. A fifteen page bibliography and in-
dex conclude the work.

622. Morgan, Robert L., Hunt, E. Stephen and Carpenter, Judith M. *Clas-
      sification of Instructional Programs, 1990 Edition.*   Washington,
      D.C.: U.S. Dept. of Education, Nat. Center for Education Statist-
      ics, 1991. 333p.
A taxonomy for use in gathering, reporting and comparing data on instructional programs. The CIP has been used by NCES in the Higher Education
General Information Surveys (HEGIS) and in its successor, the Integrated
Postsecondary Education Data System (IPEDS). The system is applicable
to all education levels and is used by many government agencies and other
organizations. Major components are the classification schedule, with
code numbers and program definitions, and an alphabetic program index.
Appendices include conversion tables relating this edition of CIP to the
last one, done in 1985, lists of schedule additions and deletions, and
a glossary of terms and abbreviations.

623. Newble, David and Cannon, Robert. *A Handbook for Teachers in Uni-
      versities and Colleges: A Guide to Improving Teaching Methods.* New
      York: St. Martins Pr., 1989. 159p. ISBN 0-312-03196-3.
The author devotes separate chapters to teaching large groups, making
conference presentations, and teaching small groups. Other chapters cover conducting labs and practical classes, planning curriculum, assessing
students, preparing materials and using teaching aids, and helping students learn. The text is amply illustrated with charts, checklists, out-

lines, samples and cartoons. Each chapter includes a list of references and suggested readings. Indexed.

624. Phifer, Paul. *College Majors and Careers: A Resource Guide for Effective Planning*. Garrett Park, Md.: Garrett Park Pr., 1987. 166p. ISBN 0-912048-46-8.
Developed as a guide for career counseling, this work explains the nature of the majors and their practical applications to provide a basic framework to future careers in the field. Further guidance is given in a list of related occupations, related skills required and personal attributes such as patience, alertness, imagination, independence, etc. Professional organizations are identified as additional sources of information. There are six appendixes: description of selected occupations; definition of skill statements; definitions of personal attributes; college majors and related high school courses; number of degrees awarded by fields; and list of publishers. A bibliography of books, directories, pamphlets, periodicals and computerized occupational information systems complements the appendixes.

625. Roose, Kenneth D. and Andersen, Charles J. *A Rating of Graduate Programs*. Washington, D.C.: American Council on Education, 1970. 115p. ISBN 0-8268-1371-2.
Appraisal of graduate programs for "supporters, producers, and consumers of graduate education". Evaluations of faculties and programs, as reflected by their reputations, are based on a survey of participating institutions. Data are organized into tables for the various disciplines and the ranks and scores of individual institutions are shown in each. Two appendices provide the questionnaire used and a list of the institutions included in the 1969 survey. Clearly out of date, but of use to those interested in the methodology.

626. Rowe, Fred A. *The Career Connection II: A Guide to Technical Majors and Their Related Careers*. Rev. ed. Indianapolis, Ind.: Jist Works, 1991. 165p. ISBN 0-942784-83-9.
A resource for counseling students for non-traditional career paths in technical fields such as carpentry, dairy-product management, electrician, hotel management, radiological technology, real estate, etc. Descriptive information begins with two- to three-sentence paragraphs outlining the nature of the work. This is followed by educational requirements, course requirements, high school courses, and related careers and their outlook. Includes separate indexes for courses, majors, and careers.

627. Rowe, Fred A. *A Guide to College Majors and Their Related Careers*. Indianapolis, Ind.: Jist Works, 1991. 272p. ISBN 0-942784-82-0.
Another guidance tool by the same author as that of <u>Career Connection II: A Guide to Technical Majors and Their Related Careers</u>. More than one hundred major fields of study are briefly described. Typical courses required in college and high school are included. In addition, career options associated with majors are given under associate degrees, bchelor's degrees or higher, including entry codes from the <u>Dictionary of Occupational Titles</u> (U.S. Dept. of Labor), ratings for the long-term outlook of the careers covered, and the average initial salary. Includes separate indexes for careers and majors as well as a bibliography.

628. Smith, Robert M., Aker, George F. and Kidd, J.R. *Handbook of Adult Education*, 5th ed. New York: Macmillan Publishing, 1970. 594p.
This work is designed for any interested person, as well as professionals in the field. Its thirty-one chapters arranged in three parts deal with

the social setting for adult education, definitions and descriptions, philosophical considerations, educators of adults, types of institutions that provide adult education (public libraries and museums, labor unions, business and industry, etc.), curriculum and content, vocational- technical education, continuing education, education for family life, to name but a few topics. Discussions of the topics by various authors are followed by three appendices which provide a directory of participating organizations of the Committee of Adult Education Organizations, general information sources in adult education, and the contents of past editions. Each chapter has a list of references. Includes a general index.

629. Trillin, Alice Stewart and Associates. *Teaching Basic Skills in College: A Guide to Objectives, Skills Assessment, Course Content, Teaching Methods, Support Services, and Administration.* San Francisco: Jossey-Bass, 1980. 327p. ISBN 0-87589-456-9.
Based on a study for the Instructional Resource Center of the City University of New York to "identify what was best in the skills programs" by examining what actually went on between students and teachers in the classrooms at the many campuses of the University. This volume provides both examples of the materials used and excerpts of students' work. Its first four chapters deal with the writing, reading, English-as-a-second-language, and mathematics programs. Each chapter reports on such things as the skill levels of students, diagnosis and placement, instructional procedures, support services, etc. The final chapter deals with program evaluation. A fourteen-page bibliography and an index are included.

630. U.S. Department of Health Education and Welfare. National Center for Education Statistics. *Educational Technology: A Handbook of Standard Terminology and a Guide for Recording and Reporting Information About Educational Technology.* (State Educational Records and Reports Series: Handbook X, Bulletin 76-321) Washington, D.C.: U.S. Dept. of Health, Education and Welfare, The Center for Education Statistics, 1975. 276p.
Presents a highly detailed, standardized system for compiling and comparing data on educational technology. The work includes a coded classification scheme, definitions of the classified terms, and units of measurement to be employed with them. It is fully indexed and includes a bibliography.

5.

ALMANACS, STATISTICAL GUIDES, AND YEARBOOKS

INTRODUCTION

This chapter includes digests and compendia of facts and statistical information, both current and retrospective, related to higher education. Included are books, monographs, and serial publications containing narrative summaries, figures, graphs, and statistical tables covering a wide range of subjects.

Whether these works are called almanacs, yearbooks, or factbooks, they are brought together in this chapter because they each provide valuable and pertinent information in concise, descriptive, or statistical form. For ease of access they are divided into a general and a special section, with the latter further divided into categories for Community Colleges, Economic Factors, Enrollments and Degrees, Faculty, Libraries, Minority Groups and Women, and Students. Included are sources that are entirely or substantially devoted to higher education.

Not included are periodical articles, pamphlets, most government publications, documents found in the Education Resources Information Center (ERIC) collection, and almanacs or yearbooks where higher education is but one of a wide range of subjects or fields of study. Other categories of publications excluded are: one-time studies or reports of limited scope or time span, titles that have been updated, or items so scarce or rare as to be generally unavailable.

Coverage of United States government publications in this chapter requires further comment. Generally, only those sources that continue to be published on a regular basis, or were published on such a basis in the past, and covered a significant time period, are included. Other works such as one-time studies or reports are excluded. Rejected as well are one-time statistical compilations covering a single year or other brief time period.

For continuing publications appearing in this chapter, in addition to a description of the present work, we include a report of a source's previous publication form and scope where appropriate. A number of these have undergone a title change or modification in title. Such former titles are indicated in the annotations. In addition, citation information includes the current agency responsible for the publication, while the starting date represents the first appearance of its earliest version.

For a listing of selected annual reports and studies in print and in computer-readable form not covered, the reader should consult the Compendium of National Data Sources on Higher Education (State Higher Education Executive Officers, 1991), described in Chapter 1.

GENERAL WORKS

631. *Almanac of Higher Education.* Chicago: Univ. of Chicago Pr., 1989- . Annual. ISSN 1044-3096.
A wide-ranging and useful selection of current statistics in a convenient format. Both the national and individual state sections include brief introductions describing background, current trends and issues. National data are presented in numerous tables and maps. State and District of Columbia sections provide information on demographics, political leadership, institutions, faculty, students, and finances, as well as miscellaneous notes. Data sources are cited in the body of the work and described more fully in a concluding section. No index; access is through the table of contents.

632. *The Condition of Education.* Washington, D.C.: U.S. Dept. of Education, Nat. Center for Education Statistics, 1975 -   . Annual. ISSN 0098-4752.
Currently offers sixty data analyses or "indicators" selected for their significance as measures of the current state of education. With the present edition, indicators cover elementary, secondary and higher education. Specific indicators included may vary, and are now arranged into six broad areas: access, participation, and progress; achievement, attainment, and curriculum; economic and other outcomes; size, growth, and output of institutions; climate, classrooms, and diversity of institutions; and human and financial resources. Indicators appear on two facing pages with text emphasizing key points and data in tabular and graphic form. A substantial part of the work is devoted to supplemental tables. Also provided are a glossary, index and an informatively annotated listing of the data sources.

633. *Digest of Education Statistics.* Washington, D.C.: U.S. Dept. of Education, Office of Educational Research and Improvement, Nat. Center for Educational Statistics. 1962-   . Annual.
Includes data on all levels of education, in terms of enrollments, population, finances, instructional staff, private and public institutions, degrees, salaries and a wide range of other topics. Information is gathered from a variety of sources, "both government and private, and draws especially on the results of surveys and activities carried out by the National Center for Education Statistics." Tables in this indispensable work are arranged into seven chapters covering respectively three educational levels, all levels in one set of tables, federal programs, outcomes of education, international comparisons, and learning resources and technology. Appendices provide a guide to the tables, a guide to sources, and definitions. Includes a subject index to the tables.

634. *Educational Rankings Annual: 1500 Rankings and Lists on*

Education, Compiled from Educational General Interest Published Sources. Detroit: Gale Research, 1991-   . Annual. ISSN 1053-1378.

A classified, annotated guide to rankings including "only data from reliable sources with defensible methodologies." This is a single-source publication of rankings, providing source information as well as actual rankings. It includes all levels of education, with substantial coverage of higher education including rankings of graduate programs in specific disciplines (eg., most-cited political science faculty, top research libraries, lowest paying institutions, etc.). Access is by means of an alphabetical outline of topics covered, and a lengthy index of rankings by personal and place name, subject, and institution.

635. *Fact Book on Higher Education.* New York: American Council on Education and Macmillan Publishing Co., 1981-   . Annual. ISSN 0363-6720.

A ready-reference source of statistical tables and trend lines arranged into subject sections currently covering demographic and economic topics, enrollment, faculty and staff, students, earned degrees, and student aid. Data are gathered from a range of governmental and non-governmental sources, with specific source citations following each table. Its user-friendly format makes this a handy source of information. A number of tables provide comparisons over long periods, with some tracing back to the 1930s and the 1950s. Includes both a detailed table of contents and an index. Beginning with the 1988/89 edition, this work includes a Guide to Sources giving background information on sources consulted.

636. Harris, Seymour Edwin. *A Statistical Portrait of Higher Education.* (A Report for the Carnegie Commission on Higher Education) New York: McGraw-Hill, 1972. 978 p. ISBN 0-07-010039-X.

The author, a leading researcher and writer on the economics of higher education, has drawn on his own work as well as on a variety of government and private sources (in particular the U.S. Office of Education and the American Council on Education) to produce this massive compilation. Some seven hundred tables, charts and graphs, along with commentary and brief summary sections, are arranged in twenty-eight chapters which are in turn grouped in five parts: Students, Enrollment, Faculty, Income and Expenditures, and Productivity and Structure. Emphasis is on economic data, but not to the exclusion of other types. Access is through a detailed table of contents and list of tables. Source citations are given for all data. A list of references is also provided.

637. *Historical Trends: State Education Facts, 1975-1985.* Washington, D.C.: U.S. Dept. of Education, Nat. Center for Education Statistics, 1988-   . Annual. ISSN 1055-6486.

Intended to be the first in a series of reports that provide basic trend data at the state level, this work is about evenly divided between public elementary and secondary education, and public and private higher education. The higher education section covers enrollments, faculty salaries, degrees conferred and expenditures. It utilizes charts to indicate percent change over the time period and tables to give figures for 1975-1976 and for each of the last five years for each state and the District of Columbia. Definitions and a guide to data sources appear in appendices.

638. Kurian, George T. *Yearbook of American Universities and Colleges.* New York: Garland, 1988-   . Annual. ISSN 0896 1034.

Organizes key data and interpretations on the condition of higher education. Most of the data have been published previously. Examples include data from the Center for Education Statistics on enrollment trends and degrees conferred; from the population census; from the American Association of University Professors (AAUP); from Barron's on college competitiveness; etc. Other previously published materials include speeches by such present or former leaders in American higher education as William Bennett and Derek Bok. Also provided are congressional reports, Carnegie Foundation report, major court decisions affecting issues such as affirmative action and faculty evaluation; and selected state reports. Includes extensive bibliographies and a subject index.

639. Litkowski, Thomas. *Free Universities and Learning Referral Centers 1981.* Washington, D.C.: U.S. Dept. of Education, Nat. Center for Education Statistics, 1983. 33 p.
Reports results of NCES's second survey of these nontraditional organizations. Narrative text and detailed tables cover survey methodology, trends, number of institutions, registrations and referrals, expenditures and revenues, staffing, and sections offered in selected subject areas. A directory of institutions is appended.

640. *Numbers of Employees in Institutions of Higher Education 1972-* . Washington, D.C.: U.S. Dept. of Health, Education, and Welfare, Ed. Div., Nat. Center for Education Statistics, 1976- . Irregular.
Covers the numbers of full-time, part-time, and full-time-equivalent professional employees by occupational activity and program function. Corresponding numbers of nonprofessional employees are presented by program function. Data are obtained from the annual Higher Education and General Information Survey (HEGIS). Basic tables are arranged in five parts: aggregate United States data for professional and nonprofessional employees, numbers of professional employees by occupational activity (by state and institution), numbers of professional employees by program function (by state and institution), numbers of instructional faculty (by state and institution), and numbers of professional employees (by employment status, sex, state, and institution). Since its first appearance in 1955, this report's title has varied slightly as has its focus. From 1955-1963/64 it appeared as issues of USOE circulars. After 1963 it continued as a separate series. Access is by means of the table of contents. Appendices include a copy of the survey instrument and information on the data collection procedure.

641. *Planning and Management Information: American Colleges and Universities* (Uniform title). Boulder, Colo.: Nat. Data Service for Higher Education.
Drawing on data from the U.S. Department of Education Higher Education General Information Survey (HEGIS) and Integrated Postsecondary Education Data System (IPEDS), College Board, the Council for Financial Aid for Education and the John Minter Associates financial database, this publisher produces a broad array of statistical reports and data analyses intended to be of particular use in institutional comparisons. The reports cover the broad areas of finance, students, staff, institutional characteristics, libraries, and academic programs. They include, among others, the following titles, many of which are updated annually:

Current Fund Revenues, Expenditures and Other Financial Data.
Financial Statistics and Ratios.
Higher Education Costs.

Management Ratios.
Survey of Student Costs and Financial Aid.
Tuition/Fees, Financial Aid Statistics.
Enrollment Management Ratios.
Freshman Class Statistics and Ratios.
Student Body Profile.
College and University Salary and Wages Outlay Comparisons.
Faculty Salaries: 9/10 Month. and 11/12 Month.
Staff Ratios.
Institutional Characteristics.

Each report is available in several versions that cover different categories of institutions, as defined by control (public or private), enrollment, and Carnegie Commission Classification, and is produced in print or magnetic disk form or both. Contact the publisher for further details and a full list of titles available.

642. *Projections of Education Statistics.* Washington, D.C.: U.S. Dept. of Education, Statistical Standards and Methodology Div., Nat. Center for Education Statistics, 1964-   . Annual.
Provides projections of statistics for all levels of education for the fifty states, and the District of Columbia. Narrative summaries, charts, and tables cover enrollments, graduates, teachers, and expenditures. Tables related to higher education cover earned doctor's degrees, estimated demand for full-time-equivalent instructional staff, estimated average charges per full-time-equivalent student, total enrollment with alternative projections by sex, students' attendance status, and institutional control type. Three alternative projections are offered in many of the other tables as well, including high, intermediate, and low alternative projections. Appendices cover methodology, classification of degrees and definitions. Access to figures and tables is by means of the table of contents.

643. *Standard Education Almanac.* Orange, N.J.: Academic Media, 1968-1984. Annual.
Covers all aspects and levels of education in the nation. This almanac is designed to provide the most comprehensive coverage of education, using data from a wide variety of sources which are meticulously cited. Its section on higher education provides statistics on enrollments, expenditures, earned degrees, and instructional staff. There is also a section listing directories of education. The information is accessible by means of a table of contents, a table of tables, a table of figures, and a subject index.

644. *State Higher Education Profiles.* 3d ed. Washington, D.C.: Nat. Center for Education Statistics, Postsecondary Education Statistics Div. Special Surveys and Analysis Branch, 1991. p. 538.
Includes thirteen basic statistical tables on higher education for the nation, for each of the fifty states and for the District of Columbia. Coverage includes enrollment, full-time faculty, revenues, expenditures, financial aid, and degrees and other formal awards conferred. Data are for fiscal year 1987, permitting comparison of each state to a national average and ranking states on selected statistics. Appendices include: a) sources of data and definition of terms, and b) classification of institutions by state, control type and degree level. Access is by means of the table of contents. Lacks an index.

645. *Statistics of Land Grant Colleges and Universities, [year].* 1870-1964/1965. Washington, D.C.: U.S. Office of Education, Bur.

of Educational Research and Development, Nat. Center for
Educational Statistics, 1870-1965. Annual.
Provides summary data for land-grant institutions as a whole, and details
for individual institutions. Coverage includes enrollment, degrees
earned, faculty and other professional staff, and financial statistics.
It began as a chapter of the Annual Report of the U.S. Commissioner of
Education; from 1916/17 to 1962/63 it appeared as USOE Bulletins and
Circulars; it then continued as a separate publication to 1965. Access
to the separate publications is by means of the table of contents with
a list of individual tables following. Appendices include data for
faculty and other professional staff, a comprehensive report on
enrollment, financial statistics, and regular federal appropriations.

646. *Yearbook of the National Society for the Study of Education.*
Chicago: Univ. of Chicago Pr., 1902-   . Annual, in two parts.
ISSN 0077-5762.
Each of the two volumes of this work is a collection of essays or studies
by a number of contributors on a topic or issue of current importance.
Over the years, subjects of general interest as well as more specialized
ones have been addressed. Among the latter, some, such as Graduate Study
in Education, The Public Junior College and Education for the
Professions, have dealt with specific higher education issues.

SPECIAL WORKS

Community Colleges

647. *Community, Technical and Junior Colleges Statistical Yearbook.*
Washington, D.C.: American Assn. of Community and Junior Colleges,
1990-   . Annual.
Provides a statistical portrait of colleges on a state-by-state and
institution-by-institution basis. Included are fall enrollment data,
number of minority students, number of faculty and professional staff
employed, and tuition and fees charged. In addition to the college-by-
college data, statistical summaries are provided on a state and national
basis.   Part one, the major section, provides information about
individual colleges; a very brief second part presents the state data.
Includes an alphabetical index of colleges covered.

648. Dickmeyer, Nathan and Cirino, Anna Marie. *Comparative Financial
Statistics for Public Community and Junior Colleges, 1988-89.*
Washington, D.C.: Nat. Assn. of Coll. and Univ. Business Officers,
1990. 68 p.
Produced in cooperation with the Association of Community College
Trustees, the American Association of Community and Junior Colleges and
the National Center for Education Statistics, this is the twelfth in a
series of annual comparative data studies. It is intended to help
institutions compare their financial performance to national and peer
group norms and includes worksheets to facilitate such an analysis in
major areas of expenditures, revenues, enrollment distributions and staff
ratios. Other chapters report the norms, as established in a survey of
544 institutions, in the form of quartile statistics for the full sample
and medians and quartiles for peer groups of colleges as defined by
enrollment size and vocational/technical orientation. Appendices provide
a description of the methodology, survey forms, a glossary and a list of
participating institutions.

649. Dickmeyer, Nathan and Cirino, Anna Marie. *Statewide Financial*

Statistics for Public Community and Junior Colleges, 1987-88.
Washington, D.C.: Nat. Assn. of Coll. and Univ. Business Officers,
1989. 150 p.
The preface describes this work as an outgrowth of Dickmeyer and Cirino's
Comparative Financial Statistics for Public Community and Junior Colleges
and the first of a series of annual studies. Data from a sample of 559
institutions are drawn from the National Center for Education Statistics
Integrated Postsecondary Education Data System (IPEDS) and supplemented
by an additional survey and analysis performed by NACUBO. Tables,
comprising the bulk of this work, present median and quartile statistics
by region and by state on expenditures, revenues, staff and enrollments.
Appendices contain a description of the survey and analysis methodologies
and a list of the participating colleges.

650. El-Khawas, Elaine H. *Community College Fact Book.* New York:
      American Council on Education, Macmillan, 1988. 167 p. ISBN 0-02-
      900941-3.
Presents current and trend data in seventy-three, one-page topical charts
and graphs, each with amplifying or elaborating text and data source
citation. The charts are grouped into a "General Information" section,
which covers community colleges and their enrollments, students,
educational outcomes, finances and staff, and a "Planning Information"
section which covers national demographic and economic data that have an
impact on community colleges. An appendix of forty-one highly detailed
tables from which the graphs and charts were derived fills nearly half
the volume. This section is not analyzed in the detailed table of
contents, nor is it included in the index.

Economic Factors

651. *Administrative Compensation Survey.* Washington, D.C.: Coll. and
      Univ. Personnel Assn., 1977-   . Annual.
Presents data on salaries of administrators in higher education. The
report presently covers more than 160 administrative positions at more
than 1,300 public and private institutions. A broad range of information
is provided in tables arranged into five units: 1) general data about
all institutions surveyed; 2) comparative data by institutional
enrollment level; 3) data by institution type (i.e., doctoral-degree
granting, baccalaureate level, etc.); 4) data by budget level; and 5)
special comparisons between males and females, minorities and
nonminorities, inside and outside hires, and median years of service.
Appendices include a list of responding institutions, special-study order
form, Carnegie classification and National Center for Education
Statistics (NCES) codes for institutions, a salary compensation
worksheet, and a copy of the salary survey questionnaire. This is an
important, timely source of salary information. Access is by means of
the table of contents. Lacks an index.

652. *College Costs: Basic Student Charges at 2-Year and 4-Year
      Institutions, [year].* Washington, D.C.: Nat. Center for
      Education Statistics, 1984-   . Annual.
Intended to be a comparative guide to expected tuition, mandatory fees,
room and board expenses for in-state and out-of-state students, this
compilation covers almost four thousand public and private institutions.
It is arranged in two sections, the first for less-than-four-year
schools, the second for those which grant a bachelor's degree or higher.
For the latter, costs are listed for both undergraduate and graduate
students. Within each section, schools are grouped by state and

listed alphabetically. Average costs for each state are also indicated.

653. *Compensation and Benefits Survey of College and University Chief Executive Officers.* Washington, D.C.: Coll. and Univ. Personnel Assn., 1984. 109 p.
Drawing on some thirteen hundred survey responses, this work's largest section consists of tabular and trend-line data on CEO salaries and other cash compensation in relation to enrollments and operating budgets at various types of institutions. Other sections briefly profile the characteristics of the respondents and their institutions, and a final section presents tables indicating the prevalence of benefits and perquisites such as housing, cars, travel and entertainment expenses, memberships, vacations, retirement plans, etc. Appendices list the participating institutions, reproduce the survey questionnaire, and describe the statistical methodology.

654. *Financial Statistics of Institutions of Higher Education.* 1955/56-1962/63; 1965/66-   . Washington, D.C.: U.S. Dept. of Education, Nat. Center for Education Statistics, 1955/56-1962/63; 1965/66-   . Annual.
Provides data, formerly gathered from the annual Higher Education General Information Survey (HEGIS) and since 1987 obtained through the Integrated Postsecondary Education Data System (IPEDS), on higher education finances. Summary tables include statistics on current funds revenues and expenditures, book value of assets and indebtedness, endowments, tuition and fees, scholarship and fellowship awards, and other expenditures and fees. Data are arranged in national aggregates, by state and region, by control type (public or private), and by level (university, four-year and two-year colleges). Access is by means of the table of contents. Appendices cover such subjects as the survey's methodology, institutions surveyed, units not responding, and a copy of the survey report with data for the fifty states and the District of Columbia. See also the related series "Statistics of Higher Education" (U.S. Office of Higher Education, 1870-1917, 1917/18-1957/58), appearing through 1917 as part of the Annual Report of the U.S. Commissioner of Education, to 1958 as a chapter of the Biennial Survey of Education, and to 1938 as the USOE Bulletin.

655. Halstead, D. Kent. *Inflation Measures for Schools and Colleges.* Washington, D.C.: U.S. Dept. of Education, Nat. Institute of Education, 1983. 183 p.
A revised and expanded edition of Halstead's Higher Education Prices and Price Indexes (Washington, D.C.: U.S. Dept. of Health, Education and Welfare, Office of Education, 1975). This work describes the background, derivation and application of the Higher Education Price Index for current operations, the Research and Development Index, the Boeckh Index (for physical plant additions) and the School Price Index (for elementary-secondary schools). Numerous tables and charts present price data and trends for the indexes and their major components for 1961-1982. Updated by the annual Higher Education Prices and Price Indexes: [year] Update (see entry below).

656. *Higher Education Prices and Price Indexes: [year] Update.* Washington, D.C.: Research Associates of Washington, 1989-   . Annual. ISSN 0148-0634.
A series of updates (formerly called "Supplements" and published by the Office of Education) to Halstead's Inflation Measures for Schools and Colleges. The 1988 issue reports and discusses price trends related to current operations, sponsored research and building construction, tracing

the Consumer Price Index, the Higher Education Price Index, the Research and Development Price Index and the Boeckh Index for construction, along with some of their major subindexes. Detailed data are presented for 1976-1988, with summary tables and charts for 1961-1988.

657. McCoy, Marilyn and others. *Higher Education Financing in the Fifty States: Interstate Comparisons, Fiscal Year 1984.* 5th ed. Boulder, Colo.: Nat. Center for Higher Education Management Systems, 1986. 546 p.
A comprehensive and detailed report that also includes trend data starting with 1980. Its first chapter contains an introductory survey of general trends, as well as tables ranking the states on a variety of financial, enrollment and faculty salary measures and ratios. A description of the methodology employed appears in the second chapter. Chapter 3, the largest section of this volume, contains reports in tabular and chart form on the individual states and the District of Columbia. Each of these reports covers state financing, public and independent institutions, appropriations, revenues, faculty salaries and characteristics of types of institutions. Appendices list institutions and data sources.

658. *Voluntary Support of Education.* New York: Council for Aid to Education, 1954/55-   . Annual. ISSN 0363-3683.
Compilation of support reported by seventeen hundred survey participants: public and private postsecondary institutions (categorized as research/doctoral, comprehensive, liberal arts, professional and specialized, and two-year) and private elementary and secondary schools. The pre-college institutions represent less than a third of the respondents. The largest section of this work is a detailed table which lists for each institution the various kinds and sources of support received. Summary and trend statistics are given both in the commentary sections and in the appendix tables.

Faculty

659. *Salaries of Full-Time Instructional Faculty on 9- and 10-Month Contracts in Institutions of Higher Education, 1979-80 through 1989-90.* (E.D. Tabs Report) Washington, D.C.: U.S. Dept. of Education, Office of Educational Research and Improvement, 1991. 42 p.
Data are presented in twenty-two tables displaying salaries by academic year and rank, control type (public or private), institutional category (four-year and two-year colleges), and sex of faculty covering fifty states and the District of Columbia. Information was collected through the Integrated Postsecondary Education Data System (IPEDS) for the academic years 1987-88 and 1989-90. For prior years, data were provided through the Higher Education General Information Survey (HEGIS). Access is by means of the table of contents. An appendix includes a copy of the IPEDS survey instrument along with instructions.

660. *Salaries, Tenure, and Fringe Benefits of Full-Time Instructional Faculty in Institutions of Higher Education.* Washington, D.C.: U.S. Dept. of Health, Education and Welfare, Ed. Div., Nat. Center for Education Statistics, 1977-   . Irregular.
Provides data by rank and sex for full-time members of the teaching faculty at institutions of higher education in the United States. Data are reported by sex, academic rank, length of contract, level of institutions, and control type (i.e., public or private). Faculty

included "those members of the Instruction/Research Staff employed on a full-time basis whose regular assignment is instruction, including those with released time for research." Access is by means of table listings on the contents pages. Data for the report were obtained from the Higher Education General Information Survey (HEGIS) reports, and in later years from the Integrated Postsecondary Education Data System (IPEDS). This published series has undergone title changes as its scope has evolved. Similar data were reported in Higher Education Planning and Management Data (1957/58- 1960/61). Higher Education Salaries appeared as issues of the USOE Circular for 1962, 1964, 1965; reports were published as a separate series under the same title for 1966/67-1967/68. It appeared as Salaries and Tenure of Instructional Faculty in Institutions of Higher Education, 1974-1975 in 1976, while two reports appeared as OERI Bulletins (1984/85-1985/86). A ten-year cumulation of salary data (1979/80-1989/90) appears elsewhere in this chapter.

Higher Education and Government

661. *Appropriations of State Tax Funds for Operating Expenses of Higher Education.* Washington, D.C.: Nat. Assn. of State Universities and Land-Grant Colleges, 1960/61-   . Annual. ISSN 0457-4361.
This report consists mainly of listings for each state for the current fiscal year showing total support and amounts allocated to individual units or institutions, agencies and programs. Degree of detail varies from state to state. An introduction reports briefly on the nature and limitations of the data and on national and state trends.

662. *Federal Support to Universities, Colleges and Selected Nonprofit Institutions.* Washington, D.C.: Nat. Science Foundation, 1967/68-   . Annual.
All types of direct aid are included in this report, which is based on data from the various Federal agencies that provide support. Over fifty tables present information analyzed and/or ranked by amount of aid received, year received (usually for the last seven years, sometimes more), type of activity, funding agency, technical and academic fields, individual institutions, type of institution, and state and geographical region.

663. Halstead, D. Kent. *State Profiles: Financing Public Higher Education, 1978-1991.* 14th ed. Washington, D.C.:   Research Associates of Washington, 1991. 220 p.
A report and statistical analysis of the states' support for public higher education for the current year, with data from previous years included for comparison purposes. Data are drawn from a survey of state higher education finance officers. The report employs a statistical model which generates ratios, rankings and indexes from basic data on population, high school graduates, public FTE enrollment, tax capacity, tax revenues, government appropriations, system support index, tuition revenues and disposable personal income. An introductory section describes the model, and an appendix provides definitions of the data and a copy of the survey instructions.

664. Halstead, D. Kent. *State Profiles: Financing Public Higher Education, 1985-86.* Washington, D.C.: Research Associates of Washington, 1986-   . Annual.
Provides current fiscal-year appropriations, tuition, enrollment, and supporting data for comparative analysis of state financing of public higher education. Data are provided by State Higher Education Finance

Officers of the fifty states and the District of Columbia. Readers are advised that the report is based on considerable estimated data. For earlier works of comparable data see also: Higher Education Financing in the Fifty States (Nat. Center for Higher Education Management Systems, 1979-1984), and How States Compare in Financing Higher Education (Nat. Institute of Education, 1982-1985). Both are authored or co-authored by Halstead.

Law

665.   *Yearbook of Education Law*. Topeka, Kan.: Nat. Organization on Legal Problems of Education, 1988-   . Annual.
Provides analysis and discussion of judicial decisions on education handed down by State and Federal courts. These summaries are arranged under eight subject chapters, each prepared by one or more specialists. Subjects covered include: employees, bargaining, pupils, handicapped, torts, sports, finance, and higher education. The higher education chapter includes such topics as discrimination, faculty employment, administration, students, liability, antitrust, patents, and estates and wills. Includes a detailed table of contents, table of cases, and a general index.

666.   *The Yearbook of Higher Education Law*. V.1-   . 1977-   . Topeka, Kan.: Nat. Organization on Legal Problems of Education, 1977-   . Annual.
Provides citations to and discussion of state and federal court cases involving higher education institutions. Six chapters cover the fields of governance, finance, property, tort liability, employees, and students. Each footnoted chapter contains an introduction to the field followed by topical sections. For example, the chapter on students covers eighteen topics, ranging from freedom of expression through resident housing, athletics, and religious matters to law school students and bar admissions. Table of cases and separate subject index.

Libraries

667.   *ACRL University Library Statistics, 1987-88: A Compilation of Statistics From One Hundred Non-ARL University Libraries*. Chicago: Assn. of Coll. and Research Libraries, 1989. 80 p. ISBN 0-8389-7288-8.
The fifth and latest in a series of similar reports that began with 1978-79. This work presents the results of a survey of institutions not belonging to the Association of Research Libraries (which conducts and publishes its own similar surveys), but classified as Research Universities I and II or Doctorate-Granting Universities I and II. The volume consists mainly of numerical data tables and institutional rank order tables covering: collections, materials types and purchases; interlibrary loans; staffing; and expenditures for salaries, materials and other operating expenses. A copy of the survey questionnaire is appended.

668.   *ARL Statistics*. Washington, D.C.: Assn. of Research Libraries, 1974/75-   . Annual. ISSN 0147-2135.
Reports data on the over one hundred member libraries of ARL. Numerical survey responses and institutional rank orders are presented in tables covering size of and additions to collections; materials types; interlibrary loan activity; staffing; and expenditures for materials,

binding, salaries and other operating expenses. Data on institutions'
Ph.D. production, faculty and enrollments are reported separately. A
copy of the survey questionnaire and directions is also included.

669. *Library Statistics of Colleges and Universities.* Washington, D.C.:
      U.S. Dept. of Education, Office of Educational Research and
      Improvement, Nat. Center for Education Statistics, 1967-   .
      Irregular.
Reports statistics on library collections, circulation and loans,
operating expenditures, staffing, salaries, and other selected management
information.   Tables include national and state summaries as well as
institutional data.   Surveys of college and university libraries were
initiated by the U.S. Office of Education a century ago. Throughout the
1940s and 1950s they appeared as USOE Circular. During the 1960s they
were divided: one part appearing as a USOE Circular: the other appearing
as a separate publication. In 1967 the first of a series of reports was
generated as part of the Higher Education General Information Survey
(HEGIS).   These appeared biennially through 1977.   Beginning in 1975
library surveys of the NCES were identified together as the Library
General Information Survey (LIBGIS), at which time the college and
university survey became a part of the LIBGIS and HEGIS. Publication has
been irregular over the years, with its last appearance in 1987 with data
covering 1985.   Access to the reports is by means of the table of
contents. Appendixes include a copy of the survey instrument and
instructions for its completion.

670. *Library Statistics of Colleges and Universities, 1985: National
      Summaries, State Summaries, Institutional Tables.* Chicago: Assn.
      of Coll. and Research Libraries, 1987. 240 p. ISBN 0-8389-7147-4.
Compiled from the Higher Education General Information Survey of 1985 by
the National Center for Educational Statistics, and updating 1982
publications by NCES and ACRL, the seventeen tables that comprise this
work report on the three levels indicated in the title. Areas covered
include volumes, titles, format of holdings, expenditures and staff, as
well as their distribution by enrollment, control and type of
institution.

671. Stubbs, Kendon and Buxton, David. *Cumulated ARL University Library
      Statistics, 1962-63 through 1978-79.*   Washington, D.C.:
      Association of Research Libraries, 1981. 163 p.
Cumulates and corrects data from the annual ARL Statistics on the
university members of ARL for the period indicated. For a fuller
description see the entry for ARL Statistics.

Minority Groups and Women

672. Carter, Deborah J. and Wilson, Reginald. *Minorities in Higher
      Education.* Washington, D.C.: American Council on Education, 1981-
      . Annual.
Prepared by the Office of Minorities in Higher Education, this work
provides data on high school completion rates, projections of high school
graduates, college participation rates, college enrollments, and degree
completions. Some data are lacking. Annual high school completion rates
and college participation rates for Asian Americans and American Indians
are not provided. The source is in two parts: narrative summaries and
tables. Tables cover several years, providing comparisons. Lacks an
index, but includes a table of contents.

673. Deskins, Donald R., Jr. *Minority Recruitment Data: An Analysis of Baccalaureate Degree Production in the United States.* Totowa, N.J.: Rowman and Allanheld, 1983. 819 p. ISBN 0-86598-145-0.

Intended to aid in identifying the pool of minority (Black, Hispanic, Asian and Native American) bachelor's recipients for recruitment to graduate and professional schools, business and industry. Data presented here are derived primarily from the 1978-79 Higher Education General Information Survey (HEGIS) Earned Degree Tapes and provide information on the numbers, distribution, institutions of origin and fields of study of degree recipients, as well as accessibility, as indicated by institutions' proximity to airports. Strategies for utilizing these data in recruitment programs are discussed briefly. An unusual and useful analysis that deserves updating.

674. Fries, Judith E. *The American Indian in Higher Education, 1975-76 to 1984-85.* Washington, D.C.: Dept. of Education, Office of Educational Research and Improvement, Center for Education Statistics, 1987. 34 p.

Following a brief historical overview, data are presented according to the following areas: population characteristics, enrollment, degrees earned, employment within higher education, and institutions enrolling predominantly American Indian students. The work includes numerous tables and diagrams, with citations to data sources. A brief but valuable source of hard-to-find information. Access is by means of the table of contents.

675. Gilford, Dorothy M. and Snyder, Joan. *Women and Minority Ph.D.'s in the 1970's: A Data Book.* Washington, D.C.: Nat. Research Council, Nat. Academy of Sciences, 1977. 188 p.

This one-time study and report presents a wide variety of data, analyzed by sex and racial/ethnic group, in three chapters: 1) the characteristics of the degree recipients themselves (such as age, marital status, family educational background, dependents, field of study, sources of support, postdoctoral plans), 2) women and minority Ph.D.'s in the workforce (including field of employment, employment sector and work activity, salary and employment status), and 3) recipients' baccalaureate and doctoral institutions (including type of institution, graduates earning doctorates, female faculty, etc.). Appendices include further detailed analyses by subject field of doctorates, samples of the survey questionnaires and a description of the sampling methodology.

676. Hill, Susan T. *Traditionally Black Institutions of Higher Education, 1860-1982.* Washington, D.C.: U.S. Dept. of Education, Office of Educational Research and Improvement, Nat. Center for Education Statistics, 1985. 112 p.

Reviews Federal statistical reports extending back to 1915, related to traditionally black institutions of higher education. Included, as well, are more recent data about these institutions up to the early 1980s. Six chapters include a statistical overview of the development of traditionally black colleges for the period from 1860 to 1970, an enrollment and residence profile of these institutions, degree awards and curriculum, traditionally black colleges in the South, finance and federal funding, and employees and facilities of the institutions. Chapters include tables and charts with the text. Appendices cover definitions, data sources, profiles of each institution, and detailed data on degrees awarded. Access is by means of the table of contents and list of tables.

677. *Historically Black Colleges and Universities Fact Book.*

Washington, D.C.: U.S. Dept. of Health and Human Services, Division of Black American Affairs, 1983. 3v.
Compiled as part of efforts to increase these institutions' participation in federally supported programs, this work reproduces and summarizes responses from sixty-nine of the 107 targeted schools and covers junior and community colleges and both private and public colleges and graduate schools. Information on each institution is presented in a standard twenty-one page format and includes its setting, control, enrollment, history and mission, curricular offerings, faculty, academic support resources, facilities and equipment. Particular attention is paid to community involvement and services, research projects and interests, evaluation experience and consortia/collaborative arrangements.

678. *Minorities and Women in Higher Education, [year].* Washington, D.C.: U.S. Equal Employment Opportunity Commission, 1983- . Biennial.
Presents the data EEOC collects on the biennial Higher Education Staff Information Report (EEO-6) which it requires of all institutions with fifteen or more employees. The numerous tables provide national and state summaries for public and private institutions, and for male and female, black, white, Hispanic, Asian/Pacific Islander and American Indian/Alaska Native groups. Categories of analysis include salary level, contract type, occupational activity, faculty rank and tenure. A copy of the form used for reporting (EEOC Form 221) is included, but no index or list of tables.

679. *Minority Student Enrollments in Higher Education: A Guide to Institutions With Highest Percent of Asian, Black, Hispanic and Native American Students.* Rev. ed. Garrett Park, Md.: Garrett Park Pr., 1988. n.p. ISBN 0-912048-49-2.
Lists over five hundred colleges in the fifty States, District of Columbia, Puerto Rico and the Pacific Territories in which at least one minority group comprises twenty percent or more of enrollment. Each institution entry provides address, telephone number, total enrollment, percent of enrollment of any minority group at or above twenty percent, highest degree awarded and representative major programs. Data are from U.S. Dept. of Education sources for 1986. A bibliography and index by major programs are included.

680. Morris, Lorenzo. *Elusive Equality: The Status of Black Americans in Higher Education.* Washington, D.C.: Howard University Pr., 1979. 369 p. ISBN 0-88258-080-9.
This study of the status of blacks in higher education is designed to throw light on the factors that affect equal opportunity. Organized around such topics as access, inequalities, black institutions, measuring inequalities, the data, in more than one hundred tables (in the text and in appendices), cover the years 1975-77. Numerous figures in both text and appendices enhance the value of this work. A bibliography of more than one hundred citations and a selected annotated bibliography of more than forty items on black student attrition are provided. Includes a general index.

681. Schantz, Nancy B. and Brown, Patricia Q. *Trends In Racial/Ethnic Enrollment in Higher Education: Fall 1978 through Fall 1988.* (Survey Report, June 1990) Washington, D.C.: U.S. Dept. of Education, Nat. Center for Education Statistics, 1990. 25 p.
Findings from the Higher Education General Information Survey (HEGIS) of fall enrollments collected biennially from 1978 to 1984 and of its successor, the Integrated Postsecondary Education Data System (IPEDS),

in 1986. The report is designed to inform policymakers, researchers, and the postsecondary education community of long-term trends. The section dealing with enrollment trends uses institution-based data from HEGIS and IPEDS, while the section on participation rates uses household-based statistics from the Census's Current Population Survey. The seven tables and four figures present data by race, ethnicity, and, in some cases, sex. Lacks an index.

682.   Touchton, Judith G. and Davis, Lynne. *Fact Book on Women in Higher Education*. New York: American Council on Education and Macmillan Publishing Co., 1991. 289 p. ISBN 0-02-900951-0.
A ready reference source of tables, graphs, and data summaries "covering all women in higher education (minority and majority) in all of their academic roles - as students, faculty, administrators, and staff." The work is divided into three parts: Part 1 highlights and summarizes data regarding demographics and economics; high school and the transition to higher education; enrollment; earned degrees; faculty, administrators, trustees, staff; and student aid. Part 2 covers these same topics more extensively and in greater detail. Part 3 contains a section on Data Issues and Sources, including a Guide to Sources, a bibliography, and source tables for topics covered in Part 2. Both Part 2 and Part 3 include sources for information cited. Data are gathered from a range of governmental sources and various postsecondary education associations. Access is by means of both the table of contents and the general index.

683.   Vetter, Betty M. *Professional Women and Minorities: A Manpower Data Resource Service*. 8th ed. Washington, D.C.: Commission on Professionals in Science and Technology, 1989. 259 p.
This work is designed to provide both current and historical statistics about the professional segment of the U.S. population and particularly the participation and availability of women and minorities in those areas generally requiring formal education to at least the baccalaureate level. Some of the data go back as far as 1967, and others include the year of publication (1989). Between editions, new data are published regularly in the periodical digest, <u>Manpower Comments</u>. The publisher, formerly called the Scientific Manpower Commission, is affiliated with the American Association for the Advancement of Science. Tables are presented in ten chapters: General Enrollments; General degrees; General Professions; General Work Force; Academic Work Force; Physical, Mathematical, and Computer Sciences; Engineering, Technology and Technicians; Agricultural, Biological, Medical & Health Sciences; Social and Behavioral Sciences; and Arts, Humanities and Education. Includes a table of contents, listing of charts, bibliography, and a subject index.

Students

684.   American College Testing Program, Research and Development Division. *College Student Profiles: Norms for the ACT Assessment, 1987-88 ed.* Iowa City: American College Testing Program, 1987.
This report is produced every three or four years from the results of the ACT Assessment Program and Student Profile Section from participating colleges. For ACT test scores and high school grades, norms are presented in terms of percentile ranks for men, women and total students by type of college chosen, region, age, family income, planned major and racial/ethnic background. The norms for the Student Profile Section are percentage distributions of responses on planned major and vocational choice, degree aspirations, factors affecting college choice, financial

aid need, need for special programs and services, and racial/ethnic background. A glossary, copy of Student Profile Survey and comments on the accuracy of the results are appended.

685. *The American Freshman: National Norms for Fall [year].* Los Angeles: Laboratory for Research in Higher Education, Graduate School of Education, Univ. of California, Los Angeles, 1971-   . Annual. ISSN 0278-6990.
Prepared by the staff of the Cooperative Institutional Research Program, this report presents the results of an annual survey of first-time, full-time college students conducted as part of CIRP's ongoing longitudinal study of American higher education. Typically, the survey samples about 200,000 students at some 350 institutions. Introductory sections explain the methodology, discuss background and trends, and list references. The bulk of each volume tabulates responses to a multitude of questions on students' family, racial and socio-economic background; political orientation; religious preferences; high school achievement; academic/career/life plans; and attitudes and opinions on social, political and moral issues. These results are stratified by gender, type of institution, selectivity of institution and geographic region. Appendices provide a list of participating institutions year-by-year and a copy of the survey form.

686. *The American Freshman: Twenty Year Trends, 1966-1985.* Los Angeles: Cooperative Institutional Research Program, Higher Education Research Institute. Graduate School of Education, Univ. of California, Los Angeles, 1987. 140 p.
Contains year-by-year national data for men, women and all freshmen as gathered by the CIRP in its annual surveys of about two hundred thousand full-time students at a sample of 550 two- and four-year institutions. After an essay overview of the data and trends, the tables which form the bulk of this work provide detailed information on freshman demographics, family backgrounds, religious preferences, academic preparation and plans, career preferences, life goals, attitudes on social and political issues, and more. A description of the methodology employed, the 1985 survey form and a list of participating institutions appear in appendices.

687. *Associate Degrees and Other Formal Awards Below the Baccalaureate.* Washington, D.C.: U.S. Dept. of Health, Education, and Welfare, Office of Education, Nat. Center for Educational Statistics, 1965/66-   . Annual.
Includes summary data and data for individual institutions offering associate and related degrees creditable toward a bachelor's degree and those degrees awarded on completion of a program of study especially granted by community and two-year colleges. Data cover states, institutional control and type, sex of students enrolled, and curriculum type and discipline. Access is by means of the table of contents. An appendix provides a copy of the survey instrument. Data are obtained from the survey instrument, "Degrees and Other Formal Awards Conferred," which is part of the annual Higher Education General Information Survey (HEGIS). During the mid 1950s and early 1960s, these data appeared as USOE Circulars. Except for the combined edition of 1965/66 and 1966/67, reports have appeared separately on an annual basis. For earlier information, see The Guide to Organized Occupational Curriculums in Higher Education, 1956-62 (U.S. Office of Education, 1965). For subsequent data see issues of Earned Degrees Conferred (U.S. Office of Education).

688. *Baccalaureate Origins of Doctorate Recipients: A Ranking by Discipline of 4-Year Private Institutions, 1920-1986 Data.* 5th ed. Lancaster, Pa: Office of Planning and Institutional Research, Franklin and Marshall College, 1988. 60 p.
Consists primarily of ranked listings by discipline for the periods 1920-1986, 1977-1986 and less detailed data for 1986 alone. This analysis draws on National Research Council files, but is limited to four-year, private, non-doctorate-granting institutions. An alphabetical list of the 877 colleges and universities included appears in an appendix.

689. *Earned Degrees Conferred.* Washington, D.C.: U.S. Dept. of Health, Education, and Welfare, Office of Ed., Nat. Center for Educational Statistics, 1947/48-   . Annual.
Provides data on baccalaureate and higher degrees conferred in the United States. Information is presented in summary tables for state and national totals and in detailed tables including degree level and sex of students, discipline and specialty, and control and level of institution. Data are obtained from the survey instrument "Degrees and Other Formal Awards Conferred" from the annual Higher Education General Information Survey (HEGIS). From its introduction through 1963, the report appeared as USOE Circulars. Thereafter it was published as a separate series, appearing in two parts: Summary Data, and Institutional Data. Access to the reports' contents is through the table of contents. Appendices include a reproduction of the survey and instructions for its completion. The 1988 issue of Statistical Abstract of the United States (U.S. Dept. of Commerce) ceases reference to the report, instead relying on the Digest of Education Statistics (U.S. Dept. of Education). Readers are also advised to see Trends in Bachelors and Higher Degrees, 1975-1985 (U.S. Dept. of Education).

690. *Fall Enrollment in Colleges and Universities.* 1947-   . Washington, D.C.: U.S. Dept. of Education, Office of Educational Research and Improvement, Nat. Center for Education Statistics, 1947-   . Annual.
Provides summary data on institutions located in the fifty United States, District of Columbia, and (in the state tables) institutions in outlying areas (Guam, Puerto Rico, etc.). Tables cover attendance status (full-time, part-time), enrollment level (first-time, freshmen, undergraduates, graduate students, etc.), student sex and racial or ethnic designation, and type of institution control (public, private). Data permit comparison by state, control type, type of institution, and other significant variables including previous years. Information has been gathered annually as part of the Higher Education General Information Survey (HEGIS) since 1966, while the enrollment reports - with some title variation - extend back to the 1940s. Appendices cover methodology, classification of institutions, comparison tables for previous years, and the survey form used and instructions for its completion. Access is by means of the table of contents. No index.

691. *High School Graduates: Projections for the Fifty States, 1982-2000.* Boulder, Colo.: Western Interstate Commission for Higher Education, 1984. 33 p.
This work updates and expands the first report which appeared in 1979. A more recent edition apparently has not been published, but the data, gathered from state education departments, as well as the projections, are not easily found elsewhere. Graphs indicate national, regional and state projected percent change at specific intervals. A year-by-year table provides actual figures for 1975-1982 and projections for 1983-2000

for each state and the District of Columbia. A concluding section describes the methodology used.

692. National Academy of Sciences, National Research Council. *A Century of Doctorates: Data Analyses of Growth and Change: U.S. Ph.D.'s -- Their Numbers, Origins, Characteristics, and the Institutions From Which They Come.* Washington, D.C.: Nat. Academy of Sciences, Nat. Research Council, 1978. 173 p. ISBN 0-309-02738-1.
Drawing primarily on NAS Doctorate Records File data, this major compilation encompasses all doctoral-level earned degrees during the century ending in 1974. Its main sections cover historical trends, characteristics of degree recipients, their post-doctorate plans and employment, and the characteristics of the conferring institutions, all presented in numerous charts, graphs and tables as well as explanatory text. Appendices present further disciplinary, institutional and geographic data. Brief selective bibliography, glossary and subject index.

693. National Academy of Sciences, National Research Council. *Doctorate Production in United States Universities 1920-1962, with Baccalaureate Origins of Doctorates in Sciences, Arts and Professions.* (NAS Publication 1142) Washington, D.C.: NAS-NRC, 1963. 215 p.
This work cumulates and greatly augments data and analyses from four earlier NAS publications which covered fewer disciplines and shorter time spans. Most of the volume consists of tables, graphs and charts, supplemented by brief commentary. The production of doctorates is analyzed by discipline, institution, time period and geographic area. For the period starting in 1957, data are also available on the baccalaureate origins of doctorates and on characteristics and post- doctoral experience of the degree recipients. No index; access only through a list of tables and figures.

694. Office of Scientific and Engineering Personnel, National Research Council. *Doctorate Recipients From United States Universities: Summary Report, [year].* Washington, D.C.: Nat. Academy Pr., 1967- . Annual.
The 1988 edition is the twenty-second in this series of reports on the results of the yearly Survey of Earned Doctorates conducted by the National Science Foundation and other bodies. These data update the Doctorate Records file and supplement earlier publications of the NRC and the National Academy of Sciences. Graphs, tables and commentary present information primarily on the numbers and characteristics of doctorate recipients and on their post-graduation plans. A copy of the survey questionnaire is appended. Access is by table of contents and lists of figures and tables.

695. Office of Scientific Personnel, National Academy of Sciences. *Doctorate Recipients From United States Universities 1958-1966: A Statistical Report.* (NAS Publication, 1489) Washington, D.C. National Academy of Sciences, 1967. 262 p.
This work complements NAS's earlier <u>Doctorate Production in United States Universities 1920-1962</u> with more recent and detailed information. Like other reports in this series, this one draws mainly on data from the annual Survey of Earned Doctorates, as compiled in the Doctorate Records File. With minimal interpretive commentary, the numerous tables and graphs analyze doctorates granted by time period, field, institution and state, recipient's country of origin and postdoctoral employment, as well as the characteristics of women recipients. Appendices include information on institutional and baccalaureate origins of doctorates,

leading degree-granting institutions and the geographic migration of recipients. Since 1967 this publication has been updated by the yearly Summary Report.

696.   *Students Enrolled for Advanced Degrees.* Washington, D.C.:   U.S.
       Dept. of Health, Education and Welfare, Office of Ed., Nat. Center
       for Education Statistics, 1959-   . Annual.
Provides institutional and summary data, including summary data by state or other geographic area, institutional control type (public or private) and level, as well as by discipline or specialty. Data for the report were obtained through the Higher Education General Information Survey (HEGIS). Tables are accessed by means of the table of contents. This document first appeared as the USOE Circular.   After 1964 it was published separately in two parts: Institutional and Summary Data. Its title has varied over the years: Enrollment for Advanced Degrees and Enrollment for Master's and Higher Degrees. It ceases to appear in the source listings of the Statistical Abstract of the United States after 1980. Appendices include copies of survey instruments and instructions for their completion. Issues of the report covering data for the period from 1966 to 1975 have appeared in the Educational Resources Information Center (ERIC) publication series.

6.

ABSTRACTS, INDEXES, AND REPORTERS

INTRODUCTION

This chapter brings together sources which systematically cite and describe the contents of books, periodicals, and other documents pertaining to higher education. These sources may cover the field exclusively (e.g., Higher Education Abstracts) or in conjunction with other subjects or fields of study (e.g., PAIS International in Print).

Excluded are indexes, abstracts, or reporters that cover only incidentally the field of higher education. Such indexes as the Reader's Guide to Periodical Literature, the Humanities Index, or the Social Sciences Index (all published by H.W. Wilson Co.) are already well known standard works cited in many guides to literature searching and library use. Researchers are advised to consult Bill Katz's Magazines for Libraries (Bowker, 1969-   .) under "Abstracts and Indexes" as a ready source to well over two hundred known and not-so-well-known periodical indexes and abstracts.

While selected for their more specific focus on education or higher education, sources described in this chapter nonetheless offer access to a range of research or scholarly interests. Among sources included is a reprint of nearly forty-four thousand citations appearing in more than one hundred issues of the Bulletin of the U.S. Office of Education (Garland Publishing, 1979) covering the earlier decades of the twentieth century. Another is an index to 130 state education journals and newsletters - sources overlooked in standard indexes.

The twenty-seven sources here described are arranged in general subject sections. These include: General Works, Administration, History, and Law. Within these sections users will find sources providing access to a wide range of materials: books and parts of books, conference proceedings, court decisions, dissertations, government publications, research reports, and other items.

Arrangement within the sections is alphabetical by main entry which, in most cases, is the title of the work. A few titles are listed by the name of the author or compiler. All works, however, are listed in separate author, title, and subject indexes at the end of the book.

GENERAL WORKS

697. *British Education Index.* Leeds, England: Brotherton Library, Univ. of Leeds, 1954-   . Annual.
An author and subject index of periodical articles "of permanent educational interest" currently appearing in approximately three hundred English language periodicals. These sources are published in the British Isles, together with certain internationally published periodicals. Arrangement is alphabetical within each section of the index. As of 1991, quarterly issues cumulate into an annual   publication. A significant number of articles cover education in the United States and some of those relate to higher education. Of value especially for its British and international perspective.

698. *Current Index to Journals in Education.* Phoenix, Ariz.: Oryx Pr., 1969-   . Semiannual.
A monthly guide, with semiannual cumulations, to, currently 760 major educational and education-related journals. A major index, it forms part of the Educational Resources Information Center (ERIC) system of indexes and abstracts. Issues are in four parts: the Main Entry section, with entries arranged by accession numbers, including complete citation, brief annotation, and assigned subject headings (Descriptors); the Subject Index, in which entries include abbreviated citations; the Author Index; and the highly useful Journal Contents Index listing the contents of journal issues covered in the index. Also includes a Source Journal Index arranged by title.

699. *Dissertation Abstracts International.* Ann Arbor, Mich.: Univ. Micro Films International, 1938-   . Monthly.
Provides abstracts of doctoral dissertations submitted to University Microfilms International by cooperating United States and selected foreign institutions of higher education. For earlier years, entries are arranged by subject field, then alphabetically by author. Entries include the title, order number, author, institution, the abstract, and other pertinent information. Each issue also includes author and subject indexes. Since the academic year 1966/67, the monthly abstracts are divided into an "A" section (humanities and social sciences) and a "B" section (sciences and engineering), with combined indexes in both issues. Since 1969/70 the index includes a "Keyword title index" and separate listings for the "A" and "B" sections. A Comprehensive Dissertation Index, 1861-1972 (Ann Arbor, Mich.: Xerox Univ. Micro Films, 1973) covers more than 417,000 dissertations in thirty-seven volumes. Cumulative author/subject indexes continue to be published. The value of the abstracting service to scholars and students of higher education is suggested by the inclusion of more than eight hundred dissertations in the Comprehensive Dissertation Index under the keyword "higher education."

700. *Education Index.* New York: H. W. Wilson Co., 1929/32-   . Annual.
A major author-subject index to, currently, four hundred English language periodicals and yearbooks. The principal portion of the index lists published articles in alphabetical order by titles under major headings and subheadings which are also arranged alphabetically. Coverage extends to all age-grade levels from preschool to higher and adult education, and

all subjects and fields. A second section includes book reviews in one
alphabetical order by author. Entries include book titles and citations
to review sources. The index is published monthly, except July and
August, with an annual cumulation.

701. *Education Literature, 1907-1932.* New York: Garland Publishing,
      1979. 25 vols. in 12.
A comprehensive index of nearly forty-four thousand citations to publications of the period. This is a reproduction of 117 issues of the
U.S. Office of Education's (formerly Bureau of Education) published
indexes to articles, books, conference proceedings, government publications, pamphlets, and other materials received in its library. All
aspects of education (American and foreign, practical and theoretical)
are represented from preschool to higher education. More than seven
hundred important journals are selectively indexed. The index, covering
a period not represented elsewhere, ceased with the introduction of the
Education Index (H.W. Wilson Co., 1929-   .) Entries are grouped into
general subject headings varying from volume to volume. Books and
conference proceedings frequently include lists of their contents. Brief
annotations are included with many entries. Unique to this reprint
edition is the addition of a cumulative index including a name index of
all proper nouns regardless if by or about the subject and a general
subject index. A gold mine of information for the historian of education.

702. Fabiano, Emily. *Index to Tests Used in Educational Dissertations.*
      Phoenix, Ariz.: Oryx Pr., 1989. 371p. ISBN 0-89774-288-5.
Includes more than fifty thousand test title occurrences since 1938 in
dissertations found in Dissertation Abstracts International (Ann Arbor,
Mich.: Univ. Microfilms Internat.) Only tests cited under the education
heading are included. Tests are arranged alphabetically by title then
by test population. Entries include title, test population, volume and
page number, location in Dissertation Abstracts International, and the
dissertation author. A substantial number of entries relate to higher
education (e.g. the test entry "College and University Environmental
Scale" includes ninety-two different test population applications). A
keyword/name index provides cross references for test authors, keywords
in test titles, or acronyms by which tests are known.

703. *Higher Education Abstracts.* Claremont, Calif.: Claremont Graduate
      School, 1965-   . Quarterly. ISSN 0748-4364.
A valuable abstracting service covering periodicals, books and monographs, proceedings and other documents related to higher education as
a field of study. Current issues regularly review about 120 higher education and related journals. Abstracts, which vary in length from one
to several paragraphs, provide research findings and exposition of other
higher education topics. Issues of the abstract, formerly known as College Student Personnel Abstracts, are divided into the following subject
categories: students, faculty, administration, and higher education.
These are further divided into useful subtopics; both are accessible via
the table of contents. Separate author and subject indexes.

704. *Office of Education Research Reports, 1956-65.* Washington, D.C.:
      Educational Research Information Center (ERIC), 1967. 2 vols.
These volumes describe more than one thousand research reports on projects sponsored by the Bureau of Research, Office of Education for the
years from 1956 to 1965. The reports appear as items in the Educational
Research Information Center (ERIC) microfiche documents collection, and
are each assigned unique accession (ED) numbers. These reports provide

information on a wide variety of topics useful to teachers, administrators, researchers, and others with an interest in education or higher education. An index volume consists of four points of access: authors, institutions, subjects, and report numbers. An abstract volume, arranged by accession (ED) numbers, includes for each report the citation, document purchase information, list of assigned subject headings, and a resume or abstract. For information about post-1965 reports, and additional information about ERIC, see the entry in this chapter under the title Resources in Education (Educational Resources Information Center, ERIC).

705. *PAIS International in Print.* New York: Public Affairs Information Service, 1915-   . Monthly. ISSN 1051-4015.

While much more than a guide to postsecondary education literature, PAIS is a highly useful source for finding information about higher education in non-higher education publications, including books, articles, government documents, pamphlets, and other sources. A recent annual cumulation lists sources under approximately sixty headings and subheadings directly related to higher education. Many other topics yield items useful to higher education study (e.g., Academic Freedom, Scientific Freedom, Faculty Participation, Black Students, etc.). This monthly source (with quarterly and annual cumulations) has been published since 1915, with some variation in title. It covers all subjects "that bear on contemporary public issues and the making and evaluating of public policy." Entries, some with brief annotations, are arranged alphabetically by topic and subtopic, giving such information as the document classification number for U.S. Government publications. Approximately seven thousand to eight thousand books per year and sixteen hundred periodicals are examined for inclusion. Particularly useful for policy study and governmental issues related to higher education.

706. Quay, Richard H. *Index to Anthologies on Postsecondary Education, 1960-1978.* Westport, Conn.: Greenwood Pr., 1980. 342p. ISBN 0-313-21272-4.

Provides author and subject access to 218 anthologies, covering a broad range of topics. Access to this source is facilitated by the table of contents which divides the anthologies into thirty-one broad subjects, including such topics as admissions, curriculum and instruction, the history of postsecondary education, legal issues, planning and students. Includes a list of anthologies covered, as well as author and subject indexes.

707. *Recent Publications of the Department of Education.* Washington, D.C.: Dept. of Ed., Office of Educational Research and Improvement, Office of Research, Educational Resources Information Center (ERIC), 1991-   . Quarterly.

A classified, annotated guide to selected, recent publications produced or sponsored by the Department of Education on topics of national importance. Documents covered include the field of higher education. All sources cited are indexed in the Educational Resources Information Center (ERIC) database, and are available from the ERIC Document Reproduction Service. Bibliographic citations include the ERIC "ED" documents number. Access is by means of the table of contents which is arranged by topic and subdivided by more specific topic areas. Titles, in truncated form, are arranged by specific topic areas which are listed alphabetically.

708. *Reporter: Clearinghouse of Studies on Higher Education.* (Nos. 1-7, Circulars 562, 611, 622, 680, 686, 720, 760) Washington, D.C.: U.S. Dept. of Health, Education, and Welfare, Office of Education,

1959-1965.
A classified, annotated list of studies received by the Clearinghouse of
Studies on Higher Education. Included are reports of research identified
and submitted by colleges and universities, and regional, state, and national agencies of higher education since 1950. Arrangement is alphabetical by college or university, organization, or state (if related to a
council, staff, commission, or other group affiliated with a state).
Concludes with a list of institutions and persons reporting the studies.

709. *Research into Higher Education Abstracts*. London, England: Society
     for Research into Higher Education, 1967-   . Triennial. ISSN
     0034-5326.
A classified guide to well over three hundred periodicals, focusing on
British higher education with coverage elsewhere as well. Of the international list of periodicals surveyed, about thirty percent have United
States imprints. Abstracts focus on organization and management, teaching and learning, staff and students, and information technology. Each
issue includes about two hundred citations, with paragraph-length annotations. Offers author and subject indexes with annual cumulations of
both.

710. *Resources in Education*. Washington, D.C.: U.S. Dept. of Education,
     Office of Educational Research and Improvement, 1966-   . Monthly.
An abstracting journal that cites and describes a wide range of published
and unpublished sources comprising the Educational Resources Information
Center (ERIC) documents collection. Each issue covers more than one
thousand items, including: books, theses and dissertations, guides, bibliographies, research findings, speeches, and other sources. Currently,
sixteen clearinghouses acquire and select documents for inclusion into
the ERIC system, now numbering substantially more than three hundred
thousand items. Entries in the monthly abstracts, arranged by document
item (ED) numbers, include a complete citation, purchase price (paper
copy or microfiche), list of subject headings, and a document summary
(abstract). Issues also include a number of indexes: subject, author,
institution, publication type, and clearinghouse ERIC ED item number
cross references. Issued separately are semiannual indexes and a
commercially published annual index (Oryx Pr.). Resources in Education
is an essential tool for research and study related to education and
higher education. This work was initially entitled Research in
Education, and reported results of studies funded by the Office of Education. For pre-1966 reports of funded research projects, see in this
chapter Office of Education Research Reports, 1956-65: Indexes, Resumes
(Educational Research Information Center (ERIC)).

711. *Social Sciences Citation Index*. Philadelphia: Institute for Sci-
     entific Information, 1969-   . Three issues per year. ISSN 0091-
     3707.
An international, multidisciplinary index currently covering approximately forty-seven hundred journals and a limited number of monographic series. It appears in four parts: 1) Citation Index (alphabetical list of
primary authors cited during the period covered by the index, with cited
works arranged chronologically along with citing authors; 2) Source Index
(alphabetical list of citing authors, with a full description of sources
followed by listed references); 3) Corporate Index (in two sections: Geographic and Organization, with relevant, current sources arranged alphabetically under each); and 4) Permuterm Subject Index (alphabetical list
of primary terms, followed by co-terms, along with the author of the item
whose title includes the primary and co-terms. This is an important
source, covering well over one hundred journals in education and

educational research. A recent permuterm index included more than five hundred co-terms associated with the primary term "college." Includes both annual and five-year cumulative indexes.

712. *State Education Journal Index and Educators' Guide to Periodicals Research Strategy.* Westminster, Colo.: State Education Journal Index and Educators' Guide to Periodicals, 1963-   . Semiannual.
Describes the contents of more than 130 state education journals and newsletter of local interest. Emphasis is on periodicals that are not indexed in other standard indexes to educational literature. Arrangement is alphabetical by subject; under each, articles are listed alphabetically by title. Brief annotations are included with titles that are misleading. Each issue of the index includes a useful guide to searching periodical literature.

SPECIAL WORKS

Administration

713. *Educational Administration Abstracts.* Newburg Park, Calif.: Corwin Pr., 1966-   . Quarterly. ISSN 0013-1601.
A classified guide to professional books, articles and other sources of interest to administrators, educators, and students at all levels of education. Focus is on such areas as management, personnel, curriculum and teaching, and community-governmental matters. Issues currently cover about one hundred periodicals, with well over two hundred entries providing complete citations and paragraph-length summaries. This source includes author and subject indexes, with annual cumulations of both.

History

714. McCarthy, Joseph M. *An International List of Articles on the History of Education Published in Non-Educational Serials, 1965-1974.* (Garland Reference Library of Social Sciences, Vol. 33) New York: Garland Publishing, 1977. 228p. ISBN 0-8240-9909-5.
Cites 2,817 articles, without annotations, in 521 English and foreign language periodicals. An introductory chapter lists articles with focus on the ancient world. Following chapters are arranged by continent then by country. More than eight hundred articles cover the United States, with many of these relating to higher education. Includes an author index. While limited in coverage, the emphasis on non-educational sources makes this a unique source for the student and scholar.

Law

715. Blackwell, Thomas E. *The College Law Digest, 1935-1970.* Washington, D.C.: Nat. Assn. of Coll. and Univ. Attorneys, 1974. 256p.
An index to reported cases, for college and university administrators and attorneys. This work summarizes litigation, legislation, and governmental regulations (both federal and state) over a thirty-five year span, and includes relevant citations to materials in other publications. Contents are organized under more than two hundred subject headings and subheadings. Access is provided by the table of contents and a table of cases arranged alphabetically by case name. This source updates a 1936 edition of the same title, which covered the period from 1819, and was published by the Carnegie Foundation for the advancement of teaching.

It consolidates works by the Carnegie Foundation covering the periods 1936 to 1940 and 1941 to 1945; another volume covering the years 1946 through 1950, published by Columbia University Press (1952); and an additional issue covering cases after 1950, which was published in 1964 by Interstate Printers and Publishers. A subsequent work, published in 1976 by Illinois State University, brings case coverage up to that date.

716. *College and University Reporter.* Chicago: Commerce Clearing House, 1965-1982. Loose-leaf.
A legal service - now discontinued - updated periodically and supplemented with a weekly report on developments in the law. This source provides coverage of federal programs of interest to college and university administrators, faculties, students, and donors. Contents are arranged by subject, each identified by a tab guide. It includes summaries of court decisions, and other information, with a table of cases and topical index.

717. *Deskbook Encyclopedia of American School Law.* Rosemount, Minn.: Informational Research Systems, 1981-   . Annual.
An "encyclopedic compilation of state and federal appellate court decisions which affect education." Case summaries (along with a citation to the court from which a decision has been issued) are arranged by subject with subtopics. Subject chapters range from accidents, injuries and death, to employment practices, freedom of speech, and student rights. Cases cited include public, private, elementary, secondary, and higher education. In addition to a table of cases covered, the work includes a classified list of law review articles, a classified guide to U.S. Supreme Court decisions, and a subject index.

718. *Education Law.* New York: Matthew Bender, 1984-   . 4v. ISBN 0-8205-1397-0.
A loose-leaf service, with updates, covering education with emphasis on topics having their basis in federal constitutional or statutory law, along with coverage of topics related to specific cases of wide interest. The work is in two parts: Part 1 covers the law in fourteen volumes, representing all levels of education. Chapter topics encompass issues of church and state, conditions of employment, students and curriculum, finance, and litigation. Part 2 consists of forms, tables of selected state statutes, a subject index, general statute tables, and a table of cases mentioned.

719. *Specialty Law Digest: Education.* Blaine, Minn.: Specialty Digest Publications, 1981-1987. Monthly. ISSN 0275-2107.
For attorneys, administrators, and educators at all levels of education. Issues include a case survey section, consisting of single-paragraph summaries of decisions, designed for quick scanning of the month's decisions. Also provided is a selected educational law bibliography of articles published in law reviews and journals, and a general commentary section. An outline of education law facilitates the location of legal rulings by subject. Includes indices for colleges and universities, schools, as well as a table of cases.

720. *U.S. Supreme Court Education Cases.* 2d ed. Rosemont, Minn.: Data Research, Inc., 1991. 238p. ISBN 0-939675-26-9.
Includes more than two hundred cases representing all levels of education. Case summaries are arranged chronologically in six chapters covering Desegregation, Private Schools, Student Rights, Employment, School District Operations, and Special Education and the Handicapped. Chapters are further divided by subtopics. While coverage extends from 1896 to

1991, more than one half of the cases were decided during the 1970s and 1980s. Each subject section is preceded by a brief introduction. Summaries range from a paragraph to a page in length and include full legal citations. Appendices include a listing of articles and amendments to the U.S. Constitution of interest to educators and a glossary. Access to case summaries is by means of a table of contents, table of cases, defendant-plaintiff table, and a general subject index.

721. *West's Education Law Digest.* St. Paul, Minn.: West Publishing Co., 1982-   . Irregular.
Digests are cumulative and published as required. They provide access to cases found in <u>West's Education Law Reporter</u>. The <u>Reporter</u> includes the complete text of education-related cases decided in federal and state appellate courts. They represent all levels of instructional institutions. Periodically published <u>Digests</u> provide cumulative indexes to the <u>Reporters</u>. Indexes include an alphabetical listing by author of articles and case commentaries, table of cases, separate topical key number outlines for colleges and universities and schools, and a key number <u>Digest</u> containing all <u>Digest</u> paragraphs prepared from the opinions and arranged alphabetically by assigned paragraph topics.

722. *West's Education Law Reporter.* St. Paul, Minn.: West Publishing Co., 1982-   . Biweekly.
Covers education cases decided in the United States Supreme Court, United States Courts of Appeals, and United States District Courts. Biweekly issues are cumulated into five or six bound volumes per year, with a separate annual index volume. Higher education is well represented with subject coverage ranging from constitutional and statutory provisions and property matters, to tenure and termination cases, and decisions related to students. Case summaries, which include texts of decisions, constitute the major part of each reporter. The summary section is preceded by an alphabetically arranged table of cases, selected articles, and selected, detailed case reports. At the conclusion of the work, brief case digest summaries are arranged by topic and Wests' Key Number for ready subject searching. These digest summaries include case and statutory citations and case names. The user notes the case name and refers to it in the table of cases, to find the case report.

723. Zirkel, Perry A. and Richardson, Sharon N. *A Digest of Supreme Court Decisions Affecting Education.* 2d ed. Bloomington, Ind.: Phi Delta Kappa Educational Foundation, 1988. 204p. ISBN 0-87367-436-7.
A comprehensive, concise, ready-reference source of 252 cases summarized through March 1988. This work covers both public and private education, from kindergarten through grade twelve. Higher education is included where cases have a direct impact on staff and students. Seven chapters cover school district governance and finance, church-state relations, student rights and responsibilities, employee rights and responsibilities, discrimination, civil rights, and illustrations of procedural prerequisities for obtaining rulings on merit. An appendix lists selected federal constitutional provisions. Provides both a table of cases and a subject index.

7.

BIOGRAPHICAL SOURCES

INTRODUCTION

Among the more difficult tasks for a librarian or researcher is that of finding background information about a scholar or college administrator. Public relations people encounter similar difficulties in preparing biographical sketches for brochures, lectures and programs or speech introductions. The fact is there are few single works to which one can turn for systematic and comprehensive coverage of past and present members of the higher education community. Sources which are available are usually limited in some fundamental way: by time period covered, discipline or field, or prominence of the subject.

This chapter describes fourteen such biographical works generally available in libraries serving those with a need or interest in education or higher education. Of the titles included, some function as secondary sources in that they provide citations to other works. Others contain the information sought. As reference works, none treat their subjects in great depth, an approach for which book-length biographies are better suited.

A less obvious distinction that needs to be made here is that between biographical dictionaries and biographical directories. The latter, offering little more than names, titles and addresses have been placed in the chapter covering directories. We have included in this chapter biographical dictionaries: those works which enumerate, often in abbreviated form, basic facts, activities, and accomplishments of their subjects' lives and careers, sometimes including photographs and lists of publications.

Users will find the chapter divided into four parts: General Works, Academic Staff, Administrators, and Faculty.

GENERAL WORKS

724. *Biography Index: A Cumulative Index to Biographical Material in Books and Magazines.* New York: H. W. Wilson Co., 1946/1949 - . Biennial. ISSN 0006-3053.

A guide to biographical information about Americans appearing in periodicals and books of individual and collective biography, and biographical information appearing in non-biographical sources. Materials covered include obituaries, collected letters, diaries, memoirs, juvenile literature, book reviews, and bibliographies. The body of the work consists of individual entries arranged alphabetically by last name. This is followed by a list of entries arranged by profession or occupation. The 1988-1990 volume includes entries for more than 360 top college administrators and 1,550 college professors and instructors. Introductory sections list periodicals and composite books analyzed. The work is published quarterly, with annual and biennial cumulations. In earlier years, cumulations were triennial.

725. *Contemporary Authors: A Bio-Bibliographical Guide to Current Writers in Fiction, General Nonfiction, Poetry, Journalism, Drama, Motion Pictures, Television, and Other Fields.* Detroit: Gale Research Co., 1962- .

A non-selective source of biographical and bibliographical information about living and deceased authors "whose books are issued by commercial, risk publishers or by university presses. Authors of books published only by known vanity or author-subsidized firms are ordinarily not included." There are three entry types: sketches, brief entries and obituaries. Entries follow a standard format covering personal information, career, awards and honors, published works, works in progress, sidelights (personal anecdotes), avocational interests, and biographical sources. The series is divided into: the Original Volumes, now numbering 134; New Revision Series, updating information in previous volumes; Permanent Series, consisting of updated listings for deceased and inactive authors removed from original volumes 9-36 when these were revised: now two volumes only.

A very useful source, as many college and university staff and faculty writers are among the entries. A cumulative index is published separately and distributed with every even-numbered volume.

726. *Who's Who in America.* Wilmette, Ill.: Marquis Who's Who, 1899-. 2 vols. Annual.

Currently providing biographical sketches of nearly eighty thousand "outstanding" individuals in Canada and Mexico as well as the United States. Long honored, this source covers prominent individuals in business, government, journalism, art, diplomacy, law, science, medicine, music, and education. Among educators represented are key administrators of major colleges and universities. They include presidents, provosts, deans, and selected department heads, as well as state university system administrators. Also included are professors who have made significant research contributions in their fields. Entries are alphabetical by last name. They cover education, career, awards, memberships, military record, professional certifications, religion, political affiliation, published works, and mailing addresses. The second volume includes a retiree index, necrology, and biographies in Marquis Who's Who regional and topical directories.

SPECIAL WORKS

Academic Staff

727. Cook, Robert C. *Presidents and Professors in American Colleges and Universities.* v. 1, 1935-36. New York: Robert C. Cook Co., 1935. 680p.
An illustrated biographical dictionary of administrators and teachers in 1,040 of the 1,170 accredited institutions of the era. The work is not intended to be all inclusive, but rather to provide a cross section of men and women in higher education. Including more than three thousand entries, this work covers school officials and teachers, librarians, officers of educational and other foundations and organizations, and publishers. A special feature is the inclusion of a substantial number of photographs of the then living subjects.

728. Cook, Robert C. *Who's Who in American Education.*   vols. 1-23. Hattiesburg, Miss.:   Who's Who in American Education, 1928-1968. Biennial.
A biographical source of eminent, living, university and college professors, superintendents and principals of schools, state and national school officials, librarians, and others.   Well over ten thousand sketches are arranged in alphabetical order by subjects' last names. Not included are college and university presidents, deans, and professors and others in scientific fields.   This group is covered in the author's Presidents and Deans of American Colleges and Universities (Who's Who in American Education, 1933-65), and Leaders in American Science (Who's Who in American Education, 1953/54- 1968/69). Entries are brief, providing essential personal facts, along with titles of dissertations and other publications. Photographs are included in all but the last issue.

729. *Leaders in Education.* 5th ed. New York: Bowker, 1974. 1,309p. ISBN 0-8352-0699-8.
First published in 1932, this work provides nearly seventeen thousand biographical sketches of officers and deans of accredited institutions of higher education, as well as covering professors of education, directors and staff of educational research institutes, state and provincial commissioners of education and selected staff, leaders in public and private school fields, officers of educated-related foundations, officials of the Office of Education and major educational associations, and selected authors. Entries, in alphabetical order, are brief and condensed covering the same points found in various "Who's Who" publications. To facilitate access, separate geographical and subject-specialty indexes are included.

730. Ohles, John F. *Biographical Dictionary of American Education.* Westport, Conn.: Greenwood Pr., 1978. 3 vols. ISBN 0-8371-9893-3.
A ready reference source including approximately 1,665 persons making contributions to American education from colonial times to 1976. Included are administrators and educators at state and national levels, as well as leaders in subject fields. Represented are persons "who had been engaged in education, were eminent, and had reached the age of sixty, had retired, or had died by January 1, 1975." Special effort was made to include women and minority groups.   Each sketch provides a short description of the subject's education, employment, contributions to education, and participation in professional activities, and selected reference works. Also included is other personal information such as date and place of birth, etc. All levels of education are covered.

Entries are alphabetical by last name. Vol. 3 includes appendices listing subjects' place of birth, state of major services, field of work, chronology of birth years, important dates in American education, and a general index.

Administration

731. Cook, Robert C. *Presidents and Deans of American Colleges and Universities. 1933-1965.* Nashville, Tenn.: Who's Who in American Education, 1933-1965.
This work has appeared eight times, with slight variation in title (1933, 1952, 1955, 1958, 1960, 1962, 1964, 1966). Each volume provides biographical sketches of executive heads and other leaders of American institutions of higher education. The eighth volume includes approximately eight thousand entries. Coverage changes from issue to issue. In 1955 the scope expanded to include chairmen and board presidents. In 1958 college and university deans were added. In 1962 trustees and chairmen of boards were dropped. Coverage is alphabetical by last name. Sketches, many including photographs, are brief, reporting subjects' education, employment, publications, and other essential personal information. Earlier volumes include a geographic index. The series is continued with an edition entitled <u>Who's Who in American College and University Administration</u> (Crowell-Collier, 1971).

732. Cook, Robert C. and Carroll, Eleanor A. *Presidents of American Colleges and Universities.* Nashville, Tenn.: Who's Who in American Education, 1952. 244p.
Includes biographical data on 1,433 presidents of colleges, universities, teachers' colleges, junior colleges, and normal schools. The first volume of this title was published in 1933 (Robert C. Cook Co., 1933). Most entries include photographs of the subjects. Among items covered are: occupation of the subject's father, the subject's ancestral history, hobbies and recreations, and names of other biographical directories and reference books in which the subject is listed. Arrangement is alphabetical by last name. Includes a geographical index arranged by states and by colleges and universities.

733. Cook, Robert C. *Trustees and Presidents of American Colleges and Universities.* Nashville, Tenn.: Who's Who in American Education, 1955. 310p.
This work continues the author's <u>Presidents of American Colleges and Universities</u>. Vol. 1 (1933-34) and Vol. 2 (1953-54). It includes biographical sketches, and, in many cases, photographs of approximately four hundred chairmen or presidents of governing boards, as well as 1,462 presidents or executive heads of American colleges, universities, teachers' colleges, junior colleges, and normal schools. An additional 395 entries include only subjects' names and addresses. Sketches include occupation of the subject's father, as well as other personal and professional accomplishments usually found in similar biographical directories. Useful as well is the inclusion of other biographical and reference works in which the subject is listed. Arrangement is alphabetical by last name. A geographical index is provided for presidents - not trustees. It is arranged by state, then by institution, and president.

734. *Who's Who in American College and University Administration, 1970-1971.* New York: Crowell-Collier Educational Corp., 1971. 681p.
Provides biographical information on about eleven thousand administrators

of higher education.   Included are presidents, deans, librarians,
bursars, and other key personnel. Entries are alphabetical by last name,
and include data that have become standard in such biographical sources.
An index is arranged by state, with subjects in alphabetical order under
institutions. This work continues Robert C. Cook's _Presidents and Deans
of American Colleges and Universities_ (Who's Who in American Education,
1933-1965). In contrast with the Cook publications, this work does not
include photographs of the subjects.

Faculty

735. American Council of Learned Societies. _Recipients of Fellowships
      and Grants, 1930-1962: A Biographical Directory._ Washington,
      D.C.: Amer. Council of Learned Societies, 1963. 260p.
Provides biographical sketches of recipients of fifteen different awards
programs with emphasis on study in the humanities.   Arrangement is
alphabetical by last name. Entries, similar to those found in most
sources of the who's who variety, are short and include such items as
publications, and membership in professional or scholarly associations.

736. _American Men and Women of Science: A Biographical Directory of
      Today's Leaders in Physical, Biological, and Related Sciences._ 18th
      ed. New Providence, N.J.: R.R. Bowker Co., 1992. 8 vols. ISBN
      0-8352-3074-0 set.
Published since 1906, this source currently provides information about
nearly 123,000 engineers and scientists, 7,021 of whom are included for
the first time. They represent 171 subject specialties from nine major
fields: Agricultural and Forest Sciences; Chemistry; Computer Sciences;
Engineering; Environmental, Sanitary, and Marine Sciences; Mathematics;
Medical and Health Sciences, Physics and Astronomy, and other fields.
Individuals must be living and "have made significant contributions in
their field." Entries include vital statistics, field of specialty,
education, honorary degrees, professional experience, awards,
memberships, research information, and mailing address. Subjects are
listed alphabetically in the first seven volumes. Volume eight includes
a discipline index arranged alphabetically by State and subject name.
The introduction to volume one lists major honors and awards recipients
and statistical distributions of the subjects. For an index to the first
fourteen editions, see _American Men and Women of Science, Editions 1-14:
Cumulative Index_ (New York: R.R. Bowker, 1983).

737. _Directory of American Scholars._ 8th ed. New York: R.R. Bowker
      Co., 1982. 4 vols. ISBN 0-8352-1476-1 set.
First published in 1942, this work provides profiles of more than 37,500
United States and Canadian scholars currently active in teaching,
research, and publishing. The work is arranged in four subject volumes:
Vol. 1: History; Vol. 2: English, Speech, and Drama; Vol. 3: Foreign
Languages, Linguistics, and Philology; Vol. 4: Philosophy, Religion, and
Law. Entries, arranged alphabetically, include primary discipline(s),
vital statistics, education, honorary degrees, past and present
professional experience, concurrent positions, memberships, honors and
awards, research interest, selected publications, and mailing address.
Each volume includes a geographic index. Volume 4 contains an index to
names in all volumes.

8.

COMPUTERIZED DATABASES

INTRODUCTION

This chapter brings together a selection of computerized databases relating to higher education, including bibliographic, full-text, and statistical compilations. These databases are available from commercial vendors, commercial or non-commercial producers, and agencies of the federal government. Except for a few of them, these files are kept current.

The databases are grouped in nine categories. These categories include: General Works, Abstracts and Indexes, Colleges, Disabilities, Economic Factors, Faculty and Staff, Grants and Scholarships, Libraries, and Students. Entries within each category are arranged alphabetically according to the database name or title. Included as well is the name and location of the producer, date of publication, and, where applicable, the frequency of publication.

Annotations provided for the databases are derived from information found in vendor catalogs and other selected sources. The annotations are generally descriptive, indicating the databases' purpose, scope, and special features. They are not meant to be users' manuals for searching the data files. Consequently, no special effort is made to describe searching options or techniques, unless such information was readily found in the reviewing literature from which the databases were selected. Also omitted are vendor names (other than producers), and information concerning the format in which the database is offered (i.e., CD-ROM, online, magnetic tape, etc.), information concerning vendors, formats, pricing, etc., is available in a number of current directories. Among these are: <u>CD-ROMs in Print</u> (Westport, Conn.: Meckler, 1987-   ); <u>Computer-Readable Data Bases</u>, now an annual printed guide distributed by Knowledge Industry Publications, White Plains, New York; and the <u>Directory of Online Databases</u> (Santa Monica, Calif.: Cuadra Associates, 1979-   .)

Our purpose, in this chapter, is to make users aware of the substantial amount of data available pertaining to higher education in electronic database form. To that end we provide this selected list.

GENERAL WORKS

738. *AV Online*. Albuquerque, N. Mex.: Nat. Info. Center for Educational
Media, Access Information, Inc., 1964-   . Quarterly.
The NICEM Center builds the bibliographic database from producers catalogs, as well as the Library of Congress, media centers and libraries.
The database covers non-print materials for all educational levels, from
preschool to graduate and teacher education as well as industrial training. All traditional media types are included. The file has approximately five hundred thousand records. Each record includes a source
citation, abstract, directory information and names of contact persons.
Data retrieval is by descriptors, keywords, producers and titles, as well
as by media code, grade level, and production year.

739. *Classification System for Postsecondary Education Courses*. Washington, D.C.: U.S. Dept. of Education, Nat. Center for Education
Statistics, 1986.
A datafile that uses an eight-digit code to identify courses of study
gathered from catalogues of undergraduate and non-collegiate institutions. This database lists about 21,500 courses. The system is developed for use with the Longitudinal Studies Program of the Center.

740. *Education Update*. Washington, D.C.: Heritage Foundation. 1983-
. Quarterly.
Corresponding to the print source of the same title, this full-text database allows users to follow trends and developments in education policy.
Emphasis is placed on issues addressed by the National Education Association such as testing of teachers and students, handicapped, finances and
other social issues. Access is by keywords.

741. *EDVENT*. Waltham, Mass.: Timeplace Inc., n.d. Weekly.
A database of educational events and continuing education seminars offered by over seven thousand organizations in U.S. and Canada. It also
lists educational media such as films, video and audio tapes. Essentially, it serves as a calendar of events for current and future conferences.
Coverage includes the current year and following three years.

742. *Institutional Characteristics (IPEDS)*. Washington, D.C.: U.S.
Dept. of Education, Nat. Center for Education Statistics, Inte-
grated Postsecondary Education Data System, 1986-   . Annual.
This series collects data for higher education, including technical and
vocational institutions. The higher education portion continues the
Higher Education General Information Survey (HEGIS) series, Institutional
Characteristics of Colleges and Universities. It is an annual count of
all private and public institutions of higher education as listed in the
Center's Education Directory: Colleges and Universities, and covers the
period from 1969/1970 through 1985/1986. When IPEDS expanded this
series in 1986 to include postsecondary institutions that offer
technical and vocational education, "Colleges and Universities" was
dropped from the title Institutional Characteristics. Data collected for
the technical institutions are obtained through a sample survey and thus
subject to sampling error. Apart from directory information such as
name, address, telephone and congressional district, this data file also
identifies type of control (public or private), level of offerings, enrollments, program types, accreditation and sex of student body.

743. *Integrated Postsecondary Education Data System (IPEDS).* Washington, D.C.: U.S. Dept. of Education, Office of Educational Research and Development, Nat. Center for Education Statistics, 1986-   .
This database is built on several surveys of all postsecondary institutions. It replaces and supplements the Higher Education Information Survey (HEGIS). The latter was implemented in 1966 reflecting annual data from all institutions listed in the Center's <u>Education Directory: Colleges and Universities</u>. IPEDS data for technical and vocational institutions are collected through sample surveys and are subject to sampling error. The following survey series provide the principal data components of the integrated system. Institutional characteristics, fall enrollment, fall enrollment in occupationally specific programs, completions, finance, staff, salaries of full-time instructional faculty, and academic libraries. Such data are annually presented in the <u>Digest of Education Statistics</u> and <u>Condition of Education</u>, among others.

744. *Inventory of College and University Physical Facilities (HEGIS).* Washington, D.C.: U.S. Dept. of Education, Nat. Center for Education Statistics, Higher Education General Information System, 1966-1979. Irregular.
Part of the Higher Education General Information Survey (HEGIS), this inventory includes data on the number of square feet of physical plant by type and function of room, organizational unit, and instructional program. The 1978 survey collected information on accessibility of facilities and programs to handicapped (as required under section 504 of the Rehabilitation Act of 1973), as well as on enrollment of, and housing for, handicapped students.

ABSTRACTS AND INDEXES

745. *AIM/ARM.* Columbus, Ohio: Nat. Center for Research in Vocational Ed., 1967-1976.
A small bibliographic database of monographs on vocational and technical education. Records include title, bibliographic information, abstract, and subject terms as provided by the <u>Thesaurus of ERIC Descriptors</u>. Useful mainly for historical research.

746. *College Press Service National Campus Classified.* Denver, Colo.: College Press Service, 1983-   . Weekly.
A full-text database that includes state and federal government reports, news releases, and articles. It serves primarily to track college trends, headline news on campuses, legislation affecting higher education, and court decisions. Access is by subject and descriptive title keywords.

747. *Dissertation Abstracts Online.* Ann Arbor, Mich.: University Microfilms International, 1861-   . Monthly.
A bibliographic database of masters theses and doctoral dissertations of virtually all American institutions and some Canadian, European and British institutions. Excluded are professional and honorary degrees. Abstracts are included since 1988. It has over one and one-half million records which are so structured as to provide multiple access by subject keywords, descriptors, title, author, institution name, year, as well as by advisor, degree, language and ISBN number.

748. *Education Daily.* Alexandria, Va: Capitol Publications Inc., n.d. Current Month.
This full-text database helps to track U.S. government actions affecting

education. Data are collected from congressional hearings, budget proposals, appropriations, documents, newsletters and court cases. The
database also includes sections of the Congressional Record and Federal
Register that deal with education. It is a shortened version of the
print source. Daily update.

749. *Education Index*. Bronx, N.Y.: H.W. Wilson Co., 1983-   . Twice
     weekly.
Corresponding to the print source of the same title, this bibliographic
database indexes over three hundred English language journals. The broad
range of subjects spans, but is not restricted to, classroom computer
trends, physical education, teacher evaluation, literacy, multiculturalism, and funding. Citations are retrieved by descriptor, subject, author, title keyword, publication type, language, periodical title, among
others.

750. *Education Research Forum*. Washington, D.C.: American Educational
     Research Assn., 1983-   . Daily.
A user-generated full-text database of articles submitted by educators.
These are non-refereed reports of studies and reviews of statistical
packages. While it is primarily used by school teachers and administrators as an electronic bulletin board for exchange of ideas, the service
is open to scholars of higher education. Articles are included as soon
as they are submitted. Access is by keyword.

751. *Educational Testing Service Test Collections Database*. Princeton,
     N.J.: Educational Testing Service, 1950-   . Quarterly.
This is a major bibliographic database of currently available standard
educational tests developed in the United States, Canada and Australia.
Included are tests in psychology, counseling, business, and education.
These tests deal with the evaluation of achievement, aptitude, attitude,
personality, skills, and measurements. Tests available from the ERIC
database are also found here. The records include abstracts and can be
retrieved by major/minor descriptors, author, title, keywords, year,
grade level, target population, identifiers, among others.

752. *ERIC*. Washington, D.C.: Educational Resources Information Center
     (ERIC), Office of Educational Research and Improvement (OERI), U.S.
     Department of Education. 1966-   . Monthly.
A major comprehensive bibliographic database of research reports, dissertations, government publications and journal articles. It corresponds
to two print sources: Resources in Education and Current Index to Journals in Education. The database is now available on CD-ROM as well as
on tape. Searchable items include abstracts, authors, titles, descriptors, keywords, accession numbers, publication years and types. The file
is approaching one million records and is updated monthly.

753. *Exceptional Child Education Resources*. Reston, Va.: Council for
     Exceptional Children, 1966-   . Monthly.
Concerned with education of the handicapped and the gifted, this bibliographic database covers published and unpublished literature. It includes citations and abstracts to books, journal articles, teaching materials, reports and government publications. Since only one half of the
citations are duplicated in ERIC, this serves as a complement to the ERIC
database. The file has close to eighty thousand records and is updated
monthly. Access is by descriptors as used in ERIC, subject keywords,
author, title, language, publication year and type.

754. *Mental Measurements Yearbook (MMYD)*. Lincoln: Buros Institute of

Mental Measurements, Univ. of Nebraska - Lincoln, 1974-   .
Monthly.
A major full text database covering reviews of educational tests and
psychological measurements. It corresponds to the print sources, Eighth
Mental Measurements Yearbook (1978), Ninth Mental Measurements Yearbook
(1985), and Supplement to the Ninth Mental Measurements Yearbook (1988).
The file is relatively small with approximately two thousand records,
Access is by fifteen fields including subjects, scores, reviewers, texts
of reviews or tests, test names, test purposes, and target populations.
The database is very useful to counselors and psychologists.

755. *Resources in Vocational Education (RIVE)*. Berkeley: Univ. of California at Berkeley, Graduate School of Education, 1978-   . Quarterly.
A bibliographic database with abstracts of state and federally administered programs and projects. These include career education, innovative
and development projects, vocational education, curriculum development,
and research, as well as end products from projects. Access is by subject terms from the Thesaurus of ERIC Descriptors, as well as by funding
source, state, congressional district, proposal number, title, author,
agency and educational level. Also includes directory information about
project coordinators, funding sources and amounts of grants. There are
over twenty thousand records.

756. *Vocational Education Curriculum Materials (VECM)*. Berkeley: Univ.
of California at Berkeley, Graduate School of Education, 1979-
. Quarterly.
Similar in format to its other product, Resources in Vocational Education
(RIVE), this database covers print and non-print curriculum materials.
Each record includes the source title, complete bibliographic information, abstract, directory information and educational level. Searchable
by subject terms from the ERIC Thesaurus, records can also be retrieved
by agency, keyword, student target population, title, state, author,
education level and format (print/non-print materials). The database
includes several thousand records.

SPECIAL WORKS

Colleges

757. *College Board's Annual Survey of Colleges*. New York: College Entrance Examination Board (CEEB), 1940-   . Annual.
A data file covering more than three thousand postsecondary institutions.
Entries include tuition, directory information, programs, financial aid,
and student profiles. Such data form the basis of the Board's interac-
tive program, entitled "Estimating your Eligibility," which provides analysis of financial needs. Several print sources are produced from these
data: College Times, The College Handbook, and The College Cost Book.

758. *College Handbook*. New York: College Entrance Examination Board
(CEEB), 19 -   . Annual.
This is a full-text database of guidance information for college bound
students. Data are based on the Board's Annual Survey of Colleges. De-
scriptive information about two- and four-year institutions is provided.
A print version is produced annually.

759. *Directory of U.S. Colleges on Disk*. Madison, Ohio: Gabriel Publishing, n.d. Biennial.

Available in MS-DOS and Macintosh versions, this data diskette provides current information on about twenty-eight hundred institutions, including their addresses, telephone numbers, enrollments and highest degrees awarded.

760. *Educational Directory.* Shelton, Conn.: Market Data Retrieval, Dun & Bradstreet Corp., n.d.
This directory provides profiles of all schools, universities, and public libraries in the U.S. In addition to addresses, names of top administrators are identified together with enrollment size, microcomputer use, budgets and expenditures. While it targets primarily the business sector for market analysis, it is also useful for anyone seeking comparative data on higher education institutions. Updated semi-annually.

761. *Electronic Directory of Education.* Shelton, Conn.: Market Data Retrieval, n.d.
Formerly known as D & B Dun's Electronic Directory of Education, this database provides names, addresses, and telephone numbers of some three thousand schools, colleges and universities, and public libraries in the U.S. Administrators, counselors, principals and librarians are identified. Includes information about budgets, enrollments, microcomputer availability, etc. The file has approximately 150,000 records, and is updated semiannually, with information verified though a telephone survey.

762. *Guidance Information System (GIS).* Hanover, N.H.: Houghton Mifflin Co., 1969-   . Semi-annual.
A full-text database of information on college selection, scholarship and career opportunities. There are six separate files covering financial aid, two-year colleges, four-year colleges, graduate and professional schools, careers, and occupations in the armed services. It is updated semi-annually and available in tape and diskette formats.

763. *Peterson's Gradline.* Princeton, N.J.: Peterson's Guides, Inc., n.d. Annual.
Compared with its print version, Peterson's Annual Guide/Graduate Study, the database provides more information on graduate fields of study. Covering accredited institutions in the U.S. and Canada, information includes college profiles, their administrative units and programs, and directory and statistical data.

Disabilities

764. *Education of the Handicapped.* Alexandria, Va.: Capitol Publications, Inc., 1988-   . Biweekly.
This database specializes in both state and federal legislation and regulations governing the handicapped population in education. It also encompasses funding, research, programs, litigation, and the Education for All Handicapped Children Act, PL 94-142.

Economic Factors

765. *APPA Comparative Costs and Staffing Report.* Waldorf, Md.: Assn. of Physical Plant Administrators of Universities and Colleges, 1974-   . Annual.
Provides a profile of maintenance costs, needs, operations, salaries,

energy consumption and staffing at campus facilities. Data are collected from four hundred institutions.

766. *Federal Obligations to Colleges and Universities and Selected Non-profit Institutions.* Washington, D.C.: Nat. Science Foundation, 1965- . Annual.
The sole source of data on federal obligations to individual institutions of higher education for research and development. Obligations are defined as funds awarded one year that could be spent in later years. These include awards for both science/engineering and other activities, fellowship/training grants, and money for construction of research facilities. Data are gathered from fifteen federal agencies and include obligations to other non-profit agencies as well as colleges and universities. All are identified by name and state. An important source for comparative data.

767. *Finance Survey (IPEDS).* Washington, D.C.: U.S. Dept. of Education, Nat. Center for Education Statistics, Integrated Postsecondary Education Data System, 1986- . Annual.
This series continues and expands the HEGIS' <u>Financial Statistics of Institutions of Higher Education</u> (1965-87) surveys. The survey instruments for data collection have undergone several changes but comparability with earlier surveys is maintained. This series aims to monitor the financial condition of postsecondary education. Some representative data are Pell Grant revenues (since 1982); revenues by source such as federal, state and local governments, tuition, and endowments; revenues by state and source; revenues received and endowment funds of one hundred institutions in rank order; and expenditures by instruction, research, libraries, etc.; and expenditures by state.

768. *Higher Education Price Indexes (HEPI).* Washington, D.C.: Research Associates of Washington, 1961- . Annual.
Covers salaries, fringe benefits and over one hundred items of equipment, supplies and services purchased. Such price changes provide a measure of the inflation and purchasing power of higher education institutions.

769. *A National Comparison: Tuition and Required Fees.* Olympia, Wash.: Washington Higher Education Coordinating Board, n.d. Annual.
Provides comparative state data on two- and four-year public institutions. In addition to tuition costs, data are collected for resident charges and student fees for both graduate and undergraduate students. Similar data are collected by the U.S. National Center for Education Statistics in conjunction with the IPEDS Institutional Characteristics Survey.

Faculty and Staff

770. *Fall Staff Survey (IPEDS).* Washington, D.C. U.S. Dept. of Education, Nat. Center for Education Statistics, Integrated Postsecondary Education Data System, 1987/88- . Biennial.
Contains statistical data on distribution of full- and part-time faculty and staff by sex in various occupational categories. These include clerical, service, maintenance, executive, and administrative, personnel, faculty, research assistants and other technical professionals. Data are collected from over four thousand postsecondary education institutions, in cooperation with the Equal Employment Opportunity Commission (EEOC).

771. *National Survey of Postsecondary Faculty (NSOPF).* Washington,

D.C.: U.S. Dept. of Education, Nat. Center for Education Statistics, 1987/88-   . Quadrennial.
Data are gathered through surveys of institutions, faculty and department chairs. Data elements consist of background, responsibilities, workload, salaries, benefits of full- and part-time faculty, recruitment, turnover, tenure and retention. This survey will be repeated in the future and renamed The National Study of Postsecondary Faculty.

772. *Salaries, Tenure, and Fringe Benefits of Full-Time Instructional Faculty (HEGIS/IPEDS)*. Washington, D.C.: U.S. Dept. of Education, Nat. Center for Education Statistics, Integrated Postsecondary Education Data System, 1966-   . Irregular.
Data were collected from individual colleges and universities for most years since 1966-67. The database allows for tabulations on average salary by professorial rank; state; total regular, part-time, and temporary faculty; sex; race; age; degree; and type of institution.

773. *ScholarNet*. Raleigh: North Carolina State Univ., 1985-   . Annual.
Developed as two, full-text files by the university, PoliNet and HumaNet, the databases are of interest to faculty in the social sciences, history, education, politics, humanities and behavioral sciences. The full-text data include syllabi, tutorials, newsletters, transcripts of conferences, etc. Approximately five hundred records are added annually in weekly updates. They can be searched by subject, keywords, author and title.

Grants and Scholarships

774. *Foundation Directory*. New York: Foundation Center. Semiannual.
One of two databases from the Foundation Center, this one provides current descriptive information on foundations with assets of at least $1 million. In addition, these foundations give $100,000 or more in grants per year. Updated twice a year, old records are replaced with current information. This accounts for the relatively small size of the database as compared with the Foundation Grants Index. There are over fifty searchable files. They each include: the foundation name, purpose, asset type and amounts, grant amounts, donors, contact name, and ZIP code.

775. *Foundation Grants Index*. New York: Foundation Center, 1973-   . Bimonthly.
A machine readable component of a print source of the same name, this database covers grants of $5,000 to $100,000 made by U.S. foundations. Only those foundations classified as private by the Internal Revenue Service are included. These grants are not made to individuals. Updated bimonthly, the file reached a record size of over 430,000 entries by 1991. This database provides historical records of funding by foundations not readily available in corresponding print source.

776. *Grants*. Phoenix, Ariz.: Oryx Press, 1978-   .
Provides information on grant programs offered by Federal, state and local governments and private organizations for research, development and training. The broad range of such grant programs is evident from the database's various print products: Directory of Research Grants, Directory of Grants in the Humanities, Directory of Grants in the Physical Sciences, and Directory of Biomedical and Health Care Grants. Approximately one thousand new records are added yearly. Searchable by keyword, title, grant amounts, abstracts, sponsoring agency, due date and organization type.

Libraries

777. *Academic Libraries Survey (IPEDS).* Washington, D.C.: U.S. Dept.
      of Education, Nat. Center on Education Statistics, Integrated Post-
      Secondary Education Data System, 1986-   . Biennial.
Collects statistical data on academic library staff, expenditures for
salaries, materials, collection size and services. Data include state
and national totals.

778. *ACRL University Library Statistics.* Chicago, Ill.: Assn. of Coll.
      and Research Libraries, 197?-   . Biennial.
A relatively small file covering 114 libraries across U.S. and Canada.
These libraries are excluded from the survey of research libraries, due
to their smaller collection sizes. Data includes holdings, collection
type, budget, and staffing.

779. *Library Statistics of Colleges and Universities.* U.S. Dept. of Ed-
      ucation, Nat. Center for Education Statistics, 1968/69-   . Bi-
      ennial.
Data for earlier years (1974 to 1979) were collected annually until 1979
when the survey was switched to a biennial schedule. This series presents data on about three thousand libraries including library collections, expenditures and physical facilities, staff educational attain-
ments, salaries, and fringe benefits. The latest figures available are
for 1987-1988. The survey taken in 1985 provided statistics for the fifty largest college and university libraries in rank order by size of
collection.

Students

780. *American College Testing Assessment (ACT).* Iowa City, Iowa: Amer-
      ican College Testing Program, 1984-   . Annual.
Taken by college bound students, this test measures their educational
achievement in English, mathematics, social studies and the natural
sciences. It is also an indicator of how well the student might perform
in college. As of 1984, test scores of all students examined are used
to compute national norms.

781. *College Recruitment Database.* Indianapolis, Ind.: Executive Tele-
      com System Inc., Current.
Available through the Human Resources Information Network of Executive
Telecom System, this database serves recruiters by providing a resume of
college students. As of 1988, a total of six institutions are included:
Clarkson College, Iowa State, Kansas University, North Carolina State,
Purdue University, University of Tennessee at Knoxville. Graduates from
other colleges and universities will be available as the database con-
tinues to expand.

782. *Completions Survey (IPEDS).* Washington, D.C.: U.S. Dept. of Educa-
      tion, Nat. Center for Education Statistics, Integrated Postsecond-
      ary Education Data System, 1986-   . Annual.
In its earlier years, this series was known as Earned Degrees Conferred
and was part of Higher Education General Information Survey (HEGIS), with
data collected from institutions. Due to revisions of degree
classification in 1970-1971 and 1982-1983, data for periods before and
after those years are not directly comparable. Data components include
degrees conferred by racial/ethnic group, major field of study and sex;
degrees conferred by level of degree and field of study; degrees

conferred by public and private institutions and by disciplines. Such information is used for manpower planning and recruitment by business and government agencies.

783. *Doctorate Recipients Survey.* Washington, D.C.: Nat. Science Foundation, Nat. Research Council, 1973-   . Biennial.
A longitudinal study of scientists and humanists who have received doctorates by field of study during a forty-two-year period. Individuals are resurveyed every two years to provide historical data on employment status, profession, academic rank, tenure status, salary, place of work, and post-doctoral activities, by sex, age, and ethnic origin. This survey project is supported by the National Science Foundation, the National Endowment for the Humanities, the National Institute of Health, the Department of Agriculture, and the Department of Energy.

784. *Doctorate Records File.* Washington, D.C.: National Science Foundation, Nat. Research Council, 1920-   . Annual.
Also known as the <u>Survey of Earned Doctorates</u> awarded in the United States, data for this file are collected from graduates on both the graduates' and their parents' educational attainment. Profiles on graduates include sex, race, place of birth, high school and college attended, field of study as well as post-graduate career plans. Five federal agencies support this survey: National Science Foundation, Department of Education, National Endowment for the Humanities, Department of Agriculture, and the National Institutes of Health. Records prior to 1958 lack the full details on sociodemographic data collected in later years. Since 1966, an annual report is published by the National Academy of Science.

785. *Fall Enrollment in Occupationally Specific Program Survey (IPEDS).* Washington, D.C.: U.S. Dept. of Education, Nat. Center for Education Statistics, Integrated Postsecondary Education Data System, 1987-   . Biennial.
Presents data of students enrolled in vocational education less than four years. Students are identified by sex, race and ethnic groups.

786. *Fall Enrollment Survey (IPEDS).* Washington, D.C.: U.S. Dept. of Education, Nat. Center for Education Statistics, Integrated Postsecondary Education Data System, 1986-   . Annual.
These data have been part of the Higher Education General Information Survey (HEGIS) since 1966 and identified as <u>Fall Enrollment in Colleges and Universities</u>. IPEDS redesigned the survey system in 1986. Comparability with earlier data is maintained by allowing the HEGIS Institutions to be tabulated separately. This series provides a measure of full- and part-time students, their undergraduate/graduate status, sex, age, ethnicity, degrees, expenses by state (tuition, room and board), and type of institution.

787. *High School and Beyond.* Washington, D.C.: U.S. Dept. of Education, Nat. Center for Education Statistics, 1980-   . Biennial.
A longitudinal survey of high school seniors and sophomores that began in 1980 and follows them after graduation through postsecondary education and employment by means of biennial updates. The database examines such areas as school experiences, aspirations, test scores, postsecondary education experiences and job satisfaction. It also identifies parents' attitudes, income, employment and their effects on students' aspiration for college. The updates that pertain to higher education are found in the following files: 1) Postsecondary education transcript file (senior 1984; sophomore 1987) and 2) HS&B Financial Aid file (seniors 1980-84;

sophomores 1982-86). Data are collected from postsecondary institutions, guaranteed student loan program, and Pell Grant records.

788. *High School Graduates: Projections by State, 1986 to 2004.*
     Boulder, Colo.: Western Interstate Commission for Higher Education
     (WICHE), 1979-   . Irregular.
Present projections of high school graduates by state, region, and the nation. These data provide useful information for college and university enrollment planning. Data are available on computer disk by state or region on request. The information has also appeared in print as High School Graduates: Projections for the Fifty States (WICHE/Teachers Insurance and Annuity Assn./The College Board, 1984).

789. *National Assessment of Educational Program (NAEP).*   Washington,
     D.C.: U.S. Dept. of Education, Office of Education Research and Improvement, 1969-   . Biennial.
Educational attainment in ten learning areas is assessed for various age groups (i.e. 9, 13, 17, 25-35.) Attainment measures include: reading proficiency, history, civics, writing, science and mathematics, geography, and literacy. Analysis can be obtained at both the national and state levels. While most data pertain to high school students, those components concerned with young adults would be of interest to research in higher education.

790. *National Postsecondary Students Aid Study (NPSAS).*   Washington,
     D.C.: U.S. Dept. of Education, Nat. Center for Education Statistics, 1986/1987-. Triennial.
Data samples of students (43,000 in 1986/1987; 70,000 in 1989/1990) enrolled as graduates and undergraduates in more than 1,130 postsecondary institutions. Focus is on how students finance their education. This is the most comprehensive nationwide study on the subject. There are four major subfiles: 1) In-school component of student data presents student characteristics and award amounts; 2) In-school component of parent data supplements the above with family information; 3) Out-of-school component of loan recipients collects data from former graduates who received Guaranteed Student Loans; and 4) Transcript Survey of Student Loan Recipients contains data on students no longer enrolled. The latter two subfiles (components) provide a means to analyze the correlation between educational activities and indebtedness, coping, or loan repayment ability. Data are collected and updated every three years.

AUTHOR INDEX

Reference is to entry number

TITLE INDEX

Reference is to entry number

SUBJECT INDEX

Reference is to entry number

About the Compilers

PETER P. OLEVNIK is Head of Information Services at Drake Memorial Library, SUNY College at Brockport. His previous publications include *The Financing of American Higher Education: A Bibliographic Handbook*, guides to the use of research collections in microform, and selected reference works on higher education.

BETTY W. CHAN is Assistant Head of Information Services and Head of Government Documents at Drake Memorial Library, SUNY College at Brockport. Her publications include *Sports and Physical Education: A Guide to the Reference Resources* (Greenwood Press, 1983).

SARAH HAMMOND was an Assistant Librarian at Drake Memorial Library and is currently associated with the Zebra Mussel Information Clearinghouse (Sea-Grant Extension), SUNY College at Brockport.

GREGORY M. TOTH is a Reference Librarian at Drake Memorial Library, SUNY College at Brockport. He was formerly an Assistant Professor of English in the Virginia Community College System and a reference librarian and humanities bibliographer at the Rochester Institute of Technology.